West Baltimore Neighborhoods
Sketches of Their History 1840-1960

Roderick N. Ryon

GENERAL EDITORS
D. Randall Beirne
Joan Henley

Prepared by
The Institute for Publications Design
at the University of Baltimore

WEST BALTIMORE NEIGHBORHOODS
Sketches of Their History
1840-1960

© 1993 Roderick N. Ryon

All rights reserved. No part of the contents of this book may be reproduced by any means without the written permission of the author.

All photographs courtesy of The Peale Musuem, Baltimore City Life Museums, except where noted otherwise.

Library of Congress Catalog Card Number 93-60361

ISBN 0-9636930-0-X

Printed in the United States of America

This book was designed and produced at the University of Baltimore by Janet Kratfel under the auspices of the Institute for Publications Design at the University of Baltimore. Art Direction was by Bert Smith. Maps produced under the supervision of James E. DiLisio at Towson State University.

For Joan and Chris

Letter

The University of Baltimore and its Educational Foundation are pleased to cooperate with the City of Baltimore in jointly publishing this book about Baltimore neighborhoods.

The University of Baltimore is proud of its century of service to the city, and of its close involvement with the neighborhoods that give Baltimore its distinctive character. The University is dedicated to serving this city and its people, and this publication is a way of expressing its dedication.

H. Mebane Turner

H. Mebane Turner
President
University of Baltimore

Contents

Foreword	ix
Preface	xi
Introduction	xiii

Mount Royal and Madison — 1

Bolton Hill	5
Madison	15

The "Bottom to Sugar Hill" — 25

McCulloh Homes	31
Murphy Homes	34
Upton	37
Druid Heights	51

Along Pratt Street — 55

Hollins Park	59
Pratt-Monroe	68
Bentalou-Smallwood and Mill Hill	71

Old West End — 83

Poe Homes	86
Poppleton	89
Franklin Square	95
Union Square & West Pratt	99
Booth-Boyd	104
Lexington	106

Sandtown — 109

Harlem Park	116
Sandtown-Winchester	124

Old Annex — 131

Industrial Hinterlands — 138
Along North Avenue — 143
Greater Rosemont — 148

Beyond the Gwynns Falls — 155

Along Frederick Avenue — 160
Greater Edmondson — 170
At the Western Edge — 176

Neighborhood Maps — 181
Index — 195

Foreword

West Baltimore Neighborhoods: Sketches of their History, 1840-1960 is the second in a series of neighborhood studies designed to provide historical and demographic data on Baltimore's official geographic subdivisions. In 1989, *North Baltimore: From Estate to Development* by Karen Lewand was published as the first. Fifty neighborhoods are portrayed here and make up a selection of approximately two hundred seventy neighborhoods defined in the U. S. Census Bureau's Neighborhood Statistics Program. The series groups neighborhoods into seven major city regions that roughly conform to Regional Planning Districts originally created by the Regional Planning Council for planning and statistical purposes. The regions exhibit continuity over time and generally reflect geographical features and historical development patterns.

Source materials include maps and atlases, newspapers, institutional histories, census data, and oral testimonies. Profiles should be regarded as brief, general portraits of neighborhoods, starting points for further historical research. In a region of suburban residential neighborhoods, streetcar and automobile suburbs, and some industry, they treat physical and social changes.

Joint efforts by the Departments of Sociology, English and the Institute for Publications Design at the University of Baltimore made this book possible. Larry Reich, former Director of the Baltimore City Department of Planning, conceived of the project. Similar data books have been produced for Chicago through joint efforts of the City of Chicago and the Department of Sociology of the University of Chicago.

The able assistance of the following individuals and organizations is gratefully acknowledged: James E. DiLisio, Towson State University, for map design; Professor Bert Smith and graduate student Janet Kratfel, University of Baltimore, for art direction and design; the staffs of the Maryland Room, Enoch Pratt Free Library, Peale Museum, and the libraries of the University of Maryland Baltimore County and Towson State University.

—D. Randall Beirne
 Joan Henley
 Editors, University of Baltimore

Preface

Fifty Baltimore City neighborhoods stretch from the Martin Luther King Expressway to the city's western boundary. Built up in a century and a quarter—from the 1840s to the 1960s—they developed mostly as suburbs, residential districts apart from Baltimore industry, commerce, and the port. Like many suburbs, they have a largely unrecorded history. In Baltimore and elsewhere chroniclers prefer old country towns within city boundaries, Waverly and Govans for example, or renowned and planned communities like Roland Park or Guilford. But the Westside was setting to a major social process within Baltimore—demographic and ethnic change over time along established residential blocks. Here especially the urban phenomenon of "changing neighborhood" was acted out and molded the modern city. Attention is overdue.

These neighborhoods are situated within the boundaries of North Avenue (once the city's northern boundary) and the Gwynns Falls on the north, downtown commercial development on the east, the B and O Railroad and parallel lines on the south, and the present city border on the west. They formed the terrain of central Baltimore County until 1816. "Neighborhood," treated here as a geographic entity, is regarded as distinct from community, which emerges both within and across neighborhoods. Baltimoreans with similar backgrounds, traditions, and beliefs or values tended to spend time together and form community relationships along a single block or alley of real estate within a residential neighborhood. Or they built them around the churches, ethnic and civic clubs, and places of employment and recreation that extended beyond neighborhood boundaries. By contrast, neighborhoods, some with identities only recently formed, comprise the shared patches of real estate of diverse inhabitants.

Sketches aim to identify architectural landmarks and landscape and to look at sociotopographical changes from 1840 to 1960. These latter involved groups of inhabitants, the built environment of public and private land and edifices, and the interaction between them. A rich array of Baltimoreans once lived on the Westside—African Americans of renown and status, middle and upper class whites, industrial workers (both white ethnic and African-American), professional people, businessmen, domestic laborers, home owners and homemakers, tenants and public housing residents. All once called its neighborhoods their home. Necessarily, home builders and first inhabitants of extant architecture figure prominently in sketches, but successive generations also receive their due. As newcomers to developed neighborhoods the latter regarded urban architecture as "inherited space"—an environment to be put to new uses. Few sketches treat more than several generations of inhabitants, but collectively they aim to document the Westside's rich heterogeneity.

Editors D. Randall Beirne and Joan Henley of the University of Baltimore, and Mary Markey, Pamela H. Simpson, Joan A. Stanne, and Joseph Zehnder offered counsel and suggestions. Grants of money and released time from teaching provided by the Faculty Research Committee, Towson State University, facilitated research and writing.

—Roderick N. Ryon

Introduction

Stand along the Jones Falls, path of today's Expressway, in 1840, and start a trek by foot to the west. The vista would spread before you as it had for centuries. Only a few roads, an occasional grist mill, and isolated estate houses dotted a landscape familiar to Native Americans, trappers, and pioneers. And only the meandering Gwynns Falls, and a few now buried streams, interrupted a topographical rhythm. Gentle hills alternated with small valleys to the present western boundary of Baltimore City.

Central Baltimore County and uninhabited parts of Baltimore City spread over the junction of the plateau of crystalline rocks and the beginning of the coastal plain. Topographically distinct from older sections of the city, the plateau sloped gently south and east toward flat land. Rock and limestone made soil ill suited to the tobacco farming that spread south of Baltimore during the Colonial Era. Rolling hillside stood above the marshiness and the stagnant wetness of the old city.

Founded in 1729, Baltimore town sat at the head of a bay and farther inland than other East coast ports and towns. Early in the nineteenth century, turnpikes and roads opened real estate west of the city to sparse settlement. Uninhabited estate land was subdivided and manor houses were put up by Baltimore gentry who extended country lanes to the Frederick Road and to newly erected turnpikes, notably the Reisterstown, Calverton, and Franklintown roads.

Estate houses served as hill-top escapes from the congested city, summer retreats for affluent Baltimore merchants. Absentee owners hired tenants to cultivate farmland and orchards. Farm laborers on the estates, and a few independent millers and farmers who lived nearby, shipped wheat, corn, and flour to the city for export. Traffic could pass into Baltimore City within a day. City institutions with needs for accessible and inexpensive real estate—cemeteries, orphanages, and asylums—also acquired property before 1850. Many are Westside landmarks today.

Wooded areas began to come down after 1840. Development was spurred by the industrial and population growth of Baltimore City, and by transportation technologies. Early suburban residences went up between 1850 and 1870. They were built on acreage close to the city next to streets and roads which intersected pikes and main roads. Omnibuses, slow-moving horse-drawn passenger vehicles, transported commuters daily to and from Baltimore. Three of them operated from Franklin Square to downtown blocks as early as 1853.

Tracks for horse-drawn trolleys radiated farther beyond the central city between 1870 and 1890, years when Baltimore's population increased more than sixty percent. Trolleys that transported thirty to forty passengers traveled six to eight miles per hour. Car lines, car barns, and depots to exchange horses on the lines took into account the hilly terrain of the Westside.

Residential settlement along the trolley routes went up as new patterns of land use emerged throughout Baltimore. Traditional patterns of undifferentiated development, that is residences, shops, and industry all built close together, gave way to permanent specialization by function. Regions developed as distinctly manufacturing, commercial, or residential districts, with residential commuting encouraged. Industrial and commercial sectors tended to concentrate in older urban sections. On their east, north, and west sides, new residential districts ringed them like a horseshoe.

Electric-powered streetcars that moved twice as fast as horse-drawn vehicles replaced horse trolleys in the 1890s and spurred a massive exodus to the outer reaches of the city. Encouraged by inexpensive trolley fares, workers commuted by streetcar to all parts of the city. Baltimore's population nearly doubled from 1890 to 1930. In the 1940s and 1950s, automobiles and buses brought with them track removal, and street widening and expressway construction programs. These facilitated both traditional and "reverse" commuting, whereby traffic flows into suburbs beyond the city. Motor vehicles encouraged the final stage of urban development, extensive residential construction at the city's western edge after World War II.

Westside development all took place within City annexes, three broad belts or partial belts of land acquired between 1816 and 1918. Along the Westside, boundaries first moved from near Howard and Saratoga Streets to Boundary (or North) Avenue and a south-southwest line along today's Payson Street. The new Westside, virtually all of it rural and undeveloped, made up thirty percent of city acreage. City Surveyor Thomas Poppleton conducted a plat survey and crafted a street plan of a rectangular grid that formed the basis of seventy years of development. An annexation in 1888 moved the city boundary beyond the Gwynns Falls west of Edmondson, and the so-called belt annex of 1918 established the present city borders on all four sides.

With each addition Baltimore incorporated essentially rural, sparsely populated acreage. But new land tended to spur rapid development. Real-estate values soared, city streets and utilities were extended, and urban institutions—schools, libraries, and churches—dotted the countryside. Older sections themselves underwent architectural alteration concurrent with a population exodus into new land incorporated to the west. The modern mixture of many neighborhoods—old and new buildings and landscape, and, sometimes, of longtime inhabitants and newcomers—thus reflects several stages of development. It arose partly from new development, and partly from multiple new uses put to old edifices and land within established neighborhoods.

Mount Royal
and Madison

Fountains, monuments, and curvilinear walkways blended with green lawn space and shade trees along Eutaw Place.

The hilltop neighborhoods which extend along Mount Royal Terrace and Madison Avenue lay west of the central part of Baltimore City and the old path of the Jones Falls, from Dolphin and Preston Streets to North Avenue. The older appellation for Bolton Hill blocks, "Mount Royal," derives from an eighteenth century estate. A Pennsylvania-born miller, Jonathan Hansen, acquired a 320 acre estate on the Falls near present-day North in 1726, naming it "Mount Royal" for no apparent reason other than its elevated location. Forges and mills next to the Falls subsequently bore the name. The property eventually passed to Samuel Birkhead, a prominent Baltimore physician, who built a summer mansion called Mount Royal, now city-owned property at Reservoir and Park (Reservoir Hill).

Birkhead's grandson gave land at the eastern edge to the city in 1860 to encourage development, the eastern-most street named Mount Royal Terrace. A reservoir, built near Boundary (North) Avenue soon thereafter, and an elegant graystone railroad station of the B and O Railroad completed in 1906, etched the name permanently. While acreage on both sides of North Avenue was once regarded as Mount Royal, a school, tavern and businesses below North tend in recent times to affix the name to real estate within the 1816 city boundary.

The name Madison derives from the north-south Avenue which bisects the neighborhood. It was designated for a downtown street, itself named in 1833 for James Madison, fourth president.

Nineteenth-century row houses and churches, built mostly for native Baltimore white businessmen and their families, went up on nearly every block of real estate of both neighborhoods between 1860 and 1900. Old edifices were demolished and new landscaping and home and commercial construction spread over one quarter of the acreage between 1959 and 1970. The new development followed a massive in-migration of African-American and white workers during and after World War II.

Wealthy bankers and investors, factory and plant owners, entrepreneurs, and merchandise magnates made up Baltimore's influential business classes in the nineteenth and early twentieth centuries. The wealth, status, and influence of the various strata of businessmen reflected the gradual shift of Baltimore from a nineteenth-century commercial port to a metropolis with a mixed base of commerce, industry, and merchandising. Businessmen included merchants and fleet owners who took advantage of Baltimore's location as "Gateway to the South"; producers of Baltimore-renowned products such as pianos, straw hats, umbrellas, shoes, garments, farm tools, steam boilers, and machine parts; executives of thriving corporations; and owners of large department stores. Officers of corporations often headed the Baltimore divisions of national companies formed from mergers at the end of the nineteenth century. So many divisions of national corporations had opened in Baltimore by World War I that the city acquired the title of "Branch Office City" for its satellite divisions and offices. Department store magnates possessed wealth and status equal to that of the executives in large companies.

When early industrial and commercial development first began to alter the landscape of older sections of Baltimore after the Civil War, businessmen initiated the early phases of suburban development. Working-class settlements overcrowded many blocks east of Howard in the old city, and noise and refuse from city plants reached urban mansions close to downtown businesses and plants. While affluent businessmen moved in several directions beyond the central city, the hilly terrain along the Jones Falls was especially alluring. Country estates and manor houses familiar by name to many city dwellers dotted Mount Royal's blocks. Only gradually subdivided, estate land affixed a reputation on newly carved streets as preferred, prestigious real estate.

As new housing was built, distinguished old architecture blended with it. Druid Hill Park, a 675 acre expanse, was acquired by the city in 1860. It lay one-half mile to the north and served as a magnet to residential development. The park possessed horse and carriage paths popular with middle and upper classes, groves of trees and meadows for picnics, and a 55-acre lake. Replete with swan boats, the last was a premier city setting for Victorian Era recreation. Writer Henry James called Druid Hill Baltimore's "gem of the town." The Citizens' Passenger Railway extended an early line along Madison Avenue to a steep arched entryway.

Perched above the old city, and the housing of their working-class employees, Mount Royal and Madison blocks symbolized the high status of the affluent. Blocks were close enough to the central city to move commuters back and forth to offices daily. Homeowners, many with newly acquired wealth, were part of the city where they worked and amassed wealth. But they also towered above it. Well-dressed men travelled horse-drawn and electric trolleys, or the slower moving, chauffeur-driven private carriages preferred by the very affluent.

The family homes of the business classes were easily distinguished from both older Baltimore row houses and contemporary ones built elsewhere in the city. Blocks contained broad twenty-two foot houses, three to four stories high, not narrow, gable-topped houses of one or one-and-one-half stories. The latter lined older workers' sections of the city such as Mount Clare, now Washington Village, and south Baltimore. And, unlike the modest, plain-faced Italianate row houses being built elsewhere in Baltimore after 1870, homes here were bedecked with ornate streetfront exteriors. Showy cornices projected from stylish mansard (two-sloped) roofs, and fancy and expensive terra cotta facing covered streetfront facades. Exterior stairways held stone balusters. To exude a sense of grandeur even in blocks of row homes, massive rough-hewn, stone-covered bases of the edifices, and rounded arches, surrounded entry ways. Gates and walls were made of brick.

Like conventional row housing, groups of homes in a line had a uniformity of scale with identical heights and widths. Many possessed the ordered simplicity characteristic of neo-Classical public buildings in Baltimore. Stylized exteriors nevertheless defined the occupants as among the city's affluent classes. Variation—block to block and occasionally house to house—as well as exterior trim and street features, green terraces, and stone facing, distinguished Mount Royal and Madison streets where exceptionally prosperous home owners lived from those of managers and small entrepreneurs (See Madison). These distinctions reflected a prevalent sense of hierarchy among white middle and upper classes. The eclecticism and asymmetry of carefully individualized homes bespoke a certain confidence in material success. Equally, however, they reflected a yen during the Victorian Era for personal particularity in home residences, and for individualized possessions at a time when identity at work was increasingly subsumed by the growing size and bureaucratization of business.

Demolition projects for new public housing in neighborhoods south and west (below Dolphin Street and along Orchard) leveled nineteenth-century housing in the late 1930s. They prompted a fan-like exodus, many African-American porters, janitors, and cart drivers moving north. Black workers had traditionally worked along busy downtown commercial streets, especially Baltimore and Pratt. Domestic workers too formed part of the exodus into Mount Royal's southern blocks. Concurrently, growing defense industries, especially steel, aircraft, and shipbuilding, drew thousands of white workers to Baltimore. Baltimore was a national center of ship and aircraft assembly, Federal government contracts alone creating 50,000 new jobs between 1937 and 1941. Distant from defense plants in East Baltimore and Baltimore County, western blocks swelled with newcomers. West of Bolton Street, row homes were converted to flats, sometimes several apartments on a floor, with ceilings lowered and floors linoleumed. Housing codes allowed six apartments within a standard three-story row house, eight and nine households sharing single three-story row homes.

Southern, rural African Americans who immigrated to Baltimore after World War II added to the neighborhood population in the late 1940s and early 1950s. Thereafter, city agencies promoted demolition and new construction as solutions to home deterioration, and the leveling of blocks of nineteenth-century housing caused a new exodus beyond Mount Royal and Madison neighborhoods. Blocks west of Bolton Street were designated the Mount Royal-Fremont Urban Renewal District in 1959, one of eight districts citywide. Eighteen hundred edifices were leveled, alleys were entirely removed, and nine acres was designated for park land. Most replacement architecture was two- to three-story brick apartments and town houses, interspersed with traditional Bolton Hill park land, and with schools and a shopping center. Next to new edifices, whole blocks or parts of blocks of abandoned nineteenth-century housing were acquired by church-sponsored non-profit organizations and subjected to massive rehabilitation.

Population in-and out-migration remolded the character of the western section of Bolton Hill and of Madison. Staid blocks of middle-aged and elderly people yielded to a neighborhood with young adults and many children. Druid Hill Park and neighborhood playgrounds became recreation centers for African-American children. Young people located jobs in downtown markets and North Avenue establishments, and buses replaced trolleys to transport commuters, as both adult men and women worked away from their homes.

Bolton Hill

Bolton Hill take its name from an estate, "Bolton," itself named for an English property called "Bolton-le-Moors." George Grundy, a Baltimore merchant who emigrated from England, built the white-pillared, three-storied landmark soon after the Revolution. It sat at the foot of Bolton until 1900, on the site of the Fifth Regimental Armory. Bolton Street was laid out from its front entryway in 1848.

North Avenue, a path west and parallel to the Jones Falls Expressway, Howard, Dolphin, and a line just east of Eutaw Place along Jordan, Jordan Street Green, and a northwest extension of Jordan form boundaries to Bolton Hill. Built atop hills that slope gently toward the central city, edifices sit one hundred feet above downtown and the port. The neighborhood has one shopping center nestled among tree-lined residential blocks (on McMechen), three corner stores and commercial establishments along one side of Mount Royal and the eastern end of North, nine institutional buildings, three urban parks, and no industry. Institutions are interspersed among blocks of row houses, eight to fifteen to a street side.

Except for new town houses along Dolphin Alley, homes in eastern blocks date from 1850 to 1900. Less ornate than Eutaw Place rows, or the elegant architecture along Mount Vernon Place also built after the Civil War, residences east of Park nevertheless had distinctive qualities in high demand by the city's affluent. Streetfront facades set them apart. Along Mount Royal, stone sills outlined windows, and a liberal use of brownstone facade, or massive gray stone at the base, suggested very grand interiors. On

The late eighteenth-century estate of "Bolton" sat on the site of the Fifth Regimental Armory for over a century. Bolton Street was carved from its front lane with the early development of Bolton Hill.

other blocks expensive iron fencing and gateways, and patches of lawn rare for nineteenth-century row houses, defined the homes as exceptional.

A stream, known variously as the Great Glade, Spicer's Run, and Frick's Run, ran along McMechen and emptied into Rutter's Run at least until the Civil War. Rutter's Run flowed into the Jones Falls. Streets were laid out in a northwestern grid pattern to the Reisterstown Turnpike (Pennsylvania Avenue) and were probably set to run parallel and perpendicular to the turnpike. They were extended to North Avenue by 1870, many named for estate and mill owners or public heroes. Rutter and Lanvale acquired names from two nineteenth-century operators of mills along the Falls. Lafayette Street derives from the French hero of the American Revolution, and John probably from John Eager Howard, Revolutionary War officer and former governor, and once owner of a vast estate west of Howard Street.

First development in east Bolton Hill spread along the blocks west of John, near farms, mill workers' housing, and outdoor, somewhat dirty, businesses. Row and alley houses lined north-south streets and Lanvale. South of Townsend (Lafayette) homes edged the Lanvale Farm located just east of John, a country estate with a grand mansion house. Owned by James R. Partridge, it was farmed by tenants who exported garden produce to the city. Mill workers' shanties, a marble works, and a stone-hauling business ringed the farm. Johnny Jump-up Hill, a wild-flowered pasture land north of Townsend, lured children who roughhoused with "Falls Roaders," Irish waifs from the mills. House maids were known to gather on the hill for the ritual of spring carpet beating. Three stone churches were completed by 1877 and horse-drawn trolley lines extended on Bolton and McMechen to a station and stables on North Avenue.

Development in the 1880s and 1890s, spurred by the opening of Mount Royal Avenue, obliterated traces of farmland and industry. Rows extended from Dolphin beyond McMechen and became known for quality city services. Homes were all connected to a city water main, blocks were cleaned by street scrapers and serviced by garbage cart drivers, and park ground was tended through private care paid for by residents. Trolleys bisected the neighborhood along John and Park. An uptown train station, Bolton Station, later replaced by Mount Royal station, sat nearby at Cathedral and Biddle. A private hospital, the Hospital for the Women of Maryland, opened at Lafayette and John in 1882. Servants' quarters, three- or four-room row houses, were built along Rutter Alley behind Mount Royal.

Height above the old city and port gave eastern residential blocks the sense of being a haven apart from Baltimore but nevertheless in control of it. The vista to the south was a reminder of the proximity of old Baltimore. Children could spot ship masts and billowing tall sails from third-story windows. Neighborhood legend holds that a bride once began her processional at Brown Memorial Church on Park as a nine gun salute sounded from a harbor fleet. Two depressions, 1873 and 1893, and an exodus of first owners to the new (1888) annex, nevertheless changed Bolton Hill even as homes were being constructed. Setbacks forced a few entrepreneurs to convert homes to rooming houses. Clerks and craftsmen rented rooms next to prosperous businessmen's houses and commuted on streetcars. Blocks became the city's well-known home in exile to once prosperous former Confederates, planters, and military officers who had lost fortunes during the War. Charles Marshall, aide-de-camp to Robert E. Lee, and Harry Gilmor, the notorious Rebel raider in Baltimore County, lived on Lanvale. Thomas Dabney, once owner of 1000 acres and 500 slaves, lived with a daughter on John Street and took in boarders.

A cultural district of Baltimore, built from Mulberry to Mount Royal Station in turn-of-the-century years, remolded the social makeup of eastern Bolton Hill after 1900. Enoch Pratt Library opened on Mulberry in 1886, the Lyric Theatre was built near Cathedral in 1894, and the Maryland Institute of Art located on Mount Royal in 1906. Private schools surrounded residential blocks, Boys Latin next to Mount Royal Station on Brevard until 1960, Bryn Mawr for women on Preston until 1933, and Friends School at Park Avenue from 1899 to 1936. Blocks sat closer to cultural and educational institutions than any other nineteenth-century suburban neighborhood. Homes were divided into flats, and new tenants included male lawyers, journalists, artists, writers, and teachers and students in nearby private and public schools. The clusters of housing constituted a preferred neighborhood for generations of Johns

Servants' houses without exterior ornamentation, like these on the 1200 block of Rutter Street (Mount Royal Station tower in background), were built behind main streets lined with elegant row homes. (Courtesy Enoch Pratt Free Library)

Hopkins faculty and students who walked the North Avenue Bridge to the Homeland campus, less than one mile.

South of McMechen and west of Park and Bolton, in southwestern Bolton Hill, nineteenth-century row houses line street sides east of Mason; post-1960 town houses, apartments, and an apartment house sit on streets in the western half. The terrain has a north to south slope peaking at Mosher. Tiny front yards and ornate entry ways distinguish a few older houses; secluded green space laid out in small plots the new housing. The latter is notable for tall-windowed town houses overlooking shrubbery and yards enclosed with iron and brick gates. Park land surrounds the three twelve-storied buildings of Memorial Towers on McMechen.

Earliest development went up south of Mosher along Garden (later Linden) and the Bolton Street Trolley line. Elegant rows, some with carriage houses located on the alleys, were interspersed with individual estate homes set back from the new streets. East-west and north-south blocks to McMechen were finished by 1900. Streetcar lines crisscrossed blocks along Park, Linden, Dolphin, and McMechen. Housing was accessible both to Mount Clare yards and offices, and downtown businesses. The blocks were solidly residential except for a small hotel, the Forbes, near McMechen and Jordan, opened about 1900. The family of city notable James A. Gary, postmaster general of the United States during the William McKinley administration, occupied a brownstone estate house at Dolphin and Linden for many years.

Five blocks west of Park between Laurens and McMechen sit on a slight southward slope from Laurens. Homes along Linden Terrace and the 1600 block of Park Avenue, built near the turn of the century, reflect new tendencies to introduce greater daylight into interiors. Linden homes have first- and second-story bay windows; Park Avenue houses have concave, so-called "swellfront" walls with windows which front on the street.

On the edge of the Bolton Street trolley line, north-south blocks built up in the 1880s, after development south and east, and after the construction of a tunnel for the Baltimore and Potomac Railroad under Wilson Street during the 1870s. Row houses had the characteristic ornamentation of Mount Royal. Streetfront facades were decorative, entryways and windows employed elaborate designs of wrought iron, and interiors included as many as five marble and brick fireplaces. Rear lots that stretched to alleys barred any major residential or institutional construction on east-west streets, and guaranteed low population density. The city opened a suburban public school, #14 at Linden and Wilson; two churches were built along Park Avenue; and a synagogue, Har Sinai, was erected on Wilson. The two triangular swaths of acreage northwest of Laurens and northeast of Park above McMechen include real estate given over to contemporary housing, the fifteen-story Bolton North Apartments on McMechen, and two-to-five-room, three-or four-story garden apartments set back from the street along Roberts and North. Three playing fields along North and Roberts cover one-third of the acreage; three- and four-story nineteenth-century row houses, two corner shops, and a tiny business district at the eastern end of North Avenue another third. Undeveloped land here situated at the city's 1816 northern boundary was occupied by farms and institutions that used the Boundary Avenue egress before the streets of Bolton Hill were laid out after the Civil War.

Civil War fortifications once sat on Boundary near present-day Park. Thomas Kensett, local inventor of canning processes and owner of a city oyster-packing plant, held property for many years along Boundary. Mt. Hope, a tiny private college, was once located north of Bolton and Laurens. In 1844 the buildings were acquired by the Roman Catholic Sisters of Charity, who operated them as a hospital, Mount Hope Asylum (later Retreat), until the 1880s. Springs on the property provided water. An institution known as Baltimore Female College, the first college for women in the state, occupied new buildings on Park Avenue from 1874 to about 1890. A Methodist Episcopal school set up on St. Paul Street in 1848 for the "liberal education of young women," it was endowed by the state after 1860, and in 1868 was rechartered as a non-denominational institution.

Northern blocks lay beyond the terminus for horse trolleys on McMechen, but close to track laid soon after the Annexation of 1888 for electric lines to North Avenue and beyond. Linden and John lines extended north and west, as blocks developed with real estate to Druid Hill Park. Three-story and four-story row houses spread across every block in the 1880s and 1890s. Stylish terra cotta and stone carvings next to modern bay windows were used on Laurens and Park. Small interior parks were built by the city within blocks northwest of Linden and Laurens, and Bolton and Laurens, on land donated by developers. With street terraces on broad north-south thoroughfares, they formed a succession of patches of green from Eutaw Place to Mount Royal. The city erected a firehouse on North, east of Mount Royal, in 1901.

Artists and writers won Bolton Hill the reputation of "Gin Belt," Baltimore's Jazz Age Bohemian district in the 1920s, and brought the section a measure of fame in the 1930s. F. Scott Fitzgerald published *Tender is the Night* from a home shared with Zelda Fitzgerald on Park Avenue in the Thirties. Christopher Morley wrote *Thorofare*, a semi-autobiographical novel (1943) about growing up on Park Avenue.

"Georgetown" replaced "Gin Belt" as neighborhood appellation after World War II, Hill homes being among the first in the City subject to historic preservation and restoration. Home owners had created the Mount Royal Protective (later Improvement) Association in 1928 to stem the tide of suburban flight, home subdivision into flats, and absentee ownership. One of the city's oldest neighborhood associations, it actively promoted demolition projects after 1930, urging the leveling of property next to the Fifth Regimental Armory for more green space. But post-war urban renewal projects west and south converted the Association to the cause of preservation with rehabilitation. The Association sponsored house and garden tours to lure buyers who would inhabit the homes, formed a rehabilitation corporation to purchase properties and resell to live-in owners, lobbied to restrict neighboring subsidized housing projects, and agitated with the city for Victorian-style street lighting.

The charm and dignity of urban living in individual houses with small quaint urban parks was extolled. Exteriors were refurbished, and kitchens and plumbing modernized. Tiny plots of exterior space were set out as hidden retreats or formal gardens for small two-parent families and single professional men and women, as rigidly enforced zoning laws barred industry and stores. Alley properties, like those on 1300 Rutter Street, were reconstructed. Eastern blocks formed the core of the Bolton Hill Historical and Architectural Preservation district designated in 1967 and extending across Mount Royal and Madison neighborhoods. They became a site on the National Register of Historic Places in 1971. The former enabled CHAP, the Baltimore City Commission for Historical and Architectural Preservation formed in 1964, to review applications for construction, demolition, or substantial exterior structural alteration.

During World War II, accessible Bolton Hill streetcar lines lured both flat-dwellers displaced from housing south and west of Bolton Hill, and defense workers new to the City. Defense workers on Linden Avenue, many transplanted West Virginians who came as single workers or in whole families of workers, briefly won blocks west of Bolton the reputation as the city's "Little Appalachia." Men commuted to the East Baltimore shipyards. The opening of the Twenty-ninth Street bridge in 1937 placed the textile mills of Hampden and Woodberry in commuting distance for women. Taverns featuring country music nestled among homes carved into flats in blocks that brimmed with people. Stoops stayed crowded at night time spring through fall. The Eutaw Place terrace even formed a kind of popular neighborhood sleeping quarters on hot summer evenings.

Blocks in southwest Bolton Hill formed the southern section of so-called Project I in the early 1960s, the first development in the Mount Royal-Fremont Urban Renewal Area. Much of Linden south of McMechen was demolished for green space and residences. North of McMechen Urban Renewal left one single block of Linden Avenue unscathed, and, sometimes called Linden Terrace, it was renovated in the 1970s. Lots were lengthened and alleys closed. The street was closed off to private parking and a Victorian gazebo of brick and marble erected by the city, as thirty-five houses were marketed to investors. The McMechen Street shopping center and a contemporary park on Laurens were formed from Project I. Blocks with egress on North Avenue were all initially projected to be leveled by Urban Renewal, but amendments to the plans, lobbied for by home owners, salvaged the eastern blocks. Three hundred low-rise units were built west of Bolton.

Within eastern blocks post-war home interiors attest to the mixed results of efforts to preserve an ethnically homogenous haven, a Victorian preserve between traffic and commercial properties east and south and contemporary residential property blocks north and west. Homes carved into flats continued to rent to students and workers. Refinished oaken doors bore triple bolts, and windowways protective iron grill work. Old and new institutional buildings blended subtly into tree-lined streets of residences, only church spires obtruding above.

The Beethoven Apartments, in the 1500 block of Park Avenue, were erected in the nineteenth century as Baltimore's first streetfront terrace, or group of houses constructed to appear as a single structure. Frank Frick, founder of the Lyric Theater and developer of streetcar lines, and a builder who was enamored of the style of English town houses, built the row of ten five-storied brownstones in the so-called Second Empire style. Elegant mansard roofs extended on several sides, ornate windows and cornices along the streetfront exterior. Several had double cellars. The project was once dubbed "Frick's Folly" by City investors who believed its location, north of urban development, would keep the houses from being sold. With City Hall, they remain Baltimore's only Second Empire public buildings.

Memorial Episcopal Church at Bolton and Lafayette was formed as a mission of Emmanuel Church and located near Park and Dolphin until a tiny structure, now the church nave, was begun in 1861. It was completed before the end of the Civil War in 1864. Named a memorial to Henry Van Dyke Johns and Charles Ridgely Howard, Emmanuel clergy, it is known for very simple ecclesiastical adornments and for paintings and wooden appointments more than stained glass. The south and north transepts were completed after 1900, and a chapel was added in the 1950s. Brown Memorial Church, named for Scottish-born George Brown, and spouse Isabella McLanahan, was built in 1869-70. A founder of Alexander Brown and Sons in 1811, Brown was reputedly one of the nation's twelve wealthiest financiers at his death in 1859. A broad gray edifice with vast Tiffany windows, detailed altar carvings, and a splendid organ, it was a gift of Brown's widow.

Strawbridge United Methodist Church, formed near the present-day Fifth Regimental Armory in 1836, moved to Park and Wilson in 1882, its new edifice's interior the shape of a Greek cross. Interior appointments commemorate Methodist evangelist Robert Strawbridge. The pulpit is made of wood from his eighteenth-century pulpit, the limb of a Maryland tree under which he allegedly preached, and a log from an early Methodist meeting house.

Corpus Christi, a Victorian Gothic edifice, was built at Mount Royal and Lafayette, 1886-1891, a donation of the children of Thomas Courtenay Jenkins and Louisa Carroll Jenkins. Designed by Patrick Charles Keely, renowned nineteenth-century architect of some 600 American churches, it is known for mosaics of Florentine glass and narrow nave windows of a style associated with English designer William Morris. A motif of pointed arches and ribbed vaults extends from the roof line throughout the church. Administered by Jesuit priests until 1976, the church was renovated in 1911 and again in the late 1970s.

(OPPOSITE) Brown Memorial Presbyterian Church, Park and Lafayette Avenues, illustrates Victorian Era ecclesiastical architecture.

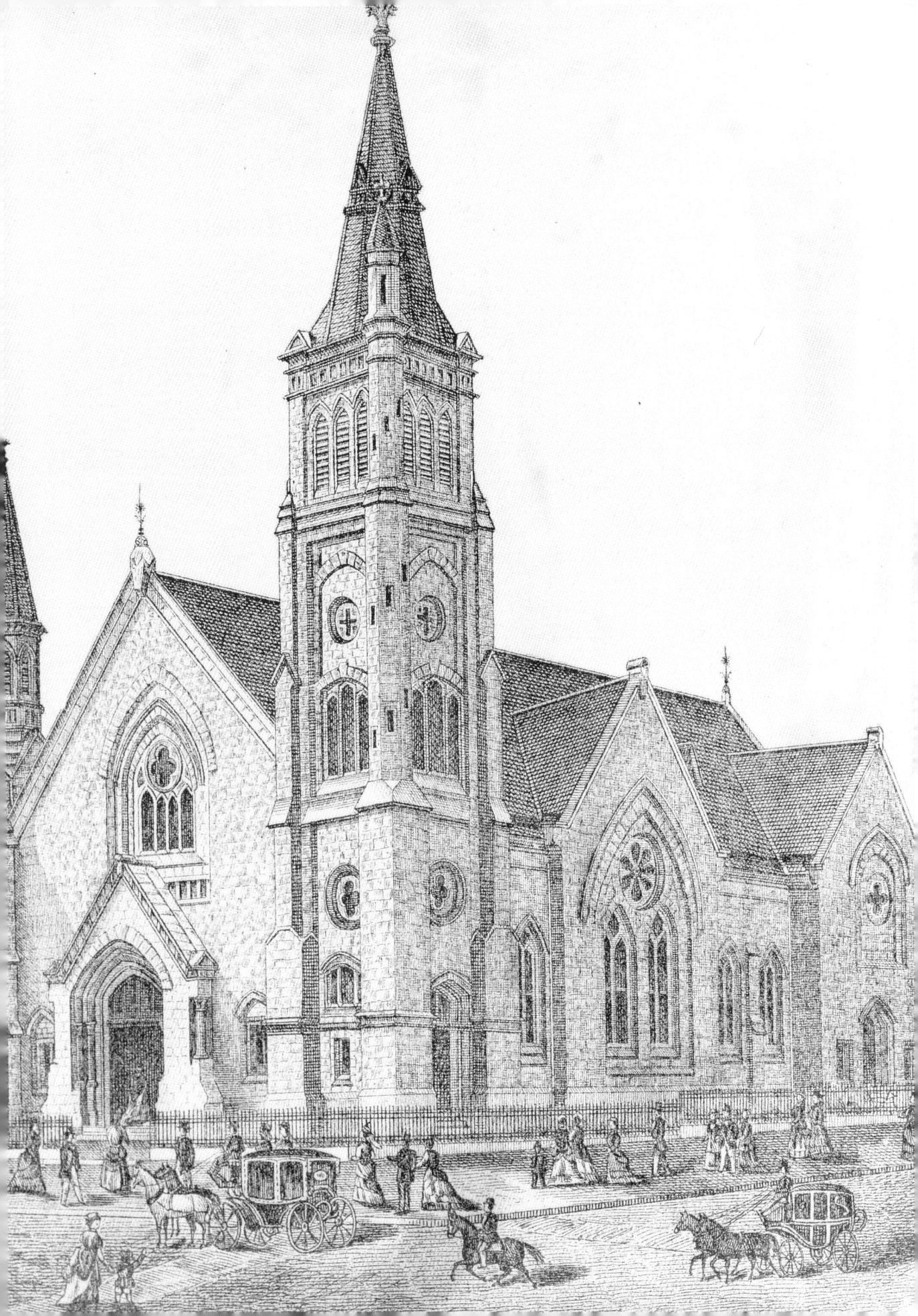

The Confederate Memorial on Mount Royal near McMechen, donated by the Maryland Daughters of the Confederacy in 1903, commemorates Maryland soldiers and sailors who served the Confederacy. It is inscribed, "Glory Stands Bending Over Grief." The three- and four-story graystone Friends Apartments at Park and Laurens was built by a Friends congregation as a meeting house sometime before 1896. Friends School, formed in rooms of a Lombard Street Meeting House in 1849, took over space here in 1899. Property was converted to apartments in 1974.

Built with contributions from the state and from philanthropists Andrew Carnegie and Michael Jenkins, the square-shaped Maryland Institute of Art building on Mount Royal Avenue dates from 1904-1907. Erected by local builder Henry Smith, it was designed by the New York architects Pell and Corbett, recipients of a Chapter of Architects of New York State award. It replaced the Market Street buildings of the Institute, destroyed by the Baltimore Great Fire of 1904.

The two- to three-storied Mount Royal Elementary and Middle School and Recreation Center buildings, distinguished by lighter brick than nineteenth century edifices, date from 1958 and serve neighborhoods north and west. The town houses of Lanvale Close, surrounding a central, landscaped courtyard, were built by the J. Jay Pecora firm and designed by Bolton Hill architects Barker, Courpas and Stauffer, for individual home owners. They displaced several thousand renters. A home owners tennis and swim club was set up on Dolphin Alley in the late 1960s.

Madison

McCulloh from Lanvale to Presstman, Presstman, Madison, North, and a line along Jordan, form Madison's west, north, and east boundaries respectively. Its southern boundary zigzags clockwise from Dolphin and a point east of Eutaw Place along Dolphin, Hoffmann, Eutaw Place, Preston, Madison, and Lanvale. It has seven churches, five private institutional buildings, two schools, and one fire hall.

Blocks south of Laurens, today a mix of contemporary and late nineteenth-century residential architecture, and built on slight hills with a southeastern slope, are site of the first development within Madison or Mount Royal. Houses at the southern edge went up as "suburbs" in the 1840's, homes built away from industrial and commercial streets. Three-storied, twenty-two by forty-eight foot row homes, novel in a city of small row housing for workers, extended along Madison from Biddle. But a grand boulevard, Eutaw Place, launched greater and more elegant home construction from the 1850s to the 1880s. City developer Henry Tiffany acquired twenty-one acres of "Rose Hill," an estate near what is now the site of the Key Monument on Eutaw Place, and owned by John Gibson before the Civil War. Tiffany petitioned the city to erect the boulevard in 1854, as he began to market lots for row-home construction. A 165-foot-wide street with 72-foot promenade in the middle, was built on the path of Gibson Street to Rose Hill. Eutaw Place commemorated the Battle of Eutaw Springs in South Carolina, a patriot victory in the Revolution in which John Eager Howard and the renowned Maryland Line participated. Howard was the eighteenth-century owner of much of the land in the 1818 annex.

Tiffany donated land for the promenade with center gardens and fountains, the street a frank imitation of the Champs Elysee of Paris and a prototype for American landscaped parkways. As monuments were erected, it became the match of other well-known urban boulevards such as Commonwealth Avenue of Boston. Ornate iron railings surrounded five block-long parks built to Wilson by 1876 and maintained by home gardeners. Park statues near Mosher depict the seasons, elderly men facing four directions. The "Children's Fountain," acquired from the Centennial Exposition of Philadelphia (1876), was built between McMechen and Wilson. The Francis Scott Key Monument, three figures and a boat at Lanvale, went up in 1911.

Stately houses, having long vertical lines of neo-classical simplicity but with ornate facades, extended along Eutaw Place to Wilson by 1880, and Laurens by 1905. The hilltop setting of some gave an added sense of height. Homes at street corners and detached estate homes were more ornate with bigger grounds. Private clubs and hotels flourished, the Phoenix, an elegant facility with a largely German Jewish clientele at 1505 Eutaw Place, opening about 1890. The Altamount Hotel at Eutaw and Lanvale, leveled by Urban Renewal in the late 1960s, served a clientage for fox hunts and Pimlico race meets. Italianate houses, with simple lines but decorative cornices, extended up Madison Avenue in the 1870s and 1880s. Rear alleys were generally erected with carriage houses, not servant housing.

The first generation of post-Civil War home owners included very wealthy merchants and manufacturers of the city, among them Hampden textile mill owner William E. Hooper, at Madison and Lafayette. Large enough for live-in servants, and built with vacant rear land rather than alley housing, these homes were living quarters to both "Upstairs" families and "Downstairs" servants. Front rooms were settings for much of the social life of the city elite, except during summer months. Festivities often involved large, extended families. Unmarried adult children often remained home in the middle-class Victorian household, men serving apprenticeships or as clerk assistants in the rapidly expanding businesses of their fathers downtown. Daughters of the wealthy, rarely schooled beyond the private academy, formed an active cadre in volunteer women's organizations also nearby in downtown facilities. Matrons selected home furnishings, planned elaborate entertainment, and chose and supervised servant help.

In an era of extensive household labor, servants, butlers, carriage drivers, yardmen, nurses, cooks and chamber maids made up one-third to one-half the residents. They roomed in basements, rear rooms, or occasionally backyard frame buildings. Adult African-American men drove carriages and waited on tables, helped by sons who maintained rear-yard stables. Black women cooked, laundered, and tended infants. White help, mostly young Irish, and occasionally German, girls—some no older than their mid or early teens—cleaned and polished. (Four floors of mirrors, glass chandeliers, and marble typically bedecked every house.) Families who lived nearby on alley blocks, or

Construction of Eutaw Place, designed as a premier formal plaza, began in 1854.

in city immigrant blocks near Mount Clare yards or East Baltimore's Oldtown, assuaged some of the loneliness of servant life in isolated, quiet urban mansions.

Alleys hidden from the main streets were as bustling as Eutaw Place was placid. Street policemen or Irish and African-American draymen, often brothers or family friends of domestic workers, traveled side and back streets. Errands or shopping drew workers to the outside world and were excuses to linger at markets or gossip on back stoops. Sundays were the servants' time away from work to attend church nearby or spend afternoons with family.

An exodus of the wealthy to new suburbs began in the 1880s, prompting the sale of large town houses to professional men, journalists, lawyers, and especially doctors. Close to east-west streetcar lines which crisscrossed the City, the 900 to 1200 blocks of Madison became known as "Doctor's Row," a prestigious office location. So many new streetcar lines crisscrossed north-south thoroughfares that offices there were accessible to the entire city. First floors were divided into waiting and examining rooms and offices. Top floors of houses on the Row and nearby were converted into spare rooms to rent, especially to students. Woodrow Wilson lived at 1210 Eutaw while a graduate student at Johns Hopkins. Blocks also became the locale of a tiny women's community, young, mostly single women in the professions who spearheaded movements for social reform and turn-of-the-century feminism in Baltimore. M. Carey Thomas, the controversial president of Bryn Mawr College, lived at Madison Avenue and Lanvale Streets, and in the 1880s raised money for the newly opened Johns Hopkins Medical School with the proviso that it enroll female students. Pioneer physician sisters Cora and Flora Brewster kept offices on "Doctor's Row."

A section of Eutaw Place to North was built with a wide carriage path, footways, and grassy plots in 1874. Encouraged by the prestige of Madison as gateway to Druid Hill Park, and by the extension of Eutaw Place, row houses spread over every Madison block north of Laurens between 1875 and 1905. Named the city's seventh historical preservation district in 1977, and sometimes called Madison Park, blocks north of Laurens, with Reservoir Hill blocks between North and Druid Hill Park, encompass Baltimore's grandest urban residential architecture. On Madison, straight-lined Italianate dwellings in the 1800 block yield to palatial structures northward. Eutaw Place homes have the uniformity of scale characteristic of row blocks, but with streetfront facades individualized home to home. Second Empire houses with mansard roofs were built in a group near Madison and Bloom, later called the Kenilworth Apartments, and at six locations beginning at house number 1912 and moving northward. Neo-Georgian brickwork was subsequently superimposed, affording an appearance of stately orderliness. Houses with facades of Queen Anne-Aesthetic and Romanesque styles were built in the 1900 and 2000 blocks of Madison. The former have an asymmetrical design with ornamentation in cut glass, terra cotta, and stone. Rough-hewn stone facings and large rounded arches characterize Romanesque surfaces. Stylized windows of careful workmanship, broad steps and decorative iron railings, door and window arches that match, and touches of brownstone and marble, recur on both Madison and Eutaw Place.

Families of German Jewish descent claimed the northern section of Madison as home before World War I, five synagogues being located within it and close by between 1893 and 1903. The first residents immigrated from downtown areas just as newly immigrating Russian Jews began to populate Jonestown and East Baltimore, home to the first generations of German Jews early in the century. These blocks became "Uptown" in the larger Jewish community, a center of ethnic leadership and a symbol of success. The Hutzler, Fried, Friedenwald, Levy, Moses, and Sonneborn families, headed by department store magnates, garment manufacturers, and civic leaders, built and owned houses. Spacious interiors, with formal as well as "family" parlors and multiple stairways, provided families luxury and live-in servants work. Elegant carriages seen in Druid Hill Park on Sundays were identified as from the neighborhood. The blocks were known to be quiet in summer when whole families—with butlers, maids, and coach and stable men—migrated to country homes in Baltimore County.

The automobile transformed Madison after World War I, professional men following their clients to new suburbs, homes converted into rooming houses and flats, and churches and institutional buildings sold to African-American congregations. Blocks became a burgeoning eastward extension of communities along Pennsylvania Avenue. For flat dwellers, the rented space was often roomier, streets less crowded than the narrow old blocks south and westward. In streetcar and later in bus and auto eras, institutional facilities were accessible to, and drew members beyond, the neighborhood.

African-American families acquired housing in northern blocks after World War I; many were headed by men of community status, notably butlers, caterers, head servants, and supervisors in upper-class clubs, hotels, and estates. Others were newspaper editors, educators, and clergy. Carved into flats during World War II, many houses reverted to individual ownership in the 1970s.

City Temple of Baltimore's congregation (Baptist) organized around first pastor William Payne to form a city ministry. It acquired Eutaw Place Baptist, a spiraling Gothic whitestone at Dolphin and Eutaw Place, in 1969. The edifice was designed in the late 1860s by Thomas Walter, architect for the wings and dome of the United States Capitol.

The three-storied, red-brick Booker T. Washington Junior High (Western High until 1931), at McCulloh and Lafayette, was designed by architect Alfred Mason in 1895 and heavily ornamented with stone and brick. An unusual bell-shaped dome caps one of two large towers.

The four-pillared Douglass Memorial, once Madison Avenue Methodist Episcopal and built on a lot donated by Henry Tiffany, has been an active community institution since the 1920s. It pioneered non-profit, community home rehabilitation in the 1970s, acquiring twelve vacant three- and four-story row homes on 1300 Madison and converting them into apartments with common yard areas for longtime residents.

The elegant Marlborough Apartments (1700 Eutaw Place), erected in 1904 on the location of a nineteenth-century mansion, the Popelein mansion, closed in 1970. Claribel and Etta Cone, friends of Matisse, Picasso, and Gertrude and Leo Stein, once housed their collection of twentieth century art there. The Marlborough re-opened in 1977, with rehabilitated living units for the elderly, funded by Federal grants.

(Overleaf) Spacious row homes, such as these at Eutaw Place and McMechen looking west on McMechen, adorned Eutaw Place and Madison Avenue.

President William Howard Taft was once hosted in the elegant Phoenix Club, organized on Park Avenue, but re-located in the 1500 block of Eutaw Place in the 1890s. An Amalgamated Clothing Workers building now occupies the site.

Allowed by Urban Renewal agencies either to restore or build institutional buildings on Eutaw Place sites north of Mosher Street, the Amalgamated Clothing Workers put up a two-story gray brick and limestone headquarters on the site of the old Phoenix Club in 1963. School 11, Eutaw-Marshburn, south of Wilson, was completed in 1970. Payne Memorial AME, a Sandtown congregation formed in 1883 and named for a denominational bishop, built a contemporary brick church with yard in 1988. It replaced the facility built by the congregation in 1927 on the site of St. John's Independent Methodist Church.

Berea Seventh Day Adventist Church acquired the Madison Avenue Temple, Madison and Robert, in 1951. The Lloyd Street congregation of East Baltimore had put up the temple sixty years before. Red and brown tiles on a dome-shaped roof contrast with the lightness of granite and decorative carvings of sandstone. With huge rounded arches and massive oak doors, and a sanctuary capable of seating one thousand, the building dominates two rows of Madison Avenue.

The "Bottom" to Sugar Hill

"You felt free there. You felt it was for you. Downtown, you couldn't try on a dress but the Avenue was ours and I tell you it was a mighty fine place to go."

"The Avenue was the onliest place we practically could go to any enjoyment, the onliest movie /there/ like everybody else at that time would go to the movies."

Pennsylvania Avenue, elegant town houses on "Droodle" (Druid Hill) Avenue and McCulloh, lawyers' and physicians' offices, fraternal lodges and social clubs, elementary schools and a high school, shops and stores, and a city newspaper, the *Afro-American*. All

Pearl Bailey in a Pennsylvania Avenue theatre dressing room, probably in the 1940s.

these indeed became black people's own during the era of de jure racial segregation within Baltimore, 1910-1960. By World War I, the Westside's oldest, and Baltimore's largest and most heavily populated, African-American neighborhoods stretched one mile along Pennsylvania. The "Bottom," downgrade and lowland south of Dolphin, formed the locale of older nineteenth-century ethnic neighborhoods; "Sugar Hill," the name taken from prestigious real estate close to the famed Harlem of Manhattan, designated extreme northern blocks. The streets of the latter extended on both sides of North Avenue.

Laid out as Reisterstown Turnpike about 1801, Pennsylvania Avenue opened up trade between the wheat farms of Baltimore and Carroll counties and the port of Baltimore. Franklin and Biddle joined the pike to the city. The land along the Avenue was entirely undeveloped until about 1840. Thereafter, residential row housing filled in the countryside in four eras of construction: town houses, mostly narrow two-story brick homes, lined streets and alleys below Dolphin before and during the Civil War; three-story rows were built from Dolphin to North from 1870 to 1900; low- and high-rise public housing replaced rows in southern sections during and after World War II; and Urban Renewal construction, a mix of apartments, homes, commercial buildings and churches, spread west of Division after 1960.

First generations of African Americans along Pennsylvania Avenue mostly descended from a community of free African Americans domiciled in Baltimore before the Civil War, and from the nineteenth-century slave families of rural Maryland and the Upper South.

The black population of all of Maryland constituted an unusual mix in the first half of the nineteenth century. As the slave population of the cotton-producing and Gulf States of the South soared, the numbers of the enslaved in the first state south of the Mason Dixon line steadily declined after 1800. Black freedmen and women in Maryland exceeded the number of every state in the union, north and south, and, at the outbreak of the Civil War, Baltimore numbered 26,000 freed people, more than any other United States city. Free men and women of African descent themselves outnumbered slaves in the city twelve to one, the latter a scant one percent of the city's population in 1860.

The urban community of antebellum freepeople traced its origins to diverse places and circumstances. French-speaking African Americans, slaves and free people from Santo Domingo, emigrated in the decade after 1793, accompanied by planters. The latter escaped rebellion in what was to become the Western hemisphere's first all-black republic. Black aliens formed a tiny urban community near St. Mary's Seminary on Paca Street. Over years, slaves among the Santo Domingoans, as well as native bondspeople in the city, ran away, often escaping to urban alleys and streets near the waterfront. Many moved back and forth between Baltimore and other port villages and cities for several years. Some eventually returned to the city and passed as free.

The slave population of the Southern Gulf states mushroomed as cotton production, spurred by the invention of the inexpensive cotton gin, spread from South Carolina to Texas from 1820 to 1860. Declining prices in the tobacco belt, the stretch of the Upper South from Maryland to North Carolina, prompted a significant minority of slave owners to emancipate slaves there after 1815. The laborers themselves encouraged the manumission process, for they formed a notoriously restless and unruly brand of property. They refused hard work, sabotaged farm equipment, and ran away when owners threatened to sell them to the deep South. Fugitives and the manumitted alike took advantage of the tributaries to the Chesapeake Bay, the York, James, Potomac, and Patuxent rivers. Many eventually made their way to Baltimore.

An anomaly in the antebellum South, city freedmen and women lived a highly precarious existence at the very edge of the system of slavery. State and city statutes alike incorporated black codes which denied them citizenship rights and severely restricted privileges: "freedmen" were barred from public schools, denied the right to vote, forbidden from owning fire arms or testifying against whites, and, if convicted of crime, threatened with sale into slavery. The codes and enforcement actually worsened in the years immediately before the Civil War. Churches shut down and free people were required to carry notorious passes certifying their status. The state even debated bills to re-enslave the manumitted as a bill to abolish "Free-Negroism" was submitted for voter referendum in 1860.

But despite restraints, antebellum freedmen and women struggled successfully for a large measure of independence and autonomy. Black men worked in diverse occupations, as cart drivers, stonecutters, shoemakers, coopers, caulkers, painters, and seamen. Women secured wages as laundresses and domestic workers. Over 130,000 white immigrants from Germany and Ireland, many of them impoverished, arrived in the port of Baltimore between 1820 and 1850. Those who stayed in the city touched off fierce competition with African Americans for jobs, often hiring themselves out for low wages in city industry. All-white unions even petitioned the state legislature to ban industrial black labor. But black craftsmen organized rival labor associations and through stiff resistance protected jobs for many years. Whole trades such as brickmaking, huckstering and stevedore work were monopolized by blacks.

Their labor needed throughout the area, African Americans lived in every section of the city, on side streets, alleys, and main streets, often near places of employment. By 1860, freepeople included men and women who worked steadily, accumulated wealth and property, paid taxes, organized schools, and supported churches and charities. After the Civil War, African Americans native to the city began to secure employment in the burgeoning service trades. More than industrial jobs, service work provided steady and reliable, if modest, incomes. Teachers located jobs in an expanding "colored" school system; clergy built up large congregations in Protestant churches, and caterers, headwaiters, and butlers acquired a monopoly of responsible positions in the homes, hotels, and clubs of wealthy whites. Such employment also guaranteed status and leadership in a growing African-American community, and influence in the city at large. Men joined the city Republican Party, voted in large numbers, and demanded and won representation in the party's citywide organization. By 1890, a share of patronage in city postal and customs services was secured to black men. Collectively, men and women in such enterprises comprised less a "middle" or "upper" class than what black Baltimoreans regarded as a "respectable" stratum. It was a rank of sober, honest stable folk with recognized responsibility. Often the third or fourth generation to have secured a measure of formal education, they were acknowledged leaders in civic, charitable, and religious organizations. Wives in homes of the "respectable" more often managed large households and organized neighborhood charities and civic and reform clubs, than labored for pay out of the home doing work traditionally undertaken by African-American women.

Status notwithstanding, rigid social and political barriers reared themselves at the end of the nineteenth century. Under the pressure of black political participation and leadership, the city and state governments had dismantled the black codes soon after the Civil War. Male suffrage, and the rights to bear arms, serve on juries, and practice law were secured. Black men enrolled in state law and medical schools, and blacks and whites often mingled at racially integrated city theatres, libraries, picnics, political rallies, and civic parades. But white segregationists gained sway in the deep Southern states after 1890, encouraging politicians in rural Maryland to spearhead a movement to re-impose controls. Statewide, proposed amendments to the state constitution nearly disenfranchised black voters through a literacy test requirement and a notorious "Grandfather's Clause." Railroad passenger and steamship facilities to and from Baltimore were segregated. Within the city, theatres confined blacks to galleries, white hotels excluded them, and the new city department stores denied them credit. The Baltimore City Council even enacted a so-called model residential housing statute in 1911. It prohibited sale of property or occupancy of houses in entirely white or entirely African-American blocks to members of the other race. Ten Southern cities passed similar legislation before the Supreme Court declared the Baltimore statute unconstitutional in 1917.

The prominent rank of city African Americans had always included dissenters and protestors, very forceful, outspoken leaders who agitated for suffrage and full civil rights. Protestors secured the removal of Jim Crow railway cars in the 1870s, and demanded educational reform—equal pay for black teachers and equal funding for black schools—in the 1870s and 1880s. But the new threats required deeper commitments and a unified community. And they in turn necessitated sufficient physical space and facilities to promote civil rights—church halls, galleries, meeting rooms, institutional offices, even streets and homes where people could convene with minimal intimidation. Solid blocks of African-American residents spread out among the neighborhoods along the Avenue after 1900.

Streetfront shops and rowhouse flats, leveled by Urban Renewal construction in the 1970s, lined Pennsylvania Avenue south of Dolphin in the heart of the "Bottom." (Courtesy Enoch Pratt Free Library)

Hard times in the tobacco belt spurred a steady migration of ex-slaves and their children to Baltimore after 1880. Emancipation had brought slaves with agricultural skills their freedom but not freedom dues, that is the money, assets, tools, or land like those won by indentured servants of the Colonial era. Postwar conditions seldom opened up new opportunities in rural areas. Sharecropping, an arrangement of workers providing laborers and owners tools and supplies, afforded rural laborers escape from oppressive supervisors and excessive work discipline. But low returns nevertheless perpetuated dependence. Banks and white planters alike were reluctant to extend credit to newly freed farm workers eager for their own land. Consequently, the trickle of "croppers," tenants, and day laborers into Baltimore swelled to a stream by 1900. The city's African-American population jumped from 54,000 to 85,000 between 1880 and 1910.

Job-seekers arrived to face a firmly implanted postwar pattern of white efforts to displace black labor from industrial jobs throughout the city. Leaders among African-American workers formed labor organizations, notably the Colored National Labor Union and the Colored Men's Progressive and Co-operative Union, to persuade industrial employers to hire black workers. East and south Baltimore craftsmen joined the Knights of Labor, a national labor organization committed to enrolling black and white workers. But some Baltimore companies dispensed with union labor entirely, hiring new immigrants from Russia, Poland, Sicily, and

Italy. By 1910, displacement of African Americans from industrial work was greater in Baltimore than in any other Southern city.

Exclusion from industry prodded newcomers and natives alike to relocate away from industrial neighborhoods, blocks which before 1880 were often racially integrated with immigrants from both Europe and the Upper South. Westside blocks close to busy commercial streets, especially Pratt, Baltimore, and Franklin, lured many. There the eager and hard-working secured jobs in the carrying trades, as cart drivers, draymen, and porters, or as street hucksters. Suburbs north and west offered jobs to laundresses, maids, and domestic workers. The new settlement here blended with that of native inhabitants in a cluster of blocks along Orchard and of alleys next to St. Mary's. That older settlement itself had been formed from Santo Domingo migration and from the migration of South Baltimore workers displaced from property acquired by the B and O railroad after the Civil War. After 1880, the in-migration of newcomers touched off expansion into blocks north of Orchard, blocks which became the Pennsylvania Avenue African-American residential district. Those streets extended to Dolphin Street and became known as the "Bottom."

McCulloh Homes

Upton Courts and the McCulloh Homes public housing project spread over twelve city blocks called McCulloh Homes. Terrain slopes gently to the southwest from Madison to a section of the Bottom near Pennsylvania. Clockwise from northeast its boundaries extend on Madison, Preston, McCulloh, King Expressway, Druid Hill, Preston, Pennsylvania, Dolphin, McCulloh, and Lanvale. It is designated by the north-west street once spelled McCulloch Street and named either for an actor, a prominent banker, or a collector of the port of Baltimore. John McCullough was a popular nineteenth century stage performer; James W. McCulloh, a Baltimore Bank-of-the-United-States cashier who figured in the monumental Supreme Court decision of McCulloh v. Maryland; James H. McCulloch, a one-time port officer and veteran of the Revolution and the War of 1812 battle of North Point. Lawn space and courtyards, the latter named for nineteenth-century alleys razed in the 1940s, abut two- and three-story brick apartments. A recreational park is situated at the northeast corner.

Biddle Street first linked Reisterstown Turnpike and the city in the early nineteenth century. Frame and brick houses of farmers and workers dotted Preston, Biddle, and Ross (now Druid Hill) before 1840; early urban housing was not built along Preston, Biddle, and Pennsylvania until the 1850s, and along Dolphin until the 1860s. Eager to market brick row houses to city merchants, developers not only carved up main streets into building lots but built narrow twelve-feet-wide alley homes behind main streets. Both slaves and white and free black servants—drivers, stable men, and domestic workers—lived on a network of back streets,

Little McCulloh, Stoddard, Little Biddle, Pear, Walnut, Tiffany, and Camel. By 1860, narrow fifteen-feet-wide row houses extended also on east-west streets, throughways wider than alleys but narrower than north-west streets. Three-story houses were built on Ross and McCulloh, brick and frame shanties in rear alleys.

Craft-workers, wagon drivers, and household domestic workers of recent German descent first inhabited the alleys and east-west streets. An ethnic Lutheran Church, St. John's on Biddle between Pennsylvania and Ross, served the community for many years. Merchants, bankers, and lawyers settled along McCulloh, which acquired local renown as home to Confederate sympathizers during the Civil War. Levi Stratton White, a notorious Confederate agent, later enlivened Baltimore lore with tales of his McCulloh home located between Biddle and Preston during the War. He published memoirs which claimed he had smuggled munitions into the South from his house. He had hidden in its secret compartments when Federal troops stormed McCulloh in search of Confederates.

Old houses were turned over to student and faculty boarders in the 1880s, blocks occasionally designated as Baltimore's Latin Quarter. Johns Hopkins, the Women's Medical College, City College, and Western High School were all located nearby. In-migration changed blocks again after 1900, African Americans moving onto main streets. The grid of streets and alleys was densely populated by a heterogenous mix of property owners and flat dwellers, workers, and professional people. Institutions followed and encircled the blocks of residences. A home for delinquent or orphaned boys, St. Mary's Episcopal, opened on Biddle near Provident Hospital, which located a thirty-five bed, black-staffed facility there in 1895. An African Methodist Episcopal chapel was built on Biddle Alley, and Grace Presbyterian Church opened on Dolphin. Taverns and a theatre, the Lincoln #2, opened on Pennsylvania Avenue in the 1910s, southern end of the Avenue entertainment district. Small black-operated businesses took over the streetfront rooms of Druid Hill town homes. The narrow, crowded houses of Biddle Alley, just east of Homes, were the subject of two studies of urban conditions that won local renown, a city poverty commission publishing the first in 1907 and the Urban League the second in 1926. Despite the cleanliness of housing units, the reports alleged, the high rent block called "Lung Block" bred disease, especially tuberculosis.

The Baltimore Housing Authority, formed to implement the National Housing Act of 1937, designated twenty-one acres as an African-American public housing project in 1939. Built east of Druid Hill by the Rosoff Company of New York, 436 units of two- or three-story brick buildings were finished in the early 1940s. Twenty-nine buildings spread over five blocks. Statuary of two children with book and harmonica bedecked a McCulloh Street entry; project courtyards took the names of old alleys and streets.

Demolition touched off emigration, and public housing rules established a pattern of rapid in-out mobility for twenty years. Old housing was leveled over one year before the projects were ready; wage increases by tenants, all one- and two-parent families until 1956, obligated them to move. Single and elderly people moved in during the 1960s. The remaining nineteenth-century housing west of Druid Hill was razed in the 1970s, replaced with Upton Courts, a mostly low-rise development architecturally compatible with the public housing.

Murphy Homes

Clockwise east to west, Argyle, King Expressway, Franklin, Fremont, George, Brune, Harlem, Myrtle, and Hoffman bound Murphy Homes. Named for civic leader George B. Murphy, son of a long-time *Afro-American* editor and a member of the city housing commission, Homes includes four fourteen-story high-rise public projects, fourteen two-story projects, and a low-rise elementary school, #30 George Street, all constructed after 1963. Park and playground land spreads over a quarter of the acreage.

Chatsworth Run, a stream near present-day Argyle that flowed into the Middle Branch, formed a natural boundary to settlement before the Civil War, when Bottom blocks eastward were first built up. But in the 1870s building and savings associations acquired estate land, the Run was filled in, and the entire neighborhood marketed as a streetcar suburb. It was regarded as apart from the bustling Mount Clare industrial district but accessible to it and to downtown. Three-story, streetfront row houses lined main streets, shanties and servant housing five narrow alleys. Baptist, Presbyterian, and United Brethren congregations all built large churches.

African Americans moved into main street housing after 1900, the new Fremont streetcar line making the area accessible to north Baltimore and downtown work places. Perkins Square Baptist Church opened on the Square; St. Barnabas Episcopal, next to the Homes on Argyle, became St. Barnabas Roman Catholic in 1907. During World War II, the blocks' population soared with the displaced of nearby housing projects. The Baltimore Urban Renewal and Housing Agency acquired

An extant decorative pagoda sits on Perkins Square, post-Civil War park formed from acreage of the "Chatsworth" estate.

real estate and constructed high rises in 1963; security guard stations with closed monitors were installed in 1973.

Homes were both the site and focus of many tenants' rights organizing projects, including rent strikes. Tenants, and Baltimore Welfare Rights and Jobs with Peace associations, lobbied for improved services and security. Among the last high-rise public housing units built in the city, the buildings found older single tenants replacing young families in the early 1980s. Perkins Square juts out at the Homes' southeastern corner, a triangular patch of green on one-and-two-tenths acres. It opened in 1872 at the behest of early home buyers. They petitioned the city to lease land next to a spring, once part of the Chatsworth estate, and now covered at the southeast corner with an eight-post Victorian pagoda with iron Moorish-design canopy. Leased from landowner Dr. Joseph Perkins, the park became an oasis in the middle of development, spring water allegedly bubbling at the rate of sixty gallons a minute and having medicinal value. A city groundskeeper housed on the Square replenished shrubbery and flowers from an adjacent greenhouse for many years.

Upton

Shaped like a Christmas tree, Upton has zigzag boundaries which extend clockwise from Dolphin and Pennsylvania along Pennsylvania, Preston, Druid Hill, Biddle, Argyle, Hoffman, Myrtle, Harlem, Brune, George, Fremont, Bloom, Division, Lafayette, McCulloh, and Dolphin. It takes its name from an extant Greek Revival country house on a Lanvale Street hilltop, built before the Civil War. Its original ornate iron work and brick walls still intact, Upton was once the property of United States Senator David Stewart, a wealthy Baltimore lawyer and vice president of St. John's College during the Civil War. Stewart's son, Charles Morton Stewart, owned a fleet of Baltimore clipper ships that could be seen from the upper veranda of the mansion. It has housed a school for special education since 1958.

Nine blocks of street space along the Bottom, developed before the Civil War when housing went up in McCulloh Homes, became a residential section for African Americans in the 1890s. With neighborhoods east and south, they formed the most expansive, densely populated African-American section of the city. Fifty-four blocks north of Dolphin and Argyle, streets which mark the beginning of a northwestern upgrade, were developed out of the Upton and Chatsworth estates. Chatsworth was the eighteenth-century property of Anne Arundel County physician George Walker acquired in 1715. During the Revolution, wealthy city rope manufacturer William Lux once hosted delegates to the Second Continental Congress there.

On terrain too steep to make commuting by omnibuses practical, horse-drawn trolley lines prompted development of a somewhat isolated post-Civil War suburb beyond Dolphin. Built close to country farms and old dairies, markets, and industries on Pennsylvania, houses extended to McMechen by the 1870s and to Bloom twenty years later. New streets were laid out, the north-south thoroughfare Etting named for Solomon Etting, local landowner and City Councilman. Hilltop houses lay close enough (one mile) to Baltimore for men to commute twice daily, but too far for short frequent trips, or for children or spouses to make regular use of older city facilities. Institutions for a distinctly neighborhood patronage therefore went up next to new residential housing within Upton. By 1884, towering Gothic graystone churches of Protestant and Roman Catholic denominations, a city market (Lafayette), a library (the first suburban branch of Enoch Pratt), public schools, a fire and police station (Northwestern), and a passenger station of the Baltimore and Potomac Railway, were built on and close to Pennsylvania.

Houses of African Americans along the "Bottom" sat on a honeycomb of springs and the buried path of the Chatsworth stream and tributaries. As whites began an exodus northward beyond Upton into the new city annex after 1890, African Americans began to buy homes on the higher elevation. They moved along Etting, Druid Hill, and east-west blocks in the 1890s, along Argyle to Fremont after 1900, and along McCulloh and throughout the Pennsylvania-Fremont corridor before World War I. By 1917 residences from Dolphin to Bloom, and McCulloh to Fremont, were home to a majority of the city's African-American property owners and most of its teachers, clergy, government workers, and shopkeepers.

Mobility into premier city housing sparked controversy with whites and episodes of violence. When Myrtle Street changed, a white street mob broke the windows of a new doctor's home. On Lanvale Street a crowd barred a black family from moving into a row house. In 1910, Yale-educated attorney George W. F. McMechen moved from a Presstman Street house to 1834 McCulloh, boundary of the fashionable Madison section. The move prompted protest from residents nearby, mass meetings of Westside whites, including white Upton churches, protesting black "encroachment." The City Council even debated bills to prohibit African-American schools and churches on predominantly white blocks.

An island for the relatively privileged next to affluent white neighborhoods and working class black ones, Upton in fact afforded new African-American residents inescapable reminders of discrimination. All-white institutions, such as Western High School for girls, bordered it until the buildings were re-designated Booker T. Washington Junior High in 1929. When large downtown department stores instituted discrimination before World War I, shops on Pennsylvania, known as Baltimore's Lennox Avenue (Harlem), provided an alternative. There, apparel could be tried on, small shops ordered clothing by mail, and clerks extended courtesies deemed improper for "colored" in downtown stores. But neighborhood patronage notwithstanding, these stores were staffed with whites. Entertainer Cab Calloway, reared in Upton, remembers that his step-father sold life insurance at home because his downtown company would provide no offices to black agents. Supreme Court Justice Thurgood Marshall, raised on Division Street, was once arrested in Upton. A delivery boy for a white merchant, he scuffled with whites on neighborhood trolleys.

But residence in Upton also stirred pride and confidence. For the "respectable" stratum of city African Americans, residence beyond the "Bottom" in Upton a scant two generations after emancipation and the notorious black codes marked financial success. And it signified very rapid progress, movement not just toward equality, but to exceptional attainment and accomplishment. Built atop gentle slopes, three-story homes towered over both the "Bottom," and the busy east-west commercial blocks and working-class housing of Poppleton, Mount Clare and the center city. Much of the housing was put up by German-born builder Joseph Cone, who also erected Harlem Park homes. Rows here lacked the elegance and grand scale of the best houses in Mount Royal, but exteriors nevertheless displayed refinement. Brick work was attractively corbelled, cornices were decorative and window trim stylized and ornate. Houses with porticos had fluted columns, while wrought iron and patches of green space, especially along Druid Hill and McCulloh, advertised housing as expensive. Grand homes on the corners had bow-shaped fronts, some with double wooded conical roof towers. These blocks were exceptionally clean and healthy. Here more than elsewhere in segregated Baltimore, African-American housing escaped the city's notorious open sewers, which flowed along alleys and even flooded flat sections before Baltimore's underground sewer system was finished in 1914.

Community leaders heralded home ownership in the Westside. Booker T. Washington once claimed that the "comfortable and attractive" housing owned by Baltimore "coloured" exceeded that of other American cities. Yet fewer than three percent of city African Americans purchased houses, and as late as 1910, according to the Federal census, home ownership lagged behind that of other cities. But property ownership was a treasured symbol in the community. Children and grandchildren of first owners held on to the family property, or acquired their own in what remained an exceptionally stable community until World War II. Improvements over the years reflected pride in ownership; innovations such as electricity, cemented cellars, and rear yard garages were added here as quickly as elsewhere.

Serving a citywide clientele, and also a sign of race advancement, professional offices, businesses, and public and private institutions—many of these last old venerable city institutions—located in Upton. They took over the first floors of large town houses while a few erected their own facilities. Fifteen doctors and lawyers offices stretched along five blocks of Druid Hill by 1916. One year later the Grand Lodge of Masons, formed from city lodges which dated from 1825, opened headquarters at McCulloh and Mosher, its annual conventions drawing many members to the neighborhood. A Colored branch of the city YMCA, organized by clergy and civil rights activists in 1885, moved to Druid Hill and McMechen in 1910, and built its four-story, neo-classical edifice at 1619 Druid Hill in 1918. It housed a dormitory and swimming pool for African Americans and operated an employment service for young people. Before World War I, the Y acquired Camp Druid Hill, a 286 acre tract on the Patuxent River for summer programs for Baltimore youth. An annex with gymnasium was completed in 1949.

Charities were represented by institutions for orphans and the elderly infirm, including the Maryland Baptist Orphanage (McMechen), St. Katherine's Home for Little Colored Girls (Episcopal, Druid Hill) and St. Mary's Home for Colored Boys (Episcopal, Biddle), all established before World War I. Provident Hospital moved from a Biddle Street row house to a 130 bed facility of the Union Protestant Infirmary (white) in 1928, establishing the city's only nurses training program for African Americans. Argyle headquartered the colored branch of the city's public baths, established before World War I, and McCulloh, at 1398, the Walter Greene Post of the American Legion organized in 1919.

Civic betterment clubs often met in institutional facilities or in the private homes of Upton. Before World War I, they provided space to chapters of the Colored Women's Suffrage and DuBois Clubs, which sponsored educational programs, and to day nursery and neighborhood improvement associations. A "Colored Law and Order League" and the Urban League, during the 1920s, took up the causes of the blocks along the Bottom—proliferation of white licensed taverns near neighborhood schools in Bottom blocks, spread of tuberculosis along narrow, dark streets, and a shortage of beds in segregated hospitals.

Public schools in the neighborhood, all facilities taken over from whites, were renamed and put to new uses. The city's only black high school was first housed in an elementary school facility opened for German immigrants, but relocated at Pennsylvania and Dolphin. New names reflected consciousness of race advancement. John Hurst Elementary, named for the Haitian-born missionary and bishop of the African Methodist Episcopal Church, took over a school at Pennsylvania and Robert; Henry Highland Garnett Elementary, the city's only so-called model school providing training for African-American teachers, opened on Division and was named for a Maryland-born anti-slavery agitator and minister to Liberia; Henry Winter Davis Elementary at Pennsylvania and Dolphin was named for the Annapolis lawyer and senator who authored the slavery abolition provision of the state's 1864 constitution.

Public events in Upton often imparted a national or even international flavor. Churches convened conventions of delegates from across the country. Fraternal orders, barred from segregated facilities downtown, met in neighborhood halls and paraded in Upton streets. Race leaders, like Booker T. Washington, W. E. B. DuBois, and Marcus Garvey, spoke frequently from church pulpits, and visiting Liberians and other black Africans were hosted at crowded public events. In the 1920s, the black-owned Deaver Smith Tea Company began to sell African goods in a Pennsylvania Avenue shop.

African-American civic institutions with city-wide patronages kept facilities in Upton or Druid Heights. St. Katherine's Orphanage, sponsored by St. Katherine of Alexandria Episcopal Church, was located on Druid Hill Avenue. (Courtesy Enoch Pratt Free Library)

Provident Hospital, chartered in 1894 and with facilities in the "Bottom," kept a 130 bed facility on the 1500 block of Division Street after 1927. (Courtesy University of Maryland Baltimore County)

Neighborhood African Americans contributed to the growing political base of city blacks after 1890. They did so even as the city-wide Republican organization sought to isolate African Americans within the Party, and as Democrats gerrymandered them out of influence in all-white wards. Lawyer Henry S. Cummings won election as Baltimore's first African-American city councilman in 1890, elected in the eleventh ward with Orchard street and Upton precincts. Also the first black elected official in the state, Cummings paved the way for a physician, John M. Cargill, and customs collector Hiram Watty, both Republicans, who with Cummings represented the neighborhood all but two years from 1895 to 1931. The Council's only African Americans for four decades, they exerted influence on educational matters, such as equalizing salaries and expanding the high-school system.

Like city African Americans elsewhere, voters here switched to the Democratic Party during the New Deal era and 1940s; Upton was the locus of a community effort to restore African-American representation on the City Council and win it in the General Assembly during the 1950s. Grand Masons required each member to secure the registration of five voters. Voter registration projects operated out of Pennsylvania Avenue shops as the "Women Power" project, a campaign of a thousand volunteers, toured churches in the heart of the Fourth Legislative District.

Early civil rights agitation centered in Upton. Nineteenth-century militants, many of them clergymen and lawyers of national renown, joined the emigration from downtown blocks, Dr. Harvey Johnson the most famous among them. A founder of the Brotherhood of Liberty, forerunner to the National Association for the Advancement of Colored People, Johnson and Ashbie Hawkins, principal of Douglass High School, organized a national race betterment movement in 1902. They helped start the Niagara movement that paved the way for the NAACP. (The Baltimore chapter of the NAACP, second oldest in the country, met in Upton.) Johnson declined white financial assistance for his church, determined that it be entirely black run, and acquired a reputation for demanding equality within his denomination. He once wrote, "There must be shown to the Negro ministry the same recognition and respect; her ministers must not be just humored and tolerated, they must be respected and appreciated with absolute equality." Johnson's Union Baptist Church moved to Druid Hill Avenue in 1905.

(OVERLEAF - LEFT) Aided by city philanthropist William Walters, Baltimore established neighborhood public bath houses before World War I. Neighborhood women did laundry at the designated "colored" bath located in the 1000 block of Argyle Avenue in 1910.

(OVERLEAF - RIGHT) An annex to the Druid Hill YMCA was dedicated in 1949.

Johnson was a power in the Ministerial, later Interdenominational Ministerial, Alliance which, while a city-wide organization, was often headed by Upton clergy and met in Upton churches. In turn-of-the-century years, it, and the neighborhood-based Maryland Suffrage League, organized petition drives, sponsored boycotts, and sent delegates to Annapolis to protest segregation. Before World War I, the Alliance collected money, printed and distributed literature, and urged black men to register to vote. Protests over segregated facilities on steamships, long patronized by large congregations for outings and excursions, prompted companies to advertise their opposition to segregation in the *Afro-American Ledger*.

The Urban League maintained an Upton office in the 1930s, and new civil rights organizations and neighborhood churches agitated for job opportunities during the Great Depression. Young people organized the City-Wide Young People's Forum, which organized boycotts along the Avenue ("Don't buy Where you Can't Work campaigns") and won clerical jobs for Douglass High School graduates. Shipyard and steel workers were urged to join labor unions at rallies at Sharp Street Methodist and Bethel AME, the Ministerial Alliance endorsing the new militant CIO unions pledged to build bi-racial unions in the city. Five hundred Baltimoreans organized at the Druid Hill Y in 1942 to participate in A. Philip Randolph's March on Washington, protesting discrimination in defense industries.

The "Avenoo" (Pennsylvania) added to the renown of Upton between the two World Wars. Famed as an entertainment district, it was a lively stretch of department stores and specialty shops crowded with shoppers from out of town. Country relatives were met at the Pennsylvania Avenue commuter station, as women packed in a day of shopping and visited together, while men kept long awaited appointments at neighborhood offices or lodges. Halloween parades for children, and a grand Easter parade for whole families, attracted hundreds. The band-led marches of Elks and Masons drew thousands. But at night the Avenue pulsated with different sounds. Loud brass blared from clubs and cabarets; long queues formed under brightly lit marquees. The revelry of crowds spilled from sidewalks into the street. South of Dolphin, two theaters, taverns, dance halls, and brothels were crowded among pawn shops and second-hand stores. Notorious city-wide, this stretch of the Avenue was "so bad, the birds sang bass," remembers one old timer. East Baltimore ragtime artist Eubie Blake performed his vaudeville debut here at the Lincoln in the 1000 block of Pennsylvania, before World War I.

Larger theatres, night clubs, restaurants, and hotels dotted the blocks northward, the Regent and the Royal Theatres dominating the 1600 and 1300 blocks respectively. First opened in 1916, the Regent was rebuilt in a still extant structure in 1920 alleged to seat over 2,000 patrons in a vaudeville and movie house. Show time won fame for musical and dance revues. It featured chorus lines in flamboyant dress stretched across the stage, tap, soft-shoe and jazz dance numbers in succession, and the big bands of the 1920s and 1930s dressed in tuxedo black. The smaller, 1,400 patron capacity Royal replaced the black-owned Douglass Theatre in

1926. It featured the city's first talkie, the black-cast motion picture "Scar of Shame" in 1929, but live entertainment won it its greatest fame. Billed as the Baltimore Appollo (Harlem's spectacular showplace), it was one on a circuit of five theatres in segregated districts of big cities. The so-called TOBA, "Theatre Owners Booking Agency," regarded by entertainers as "Tough on Black Artists / or Asses/" booked it. Patrons packed the Royal for nationally renowned artists and rising stars. Crooner Ethel Waters made her debut at the Royal, Pearl Bailey once sang in a chorus line, Louis Armstrong and Fats Waller worked as accompanists, and Billie Holiday, Ella Fitzgerald, and Earl "Fatha" Hines drew sell-out crowds in the later 1930s and early 1940s. Nat King Cole, the Platters, the Temptations, and the Supremes all performed there before it closed in 1970. Pearl Bailey remembers, "The first time I played the Royal in Baltimore, I rushed out front to see my name on the billboard after the first show." The Royal was razed in 1971 for urban renewal construction.

Smaller cabarets, night clubs, and ball rooms also lined Avenue blocks for half a century after World War I. Perry's Inn and Gamby's stirred race pride in the 1920s, for the novel New Orleans brass sounds, played in African Americans' own neighborhoods, soon rivaled prewar ragtime and the reed jazz of whites popular in the city before the War. Jazz revues featured six or more bands at the New Albert, the Savoy, named for New York's famous Savoy ballroom, and the Strand, located next to the Royal. Jazz drummer Ike Dixon, founder of a traveling jazz band in 1920, opened his comedy club in 1934 at 1440 Pennsylvania Avenue. Royal stars gathered there after show time and bit players tried new acts or "jammed" during afternoons before show time.

Clubs afforded relief for young people—escape from the rigid work roles in places of employment and from the home environment of the respectable classes of Upton. The uniform of redcaps, waiters, butlers, and maids, or the formal dress for dinner, was entirely forsaken. Patrons displayed the attire of choice in an informal setting of food, drink, and dance. Fantasies of the young were stirred at Avenue showplaces, where live matinees and even auditions on Saturday afternoons introduced children to the world of entertainment. A few dreams came true. As Blanche Calloway played the lead in the Royal's production of "Plantation Days," in 1927, a revue with an Old South theme, brother Cab auditioned for a tenor vacancy. From a slot on the traveling circuit, he won stardom at Harlem's Cotton Club, launching a career of singing and writing Dixieland and blues. It culminated in the 1950 revival of "Porgy and Bess."

A monument to African-American artistic achievement, Avenue establishments nevertheless carried costs. As segregation confined the respectable stratum and humble folk alike to housing close by, and as residential covenants, widely attached to new housing in the 1920s and 1930s, reinforced confinement, the Avenue's heavy drinking, loud noises, and exotic temptations were only doorsteps away. That the church going elderly and peddlers of "hot" goods alike, were housed in the same blocks encouraged parents to be solicitous and the young to experiment. Cab Calloway recalled an Upton childhood.

> *"One year I was spending three or four hours in church every Sunday plus Bible classes during the week, Bible school every day during the summer, and singing in the junior choir, and the next I was part of a gang of guys who were basically young hustlers. . . . I guess I grew up quickly. . . . On the one hand, my family and my music teachers, whom I loved and respected, were rather puritanical people: churchgoing, middle class, strivers. On the other hand, I spent a lot of my time in that rough and raucous Baltimore Negro night life with loud music, heavy drinking, and the kind of moral standards . . . that my parents looked down on. I managed pretty well in both."*

The residential covenants, and jobs in defense industries that dramatically increased Baltimore's African-American population during World War II, swelled Upton's population. Homes were divided and subdivided and Saturday night crowds along the Avenue soared to 20,000 and 25,000. Sailors and soldiers from nearby military installations added to the patronage. But an exodus of perhaps thirty percent from 1950 to 1970, and Urban Renewal projects thereafter, wrought lasting changes. The neighborhood-based Upton Planning Committee and the city Department of Housing and Community Development secured Federal approval in the early 1970s to designate 168 single street blocks from Pitcher to George, including much of Upton west of Etting, as the City's largest Urban Renewal area. Fifty percent of projected new construction was never completed, but playgrounds, low-rise housing, markets and churches spread over fourteen square blocks by 1982. Most of it went up west of Pennsylvania, a new post office and multi-purpose recreation center built next to old shops in the Avenue's northern blocks.

Renewal encouraged development by non-profit institutions; Greenwillow, Boone Manor, and the seventeen story Zion Towers were built in the southern blocks. Erected through provisions of the Federal Housing Act of 1968, which provided mortgage interest subsidies to non-profit sponsors, Greenwillow Manor was instigated by Mount Royal and Upton churches and built by Rouse-Waites Co., a Rouse Company subsidiary. Along the un-razed east, the 400 block of Mosher and 1500 blocks of Druid Hill and McCulloh were declared historic and architectural preservation blocks in 1985.

Upton's large Protestant churches form the most visible reminders of a century of neighborhood history. They range from century-old edifices built by African-American congregations; fashionable Gothic graystones acquired from white congregations; other landmark buildings converted to use by new postwar evangelical denominations; to modern brick churches which went up with Urban Renewal housing. Together they recall the rich traditions of African-American religion in an urban setting. Spiraling over new and old housing, they molded distinctly heterogeneous congregations--janitors and bankers, public housing and home-owned town house residents in the same pew--unified by faith and ethnic experience. They form reminders of the exceptional vitality and leadership within and beyond the neighborhood.

The oldest congregations originated in older parts of the city. Methodists, dissatisfied with worship in a white city church, founded Sharp Street Methodist Episcopal in south Baltimore at Sharp and Pratt soon after the American Methodist movement separated from the Anglican faith in Baltimore, after the Revolution. The congregation operated a church and school until the 1880s when cramped quarters prompted it to buy a lot and build a church at Dolphin and Etting in 1896. Made of light Woodstock granite laid according to a perpendicular Gothic design, it was built with gables on each of four faces. It houses a circular gallery seating 500 which, in Protestant fashion, allowed maximum vision of preacher to pew sitter. It is Baltimore's oldest church built by and for African Americans.

Union Baptist, organized on Lewis Street in 1852, moved from a sanctuary on North Street (downtown) into a new $50,000 structure at 1219 Druid Hill in 1905. Sponsor of ten Baptist missions and churches in Baltimore and Carroll and Frederick counties, it bought adjacent land and housing for Sunday School and service work in 1921 and 1940, facilities provided for day care and counselling, as well as a coffee house and secondhand store in recent decades. Union assumed denominational leadership through the presidency of pastor Vernon Dobson in the Baptist Alliance, and with the headquarters of the Union Baptist Ministries Convention and Auxiliaries located nearby at Mosher and McCulloh.

Bethel AME dates from the 1780s and purchased fashionable St. Peter's Episcopal on Druid Hill in 1911. First convened on the city's outskirts, Fish (or Saratoga) Street in 1785, it affiliated with the new AME (African Methodist Episcopal) denomination in 1816, and built a new church building on Saratoga in 1848. Street widening prompted a move to the northwest. Its new edifice was regarded as one of the city's most elegant nineteenth-century Gothic churches. Built of white marble in the style of Norman Gothic, it had a vast five-storied bell tower capped by a high towering octagonal conical spire. The spire was visible from east and south Baltimore. Known as the "church of bishops" (for pastors who assumed leadership in the international denomination), Bethel has had congregations that dwindled (between the World Wars) but expanded and revitalized in the 1960s and 1970s. Unused galleries reopened then to a congregation of several thousand, and a host of educational, musical, and outreach activities were sponsored.

Organized by members of Union Baptist in 1874, Macedonia Baptist was first housed in a stable loft on Vincent near Saratoga and in two separate small churches at Saratoga and Gilmore streets. A congregation of over one thousand purchased the graystone on a hill at Fremont and Lafayette in 1925. A large gallery and a ceiling thought to be one of the highest in the city lent a sense of grandeur.

Newer denominations in older facilities are represented by the Spirit of Truth Church of God in Christ, which refurbished the Enoch Pratt branch at Pitcher and Fremont in 1974; new church architecture by Providence Baptist, Pennsylvania AME, and Immaculate Conception Roman Catholic. Founded in 1928 at Edmondson and Fremont, Providence built one of the city's few solar-heated edifices, a

500-seat brick sanctuary in 1976. Rooftop glass panels caught the sun and collected heat then blown through rock bins. Designed with tower by local architect Peter Powell, it incorporated stained glass from the older church and was built on Lafayette, next to the old Diane theatre used by the church as a service building. Pennsylvania AME Zion's new building went up in 1977; the new Immaculate Conception was built of white stucco in curved forms designed by Ferdinand Kelly in 1972.

More than elsewhere, church congregations in Upton promoted the black consciousness movements of the 1960s and 1970s. New Shiloh, set up in 1902 on George and occupying a stately Lanvale Street edifice since 1926, acquired fame for revival and gospel tent services, and mass baptisms at Druid Hill Park lake until the 1970s. Biblical murals were then replaced with "Pilgrimage, in Word, Song, and Prayer," an elaborate mural which depicted the separation of American slave families, singing bondspeople, and migration to the North. Bethel kept alive a Pan-African movement, hosting African ambassadors, sponsoring educational programs, and agitating against South African apartheid.

Other institutions and a landmark monument likewise mirror a century of Baltimore African-American heritage. Three schools, Samuel Coleridge-Taylor, Joseph Lockerman, and Furman Templeton, are named for a composer of European-African descent whose works have been widely sung in Baltimore, a prominent educator, and civic leader, respectively. East Baltimore-born "Lady Day," Billie Holiday, is commemorated with an eight-and-one-half foot bronze statue, arms characteristically outstretched toward an audience, sculpted by James Earl Reid, in a city mini-park, at Lafayette and Pennsylvania. It was built footsteps from the clubs and theatres where haunting melodies and an unusual vocal stylization made her a legend.

Druid Heights

Druid Heights' boundaries extend clockwise from North and Madison Avenues along Madison, Presstman, McCulloh, Laurens, Division, Bloom, Pennsylvania, and North. Before development, southern blocks formed part of Chatsworth, northern blocks a section of Hap Hazard, eighteenth- and nineteenth-century property of the Lawson family that extended to Druid Hill Park. Alexander Lawson Sr., Baltimore county iron master and one-time manager of the Nottingham Iron Works, acquired it in 1741. His Oxford-educated son, Lawson Jr., once served as clerk of Baltimore County. A stream, Spicer's Run, once ran between Druid Hill and Division to Laurens and thence eastward.

Distant from markets, schools, and churches in the era of the horse-drawn trolley, Druid Heights developed with the northern blocks of Upton but with fewer public and private institutions. Residential development extended gradually across twenty-eight blocks from 1870 to 1900. A city railway company kept stables and passenger car repair shops along the city boundary at Cumberland from the 1870s to World War I. Two chapels, St. Bartholomew's Episcopal, and Ames Methodist Episcopal on Division Street between Gold and Baker Streets, served rural congregations, the latter Baltimore County African Americans. In the 1880s developers built smaller two-story Italianate houses along Division and Etting and east of Pennsylvania north of Bloom; in the 1890s, ornate, grander houses in northeastern blocks were erected as housing went up in Madison North. When trolley repair shops were torn down in the 1920s, modern, shallow-depth row housing, with front porches, was introduced along Cumberland. Two commercial stretches of shops and stores, eight blocks along Pennsylvania and North Avenues, have capped Druid Heights at the northwest edge ever since.

Heights blocks were first populated by affluent whites, but electrified trolleys encouraged both out-migration and the extension of Upton as a largely but not exclusively African-American residential section. Shopkeepers' families, many second-generation Greeks, Russian Jews, and Chinese, moved in atop street-corner laundry and grocery stores, and on Pennsylvania Avenue. But with no large markets or schools and few churches in the neighborhood, and with a North Avenue commercial district which catered to a white clientele, residents relied heavily on trolleys and patronized Upton and downtown institutions. Three lines ran north and south, an all-night line east and west, with every neighborhood block within two blocks of a car line. Tenants replaced homeowners in most residential property between 1960 and 1980.

These blocks contain two old churches and one new branch library and post office. St. Katherine's of Alexandria Episcopal, organized as a "colored" mission of Mount Calvary, moved into a stone, brick, and wooden chapel at Division and Presstman in 1911, a building which had been built for the white congregation of St. George Episcopal in 1882. The congregation was accorded parish status in 1975. Its rector and congregation spearheaded formation of the Druid Heights Community Association which met at the Church in the mid-1970s. Madison Avenue Presbyterian, the oldest black Presbyterian Church in the city, relocated in an edifice built by the Evangelical Lutheran Church of the Incarnation in 1927. Begun by blacks who refused segregated worship in the congregation of First Presbyterian, and headed by clergymen active in freedmen's aid work, the church was formed on Madison Street near Park about 1848.

Enoch Pratt's Pennsylvania Avenue branch, one of the city's largest, opened in 1953 and was designed by architects Smith and Veale. It featured innovations in library design. Glass panels made up the two-story wall on the entry sides, thereby maximizing natural light and making books and readers visible from the street in order to lure patrons. Fire Engine House #25 was opened as a suburban station for horse-drawn vehicles and equipment on Druid Hill next to North in 1903.

This structure was the entrance to the south side of Druid Hill Park c. 1910.

Along Pratt Street

Outside stalls of Hollins Market next to Hollins Hall, second floor of the market building. Hollins Hall was setting to Westside political rallies, community dances and recreation, and briefly, an armory and temporary home of the Maryland Institute of Art.

Steel, iron, and shipbuilding, Baltimore's heavy industries, have long identified eastern and southern parts of Baltimore as the city's industrial sectors. But blocks with industry on and off Pratt Street west of Poppleton, intermixed among residences, actually antedate them by decades. Sights, sounds, and smells of slaughterhouses, factories, and warehouses long exuded a peculiar mix. Grunts and squeaks from the stockyards, the clop clop of horse and wagon on cobblestones, and plant whistles at noontime blended with the waft of factory odors from the mid-nineteenth to mid-twentieth centuries. Here, a mix of industrial and home architecture forms an exception to the Baltimore pattern of geographic segmentation into distinctly residential or commercial-industrial districts.

Development along the Pratt and Frederick Avenue corridor first went up directly on the east-west thoroughfares as industries took advantage of arteries that stretched west into rural Maryland and east into the city. Frederick Road extended as a dusty trail out of Baltimore town before the Revolution. Farmers emigrating to the West, and probably even Native Americans, traveled it. A turnpike opened on its path about 1804. The first and short leg of the Baltimore and Ohio Railroad trunk line to the West was built to the Gwynns Falls in 1832, soon after the Road was chartered. Wilkens Avenue, opened in the nineteenth century, became a busy southwest artery after World War I.

Before 1800, working-class settlements of American cities often sprang up not in the heart of the tiny metropolises but beyond city borders close by. They were often built on streams or rivers. The Gywnns Falls and Frederick Road gave rise to such an early settlement beyond Baltimore and at the juncture of the stream and road on the edge of presentday Mill Hill. Stone and frame houses went up for millers and craftsmen and their families. Wheelwrights, drivers, repairmen, and tavern and inn keepers who served the busy traffic of wagons along the Road, lived close by, east of the Falls. No traces of this first settlement survive.

Railroad yards and related industries south of Pratt along Parkin and Scott spawned a far larger settlement on streets and alleys between Fremont and Carey and north of Pratt two decades before the Civil War. Before trolley lines were laid, the terrain here was more accessible to the city than hilly land west and north. Narrow and very shallow row houses, often irregularly aligned, were built on low flat land. Ten to thirteen feet wide with three to five rooms, the buildings stood one-and-one-half to two-and-one-half stories high. They went up over dirt cellars, often damp or flooded by storms and showers. A small dormer from a pitched roof, or a pair of tiny windows extending from an attic, fronted on the street. Privies and small sheds often lined tiny back yards.

Households of white and of African-American workers, often individual families with adult relatives and boarders, occupied the small houses until World War II. Immigrants—Irish and Germans before 1900, and Serbians and Croatians thereafter—predominated among the former. Hard physical labor defined the lives of all the workers. White men toiled as craftsmen, train firemen, brakemen, machinists, and iron forge men, and as unskilled and semi-skilled laborers, diggers of railway lines and porters and haulers of heavy equipment. Only slowly organized into labor unions, they worked ten- to twelve-hour days, in six-day work weeks before 1900, and only slightly less until the post-World War II era. Wage cuts, so characteristic of American industry in the nineteenth century, took a toll, as did periodic recessions and depressions. Thousands of industrial laborers lay idle in three major setbacks, the Depressions of 1873, 1893, and the 1930s. In good times and bad other adults and even children in workers' homes contributed wages out of necessity. Wives took in laundry and boarders, and daughters

The Carrollton Viaduct, allegedly oldest stone railroad bridge in the United States, spanned the Gwynns Falls at the southern edge of Mill Hill. The first leg of the Baltimore and Ohio Railroad was built over it to Ellicott City in 1829. (Courtesy Enoch Pratt Free Library)

worked as maids or factory operatives. Sons quit school to drive carts or huckster vegetables until they were old enough to work in factories; boys and girls raked coal from tracks and trains. In good times some joined the exodus to the suburbs, and to the middle class. But generations stayed in the neighborhood, blocks regularly replenished with new arrivals from Europe and the Upper South.

African-American men did much of the street vending in these older sections. After 1880 they peddled in the new blocks of middle-class housing built north and west. Cart drivers loaded wares at the Hollins Market, or drove out to nearby farms for produce. Tools and household wares, and meat, fish, farm produce, and ice were sold from pushcarts and wagons. On week days, vehicles formed a solid line along neighborhood streets and in the rear alleys of middle-class blocks north beyond Baltimore Street. By 1900 many flats were equipped with wooden ice boxes that stored perishables and needed constant replenishing from peddlers' wares.

Work within the households of both races required the hard, exacting labor of women, labor only gradually alleviated by technological changes and appliances. Not until the three decades after 1920 were electricity, and indoor plumbing and water, installed in many houses built before the Civil War. Nineteenth-century women hauled water used for cooking, dish washing, laundry, and bathing from urban hydrants and pipes located blocks from their homes. In a part of the city too crowded for other nineteenth-century urban amenities--space for a little garden n pasture and shed room for a cow-- secured all their food from outside. Before the advent of processed foods, women were required to do the preparation of market fare. They killed and plucked chickens, scaled fish, sifted impure flour, and nurtured their own yeast. Cooking stoves only gradually replaced fireplaces that required the constant attention of stoking and refueling fires, and moving heavy iron pots and pans. The small size of houses here was counted as a blessing, for fireplaces and kerosene lamps required constant attention as they coated walls with soot and grime floor to ceiling.

Working women often sandwiched the chores at home between demanding labor for wages outside. Neighborhoods included both the familiar Bridgettes, Irish girls as young as eleven or twelve, and the Beulahs, African-American women of every age, who worked as live-in maids, or as day domestic workers or laundresses. Many walked to work places in nearby middle-class neighborhoods.

The social life of men and women revolved around the streets and corner stores and taverns. While whites and blacks both inhabited alleys in early years, segregation mores prevailed by the early twentieth century. Whites lived on main streets, African Americans in the alley housing until after World War I when whites began to emigrate. Parks, playgrounds, and parlors formed the habitat of urban middle classes more than of the workers, for landscaped green space was not generally used for play and recreation until World War II. Typical of working-class neighborhoods, street intersections with corner shops, and mixed commercial-residential streets such as Baltimore, Frederick, and Pratt, bustled throughout the day. Shopkeepers at their doorways, customers, loiterers, and young people—the flirters and flirtatious alike—spent social time here. White men crowded corner bars, neighborhood "beer and boiler maker" places, after work. In street and alley alike, stoop sitting, a habit everywhere in Baltimore of working classes, was a before-bedtime ritual in good weather.

A few working-class sections along Pratt developed, and remained, as ethnically homogenous sections over generations. Highly skilled craftsmen, carpenters, masons, printers, and machinists, most of them native whites, moved into new simple, small Italianate houses located west of the Mount Clare industrial yards after 1880. (See Pratt-Monroe.) Individual families occupied whole two-floor streetfront row houses bought by the family. Women were active homemakers but seldom wage earners outside of the household. German-descent workers labored in breweries, slaughterhouses and the "hair" factory west of Stricker. Lithuanian garment workers took jobs in the city's massive garment plants, which steadily edged westward from Howard Street close to Fremont after 1910. Men hired on as tailors, cutters, and pressers, wives and daughters as buttonhole finishers and stitchers. The culture of such workers' settlements varied over time and according to ethnic tradition and custom, but everywhere proximity of home to work place molded it.

Hollins Park

Fremont Avenue, King Expressway, L Scott, Pratt, Carey, and Baltimore constitute the boundaries to Hollins named for John Smith Hollins, an estate owner in west Baltimore and mayor of the city in 1832. Active in many civic affairs, Hollins was an early promoter of a municipal water system for the city. Row houses spread over most blocks, half of them narrow, slant-roof, pre-Civil War dwellings, half three-story brick Italianate homes built late in the nineteenth century.

Neighborhood property was variously owned by Charles Ridgely, a member of the Maryland House of Delegates during the Revolution and owner of the Hampton estate in Baltimore County, Ramsey McHenry, who speculated in West Baltimore real estate, and Thomas D. and Ross R. Winans. The area includes a market, a church, a factory complex, one public school, and one mixed residential-commercial street, West Baltimore.

Residential blocks south of Lombard built up around the vast B and O Railroad Yards of Mount Clare (Washington Village) which stretched from Parkin to Carey. The B and O Railroad was built to open up trade between Baltimore and the Ohio Valley. After the War of 1812, thousands of Easterners trekked to the trans-Appalachian West, far from the manufactured and imported goods of Eastern cities. Baltimore's location at the head of the Patapsco placed it 150 miles closer to the West than other Eastern cities. Eager to tap the trade, and to outbid New York and Philadelphia whose trans-Appalachian commerce relied on canals and rivers, Baltimore merchants and speculators invested money in the Iron Horse. They were also eager to compete with a local, rival project, the Chesapeake and Ohio canal along the Potomac River.

The railroad had only recently been invented and demonstrated in England, and the state legislature chartered the B and O as the nation's first railway in 1827. The B and O's station, and its first construction and repair yards, required more acreage than was available in built-up sections of the town. But they equally needed to be close enough to the port so that wagons moving over flat land could transfer goods from wharf to rail car. Land along Pratt Street, some acquired from the estate of John Carroll, was ideal. The venerable Charles Carroll of Carrollton, Revolutionary War patriot, signer of the Declaration of Independence, and devotee of railroad technology in his octogenarian years, turned over the first spadeful of dirt, on July 4, 1828. He claimed the day ranked with the first Independence day. First passengers rode the train thirteen miles to Ellicott Mills in 1830.

The B and O spurred commercial and industrial development along Pratt Street between Parkin and the city. For a few years east-west streets hummed with the traffic of porters, draymen, wagon drivers, and teamsters, who carried goods to and from the old City. But lines were gradually extended to downtown docks and wharves and to waterfront property and terminals acquired and built by B and O. As street traffic to the city slackened, the yards themselves became busy and famous. Self-taught engineer Peter Cooper had built his "Tom Thumb" engine, the nation's first steam locomotive, only a few feet long, in 1830. Engines for other railroad lines throughout the East were constructed here in the 1840s. Samuel F. B. Morse sent his first telegraph message over wires laid along the B and O right-of-way from Washington to Mount Clare in 1844. Tsar Nicholas of Russia visited the plants in 1847 to plan rail construction across the two continents of his empire. The B and O supplemented the trunk line with lines to five other West Baltimore stations, hastening Westside suburban build-up.

An iron foundry, a locomotive plant, and the Bartlett and Hayward heavy machinery company, the last a Baltimore pioneer in structural iron, Latrobe stoves, and munitions, opened along Scott and Pratt after the Civil War. Bartlett and Hayward provided supplies to the B and O. During World War I the Bartlett and Hayward plants made ammunition. For many years, the yards and adjacent plants comprised the city's largest, most concentrated industrial sector.

The B and O yards employed 1,000 workers by 1852, 2,000 by 1860 with many of them Hollins Park inhabitants. In boom times the plants operated night and day. Yard workers during the Civil War labored round the clock, doing most of the rail repair work of the Union and replacing bridges, rails, and rolling stock destroyed by the Confederates. Both the B and O and companies which supplied the yards nearby relied mostly on Irish and German workers. To expand the work force, the B and O even extended a line after the Civil War to Locust Point, south Baltimore debarkation depot for immigrants. New immigrants were transported directly to blocks which surrounded Mount Clare yards.

The shifting fortunes of the B and O nevertheless spawned employer-employee conflict. As the road was built westward, new "branch" repair shops competed with Mount Clare, forcing lay-offs and new overcrowding in tiny houses. Skilled yard craftsmen in craft unions (machinists, boiler makers) waged bitter strikes, many joining the particularly bitter uprising of 1877, a nationwide shutdown of rail lines. In this strike precipitated by wage cuts, Baltimore B and O workers derailed an engine, stalled freight cars, and mobbed city streets.

Poverty, especially among the many common laborers who occupied damp basements on the low flat land surrounding the Yards, won the attention of immigrant aid societies. Among the Irish, the Hibernian Society, a middle-class male association formed in 1818, gave provisions for new immigrants, and secured domestic jobs for young daughters.

Before the Civil War, blocks between Baltimore and Lombard—in proximity to both downtown and Mount Clare, and to rural farms west of Carey Streets—spawned several distinct semi-urban settlements. Vendors, hucksters, and wagon drivers, probably white farmers who moved in from Baltimore County, formed a tiny community northwest of the Hollins Market. They transported produce from country to market; earliest traffic passed along Wandsbeck Street (now Arlington), which formed a link between Pratt and Baltimore Street in 1820. A few gabled-roof, two-and-one-half story workers' dwellings survive on Arlington and Baltimore.

The Mount Clare industrial distr... housing east of Poppleton and nort... timore Street after 1840. Craftsmen t... to rent whole houses along north-sou... streets, while common laborers with their families let the flats and simpler, smaller houses along Booth and Boyd. Families of Baltimore and Lombard Street shopkeepers settled in three-story houses east of Parkin. African Americans also lived along Booth, Boyd, and Stockton from the time of the Civil War.

Institutions, most of them since demolished, reflected the early heterogeneity of northern blocks. An elegant Protestant Episcopal Church, St. Mark's, was built on Lombard in 1850, close to Allen African Methodist Episcopal. The latter, today one of the oldest congregations in the city and now located on West Lexington, was housed in a frame chapel on Stockton between Carey and Carrollton. A vast estate, Alexandrofsky, spread over thirty-four acres off Fremont, Hollins, and Baltimore between 1847 and 1927. Thomas Winans, the eldest son of railroad builder Ross Winans, occupied it. Named for the Tsar of Russia, where Winans also built railroads, twenty buildings included greenhouses and a giant aviary of over a thousand exotic birds. Some buildings were Baltimore's first centrally heated edifices. The property and its

(Overleaf) Locomotive and car repair and construction shops spread west of the B and O Roundhouse beyond Poppleton Street ("Washington Village") and next to Pratt Street neighborhoods in the late nineteenth century.

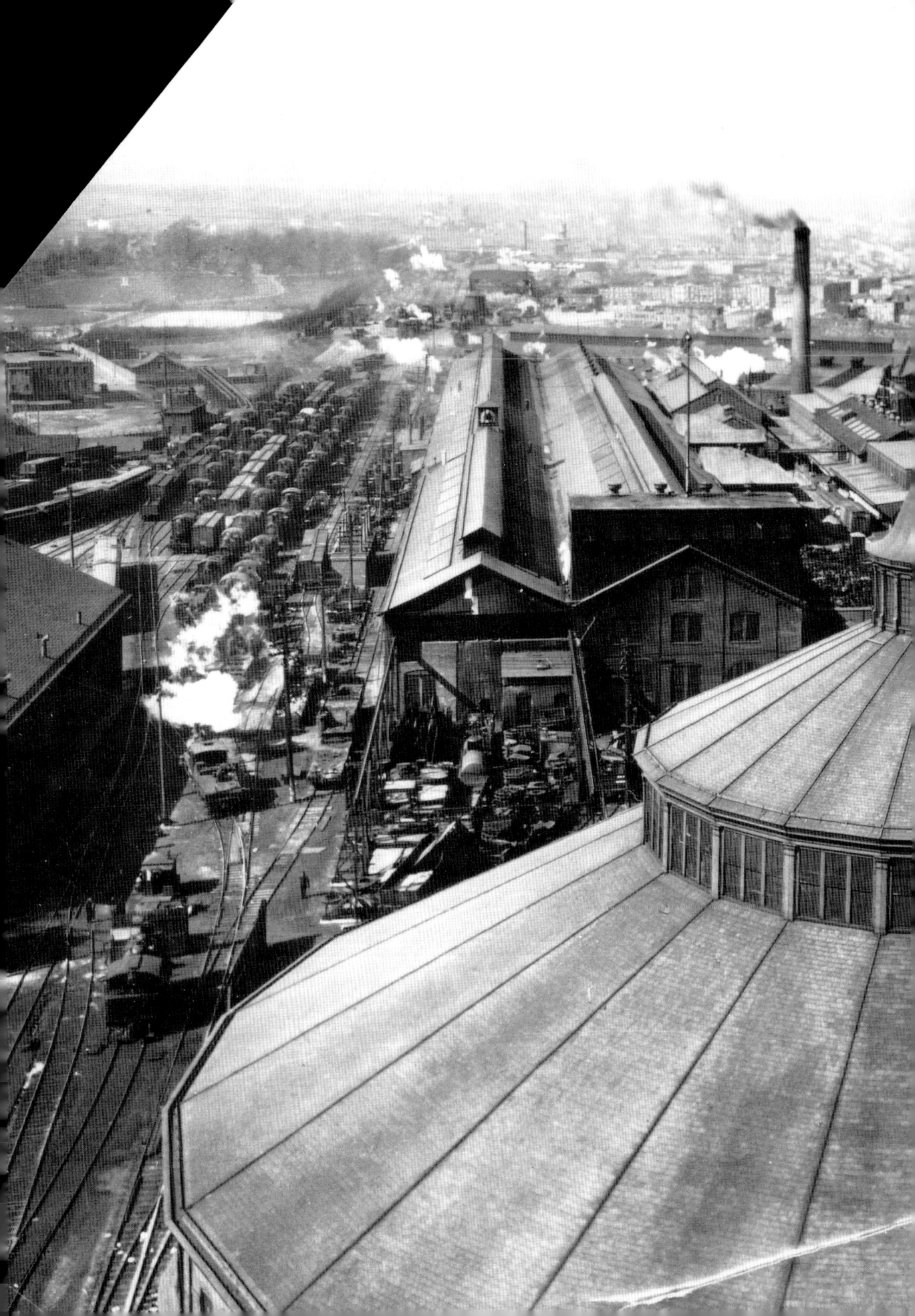

The estate house of Alexandrovsky, named for the Tsar of Russia, was kept by the Winans family near the B and O yards west of Fremont along Baltimore and Hollins Streets. Its front entrance was on Hollins Street.

inhabitants both inspired neighborhood legend. A twelve foot surrounding wall lent an air of cloistered seclusion and was erected after neighbors protested the undraped statues of Olympic gods and goddesses that dotted outside grounds. One building with a forty foot ceiling housed the world's largest organ (heard one mile away). Winans' French-born spouse, Mlle. Revillion, a familiar figure on West Baltimore Street during the Civil War, supplied food and milk to a streetfront soup kitchen and fed the neighborhood poor herself.

Immigrants transformed eastern Hollins Park into a pedestrian community of whole families of garment workers before World War I.

The city's largest industry, men's garment manufacture, slowly mushroomed from East Baltimore sweatshop enterprises in the 1880s to huge factories along Howard Street by 1914. Lithuanians, who first settled on the Eastside in the 1880s, moved along Hollins and Parkin, within walking distance of the factories; women with young children often went back and forth between home and plant throughout the workday. A settlement house, Lawrence House, opened at 814 and 816 Lombard about 1912 and sponsored athletic and social activities until the Lithuanian Democratic Club acquired part of it in 1934. Benevolent and fraternal societies flourished, and pooled funds to erect Liefuviu Tautinis Knygynas, Lithuanian Hall, at Hollins and Parkin in 1921. It was built on the site of what had been the Knapp Institute, variously a private school once attended by Henry L. Mencken, and a school for the deaf. The private institution had been opened by a nineteenth-century political refugee from Baden, Germany. Language schools, political and veterans' clubs, and sports, choral, and dance groups in Lithuanian Hall all kept alive Lithuanian culture, identifying Hollins Park as an ethnic city base. After World War II, that identity prompted many elderly people to stay, and led fourth generations from the suburbs to relocate back to the City.

West and south of "Little Lithuania," the railroad continued to stamp neighborhood life after 1900. Streets busied at noontime with workers bound home for lunch, or women carrying pails to the yards. Taverns crowded after 7 P.M on weekdays. Pratt and Baltimore Street shops drew patrons late on Saturdays, pay time at the plants. In slack times, corner markets served the workers as banks, extending credit and paying bills. Gentle breezes carried "soot storms"—dust of the railroad coal—over back yards, ruining the laundry. The sight of huge steam shovels and cranes, and the sounds of engines hooking with cars, stirred fantasies among the neighborhood young.

Neighborhood shops and taverns, as well as work in the "yard" and other plant floors, tended to break down the isolation of white ethnic workers. Children of Irish, German, new immigrant and native white "yardsmen" began to intermarry; Amity and Lemmon, once integrated with the poor of both races, became an African-American habitat. Yardsmen and their families began an exodus down the line to Lansdowne, Halethorpe, and Laurel in the 1930s, commuting to the yard by train or auto. Trucks and aircraft gradually forced the closing of repair shops in the 1940s and 1950s. The Koppers Company, which replaced Bartlett Hayward in 1927, moved many of its facilities to Baltimore County. New inhabitants remained heavily represented in nearby transportation trades, but in warehousing and trucking enterprises along southwest arteries, not in railroading.

A mix of university students and industrial and service workers moved into the flats and houses all over Hollins Park after 1950, many of them eventually active in the neighborhood-based Southwest Baltimore Citizens Planning Council, formed in 1969. With other civic groups it lobbied against neighborhood demolition projects. Blocks west of Schroeder were designated part of the Union Square Historical and Preservation District in 1978.

The complex of St. Peter the Apostle Roman Catholic Church (Hollins and Poppleton), known as the "workers' church," was built in 1842 for a parish designated by the Archdiocese to stretch from Howard Street to Elkridge, Maryland. The only ecclesiastical building of the faith between the Cathedral and Ellicott City, it eventually became the mother church to churches and parochial schools all over the Westside. Baltimore architect Robert Carey Long designed the sanctuary to recall the Athenian Temple of Hephaestus, god of fire and metallurgy. It created a fit place of worship for the stokers, welders, and boilermakers associated with the iron foundry and the B and O. Common laborers figure in its history, as Irish tunnel diggers, laborers for the B and O by day, shoveled foundations for it at night. The simple stately structure with unobstructed interior soon contrasted with the spiraling Gothic graystones that went up on higher ground nearby. Long also designed the parish presbytery, an early Baltimore Italian Renaissance edifice, on Hollins in 1849.

A mostly Irish parish for a century, St. Peter's sponsored the city's first Catholic temperance society in 1849, the first Southern residence for the Sisters of Mercy in 1855, two schools, Good Shepherd and St. Mary's, for "needy" and "neglected" children in 1865 and 1866, and the city's first parochial business schools around 1900.

Hollins Market opened in 1836 on land donated to the city. It was rebuilt in 1838, and subsequently expanded to a high-ceilinged red brick edifice. With arched entryways it resembled medieval English market halls. By 1900 it stretched four blocks with 160 inside and 180 outside stalls, and served as a common meeting ground for a rich diversity of shoppers and shopkeepers. County farmers, country women who peddled home-produced wares, West Baltimore butchers, immigrants with vendor traditions, African-American drivers and servants, all sold and purchased wares. A wooden stall at one end acquired local fame as Baltimore's Hyde Park. High and low brow alike debated politics and world affairs on Saturday nights. The market building was used successively as a temporary home of the Maryland Institute of Art (after the Great Baltimore Fire of 1904), an armory, and a setting for political rallies and public recreation. The 750-student-capacity James McHenry Elementary School opened on Schroeder in 1969.

Hollins Market in 1929. The market has functioned without interruption since 1839; at its busiest it numbered 160 inside and 180 outside stalls and stretched from Poppleton to Carey Streets.

Pratt-Monroe

Regarded both as the northern outskirts of Pigtown and the southern edge of Steuart Hill, Pratt-Monroe was first settled as a workers' suburb after the Civil War. The residential haven sat on a slight incline, apart both from the low flat land of Mount Clare Yards, and from the breweries and slaughterhouses along Frederick west and north. Carey, the B and O, Pulaski, and Pratt bound its east, south, west, and north sides. It takes its name from two east-west streets, the former a downtown waterfront byway named for Charles Pratt, Earl of Camden. The latter was designated for James Monroe, fifth president. Pratt fought in the House of Lords to repeal the notorious Stamp Act and opposed England's efforts against the colonists during the Revolution; Monroe was president when the Poppleton survey of the 1816 annex was completed.

Row houses, with commercial places at street corners, spread from Carey to Pulaski. Older ones from Carey to Stricker are distinguished by modest size and ornamentation. Two stories, and made of formstone-covered brick, they are bedecked with narrow cornices. Entryways are short and made of wood or brick, not marble, steps. Built before 1900 on narrow streets with wide sidewalks, home exteriors advertised houses as larger than pre-Civil War workers' homes but less costly than middle-class residences. Western blocks reflect popular construction styles from 1900 to 1920, notably light tan brickwork that blends with sunlight, and modest porches and yards. The neighborhood includes a school, health care clinic, city government building, and one mixed commercial-residential street, Pratt.

Late nineteenth-century industrial growth and construction throughout Baltimore placed a premium on exceptionally skilled, trained industrial labor in the city. A generation of men, most of them natives who acquired training as apprentices, and many enrolled in labor unions, managed to purchase individual houses. Carpenters, brick-makers, masons, printers, brewers, butchers, and can-makers moved from south Baltimore and east Baltimore into housing that edged country farms for a generation. Two simple Methodist chapels, Parlett (or Chenowith), built at Monroe and Ramsey on land donated from the Carroll estate, and Wilkens Avenue ME, Wilkens and Vincent, served a neighborhood working-class population for many years.

But the location and open space also lured industry and soon eroded the idyllic setting. Stockyards, slaughterhouses, and breweries opened near Frederick, brickyards near the B and O. Wilhelm Droveyards, one of the city's largest stockyards at Pratt and Payson, and a garment factory close to Wilkens, hired neighborhood workers whose isolation and distance from the rest of the city restricted their opportunities for work.

Wilkens Avenue, a broad thoroughfare cut southwest from Gilmore after 1876, encouraged development in the western blocks. West Baltimore industrialist William Wilkens (see below) donated thirty-three acres to the city to erect a kind of fashionable Charles Street for Westside workers. It was to be a broad avenue with parkland in the middle. The Westside's only terraced street beyond Eutaw Place, it was ornamented with decorative pewter urns, cupids, and fountains, and white maple and silver poplar trees. The first section extended over seven blocks built eastward from Monroe. An aura of modest refinement attracted new home buyers, and the side streets to Pulaski were lined with row houses by 1900.

Serbs and Croats moved along Woodyear after 1900, forming, with southern Hollins Park, a little neighborhood sometimes dubbed Baltimore's "Hells Kitchen." Many immigrants were neighborhood shopkeepers. Before World War I, trolleys converted blocks beyond Woodyear into a suburb of commuting workers who traveled to downtown offices and plants in East and South Baltimore and along Frederick Road west of the neighborhood. Between the World Wars, the city Industrial Bureau and Chamber of Commerce, both organizations of businessmen, persuaded the city to widen main arteries out of the city in order to lure new companies to Baltimore. Wilkens was among them. Raw materials and small product parts once brought in by wagon or rail would be hauled by van. A link to the south, Wilkens was designated a major cross-city highway with the median parkland across Pratt-Monroe reduced to a curb.

Put up near one of the busiest Baltimore thoroughfares, World War II era factories along the Avenue were converted to warehouses, distribution outposts for goods moved by truck to all parts of the city. A neighborhood mix of old row houses, storage facilities, truck parking lots, and of auto and van traffic survived into the 1980s. Periodically after World War II, the blocks also formed a city place of settlement for new white workers in Baltimore from Appalachian Kentucky and West Virginia. Pratt-Monroe's ethnic and class make-up—so distinct from blocks north of Pratt where African Americans and professional people lived—together with a community school complex on Pulaski, long provided a sense of neighborhood identity. Samuel F. B. Morse Elementary built in 1979 replaced an elementary school and one of the city's first vocational schools erected in 1904.

Bentalou-Smallwood and Mill Hill

Clockwise from Frederick and Pulaski, Bentalou-Smallwood's boundaries extend along Pulaski, the B and O, Catherine, Ashton, Bentalou, and Frederick. It is named for two streets in the Poppleton plat, the first commemorating a French cavalryman who accompanied the Marquis de Lafayette to America during the Revolution, and who was wounded at the Battle of Savannah. Paul Bentalou settled in Baltimore as a successful shipping merchant after the Revolutionary War. Smallwood derives from a state governor who was the Southern Maryland commander of the Maryland Line during the Revolution.

Unadorned two-story Italianate row houses, with many corner markets, extend to Bentalou Street; "daylight" row houses with yards on property where animal hair was once dried mark the west side. The neighborhood includes several churches and mixed commercial-residential development along Pratt and Wilkens.

Clockwise from its northeast corner, Mill Hill's boundaries are formed by Bentalou, Ashton, Catherine, the B and O, Dukeland, Wilkens, the Western Maryland Railroad, and Frederick. All but several eastern blocks lay in Baltimore County until 1888. It features two-story nineteenth-century row housing on side streets, twentieth century daylight homes with marble steps on Wilkens, a few of the typical "country" Italianate duplexes (row houses built in a pair) on Frederick, two churches, and the Westside Shopping Center.

The Wilkens Hair Factory, what Henry L. Mencken called a Baltimore "abomination," instigated urban development in both neighborhoods. German-born William Wilkens, one of Baltimore's most prosperous and influential nineteenth-century businessmen, immigrated to the United States and Baltimore in 1833. He opened a downtown plant to process animal hair but moved it to Frederick Road just beyond the 1816 city boundary in 1845, near the present-day boundary between Bentalou-Smallwood and Mill Hill.

Used first in chignons and curls popular early in the century, natural hair had a resiliency suited, after treatment, for stuffing in mattresses and hospital beds, and eventually in upholstery and automobile seating until the invention of synthetic fibers. Wilkens acquired a national market for his product, scouring the world for usable hair. His agents followed the cavalries of European armies during the Crimean War and the Union armies during the Civil War. Branch offices to secure and market the product were opened in New York, Chicago, and St. Louis.

Hair processing demanded space to scald, dry, and store, and Wilkens, who first rented Frederick Road buildings, eventually bought 150 acres on both sides of Frederick and erected buildings over fifteen acres. Many went up along Snake Hollow, named for the reptiles in a stream which emptied into the Falls, today site of the Westside Shopping Center.

After curling and scalding, hair was dried on nearby hills, some of it bagged and transported to bristle plants close by. Wilkens' first buildings, notably brick plants with kilns, horse-powered mixers, and drying sheds, themselves facilitated construction of new plant buildings and nearby residences. A small operation had mushroomed into a major enterprise by the 1880s. The factory complex resembled a medieval fortress, buildings erected of massive gray fieldstone with a bridge and a branch of the Gwynns Falls appearing as a drawbridge over a moat. Dormitories on the complex housed German and Austrian immigrants at work on their first American job in a work force that numbered 1,000.

In an era of industrial magnates—the advent of the age of Andrew Carnegie and John D. Rockefeller—Wilkens reveled in a reputation as neighborhood patriarch, building an estate house north of the plant on Frederick in Shipley Hill. He subsequently built and rented frame and brick housing along McHenry, Ramsey, and Ashton, buildings replaced by brick rows after 1900. Factory-issued scrip circulated in stores throughout southwest Baltimore. A dabbler in other investments, he financed a rail line from Baltimore to Catonsville and set up Baltimore's first telephone line between the plant and his Pratt Street warehouses.

Wilkens died in 1879, but his sons operated the plant until the 1920s. Neighborhood legends outlived him. He gave turkeys at Thanksgiving, gifts at Christmas, and converted Whitmonday, Dutch (German) Fourth of July, into a neighborhood holiday replete with parade, cannons, artillery, and employees' picnic. On a magnificent white horse ridden through neighborhood streets, he dispensed pennies to children. (A monument to the horse, with iron railing, stood on Wilkens Avenue for many years after his death.) No elderly neighborhood man was ever too old to sign on at the hair plant. Grateful workers once gave him a gold watch which he wore to his death.

The patriarch's reputation notwithstanding, the neighborhood hair factory workers were part of the labor unrest which swept the city in the 1880s and 1890s. Many joined a union of hair spinners and struck Wilkens' plant.

Blocks in Bentalou-Smallwood built up as a German section before 1900, men employed at the hair factory or a McHenry Street slaughter house or brewery, wives and daughters at the hair plant. Thomas Seeger, allegedly the first Baltimore brewmaster of lager beer, operated the Baltimore Brewing firm between Bentalou and Smallwood for many years. A more ethnically varied population of white workers moved into the blocks after World War I, commuting over streetcars and buses: Pratt developed as a commercial street; Wilkens Avenue became a locale for doctors' and lawyers' offices. After World War II, side streets too narrow for truck traffic discouraged warehouse and plant construction, and preserved old residential housing and stability.

As late as 1980 one-sixth of the neighborhood inhabitants claimed German ancestry, and a church and school were reminders of the ethnic past. St. Thomas's, Pulaski and Ramsey (Pratt-Monroe), was built for German-speaking Lutherans in 1896. School #96, Nathaniel Ramsey, at Ashton and Smallwood, opened in 1895 as German-American School # 6, part of the separate ethnic school system which Baltimore City maintained from 1869 to about 1910. Moses Montefiore Orthodox Jewish synagogue, named for a late nineteenth-century philanthropist, was located variously on Wilkens, Pulaski, and Smallwood within the neighborhood and Pratt-Monroe from 1889 to 1957, when it became part of the Woodmoor Hebrew Congregation of Baltimore County.

Known as Millington Village before the Civil War, Mill Hill blocks beyond Snake Hollow underwent two stages of development. Mill owners from the colonial village of Ellicott City opened at least three mills along the Gwynns Falls north of Frederick sometime after 1798. Multi-story stone buildings for the milling of flour, eventually converted to textile mills, took advantage of the Falls' water power, and a mill race was built near what is today Edmondson Avenue. Flour was shipped three miles to the wharves of Baltimore, where it was exported by ship. Functioning as merchant mills, or processors of large volumes of corn, mills were equipped with large, labor-intensive corn kilns, the flour transported by wagon over Frederick Road. Millers lived in frame cottages south of the Road.

Railroads alleviated reliance on wagon trade, millers' settlement dwindled, and new dwellings rapidly spread over narrow streets after the annex of 1888 incorporated this land into the City. Old streets, Catherine, Maryanna, Wilhelm, and Christian, derive their names from Wilkens' wives and sons. For many years the blocks were a heterogenous mix of hair-factory workers, Frederick and Brunswick shopkeepers, farmers, and stock and brickyard workers.

German-born William Wilkens, who kept an estate house north of Frederick Road in Shipley Hill, cultivated a reputation as neighborhood benefactor and patriarch.

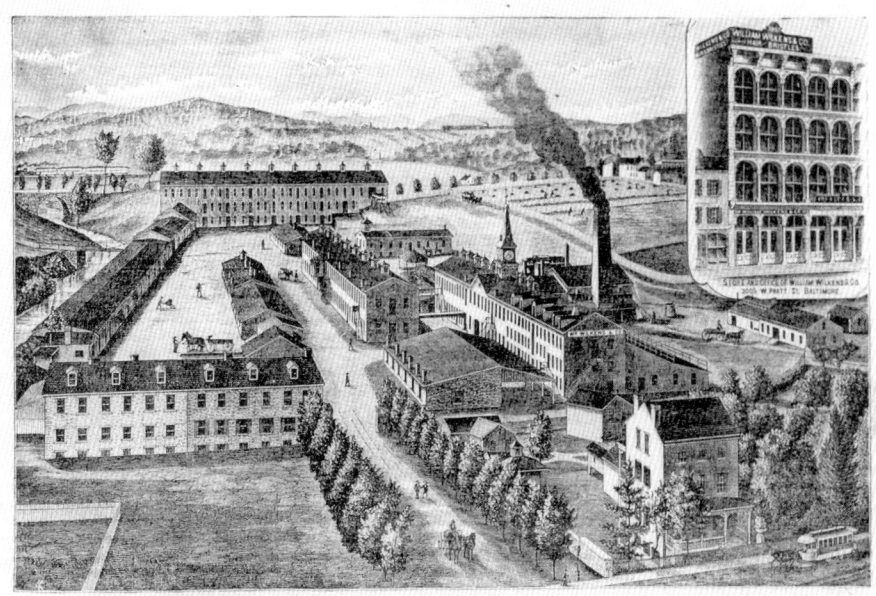

The William Wilkens Co. kept offices in large cities but maintained hair processing plants in Snake Hollow, along the boundary between Bentalou-Smallwood and Mill Hill, today site of the Westside Shopping Center. Its workforce numbered many male and female German immigrants.

Stockyards at the foot of Brunswick south of the B and O gained adjacent blocks the reputation of Baltimore's cattle town. The B and O and the Pennsylvania Railroad combined in 1881 to build pens for cattle, forcing the closing of other droveyards put up before and after the Civil War for animals driven to the western edge of Baltimore. A consolidation of older yards (including the Wilhelm Droveyard) in southwest Baltimore, these yards served sellers citywide and eventually in fourteen states. Trains and, after 1930, trucks transported most of the stock, but animals were also driven through neighborhood streets. Western Maryland farmers' wagons, loaded with pigs and with cows following behind, lined Brunswick Street and Wilkens Avenue. City buyers drove purchased animals from stockyards to slaughterhouses in all parts of the city. Neighborhood men and school-age boys worked as pen men, weighers, blacksmiths, and drivers; a so-called jerkwater streetcar ran from Mill Hill to the yards for many years. Stock buyers and auctioneers, commission agents of meat-packing companies, and western-hatted cowboys were familiar sights in the stores and taverns of Brunswick until World War II.

Prominent city builder Walter Westphal built what is now the longest row of row houses in the city, the 2600 block of Wilkens, about 1912. Row homes fanned out between Wilkens and Frederick thereafter. City street-widening programs of the 1930s spurred the renaming of Wilkens as Sunset Boulevard (1932), and then Crozier (1939) for a City civil engineer, but a strong sense of neighborhood identity prevented renaming on both occasions. When "THIS HOUSE IS ON WILKENS AVENUE" signs appeared in front windows in 1939, the City Council revoked the latter name change. Electronics, radio and scrap metal businesses, and workers' union halls replaced the breweries and slaughterhouses during and after World War II as residential blocks evolved into an automobile suburb in the 1950s. Many workers, most in individually owned homes, commuted to jobs along the Baltimore-Washington corridor. Characteristic of contemporary fringe sub-divisions, home owners relied on County suburbs for parochial schools, hospitals, large shops and theatres and forged for the Hill an identity as a space between city and county, a combination of both.

An old landmark, Holy Cross Episcopal Church, Millington and Ashton, was formed as a mission of St. Luke's Parish, Franklin Square, in 1858. Sunday School classes met in a hair factory carriage house near the present location until 1867. The first edifice on the present site was built as a country chapel in 1871. Between 1900 and 1930 the church was enlarged, remodeled, and a bell tower added, and a new mission, St. James of Irvington, was supported with religious and Sunday School services. St. Benedict's, at Millington and Wilkens, was opened by the Roman Catholic Archdiocese in 1893; a bell from a neighborhood engine house was installed in the church belfry. The parish began a school in 1903, erected a saints' shrine modeled on the grotto of Lourdes in 1907, and built a new basilica-like, Italian Romanesque structure in 1933. Atop a hill, covered by an unusual pinkish-tan, iron spot brick, and designed by Benedictine monk Michael McInerney, it dominates the flat landscape south of Wilkens Avenue. Frederick

Elementary, #260, which opened in 1983, replaced School #68 built in 1892 on Millington.

Old West End

1000 block of West Baltimore Street, 1904-06. Long a commercial thoroughfare with residential flats, West Baltimore Street was a setting for civic parades.

Old neighborhoods which huddle close to Baltimore Street beyond Fremont were stamped early and permanently by their topography and proximity to the old city. Built to the western boundary of the Annex of 1816, they stretch over land flatter and on lower elevation than blocks north. But at the same time they sit above the wet, marshy stretch southwest of downtown. A path that became Baltimore Street, extending farther west than northwest or southwest arteries out of Baltimore, first carried wagons from Frederick Road. They moved along a short, very direct route into the city soon after 1800. Blocks next to the eastern section of Baltimore Street, land accessible to downtown via horse-drawn vehicles, were developed before the Civil War. With no steep hills to negotiate, wagons, omnibuses, and horse-drawn trolleys moved in and out of the city quickly. Thereafter, development on and off Baltimore tended to form lengthy, distant penetrations, a succession of "West Ends" into the rural countryside.

Acreage east of Franklin Square lured early developers of residential real estate, but the flatness of the terrain also encouraged commercial and industrial construction. With a grid plan providing for wide streets, and for connected ones, the Poppleton survey of the 1816 annex facilitated the early location of small stores and factories close to downtown and to the Mount Clare industrial district. The streets were broad enough for the traffic of freight and of store patrons transported by horse-drawn vehicles, and for adequate building space. A succession of businesses and mills located east of Franklin Square nevertheless encouraged out-migration of residents as blocks of housing to the north and west were developed. Old residents joined the city-wide exodus of suburban dwellers from 1870 to 1900. White middle classes moved again beyond West End neighborhoods in the 1920s and 1950s. A succession of newcomers into the neighborhoods, often renters with a need for inexpensive housing, located in flats formed from the old single-family dwellings. In- and out-migration, done periodically, consequently molded two familiar patterns of Baltimore residential settlement that permanently influenced residential neighborhoods: white middle-class home buyers and families, first inhabitants of many blocks, determined the architectural character of residences; and a succession of tenants in alley houses and main street apartments adapted buildings, as well as street and park landscape, to new uses.

In 1844, the Baltimore *Sun* predicted that omnibuses—heavy, twelve-passenger boxlike vehicles—would revolutionize intra-city travel. For the first time citizens could "reside at a distance from their places of business in more healthy locations without loss of time and fatigue in walking." Stretches of suburban development appeared along Baltimore Street before the Civil War, but extensive development awaited the horse-drawn trolleys. At seven to ten miles per hour, they traveled twice as fast as omnibuses. They were well suited to the slight inclines along Baltimore, but not the steeper terrain of the northwestern sections built up later.

Land speculators began to acquire and subdivide estates on both sides of Baltimore in the area of Franklin Square. Development took place slowly, and the continuing presence of old estates there and nearby defined the region as prestigious real estate and encouraged the maintenance of high property values. Although isolated, middle-class housing nevertheless lay close to industry and working-class neighborhoods. The status-conscious Westsider Henry L. Mencken remembered periodic "invasions" into Old West End blocks in the 1880s. "Gangs" of working-class Irish lads, from what he regarded as "subterranean" parts of West Baltimore (south of Pratt), roamed through middle-class turf on and off Baltimore Street. Foul odors from the Wilkens Hair Factory also wafted through it.

Development between 1870 and 1900 reflected the emergence of a prosperous class of Baltimore businessmen and professional people before the era of corporate consolidation. Financially secure but not wealthy, the class included the owners and managers of several thousand small factories and distribution plants, wholesalers and salesmen, and many lawyers, doctors, journalists, and civil servants.

Like Victorian Era middle classes elsewhere, these home buyers held strong convictions about men and women, the family, and social class. Men, and to a lesser extent women, tended to believe in a rigid division of roles between the sexes. Males, almost "naturally," bore responsibility for outside work and public life, women for domestic life and the rearing of children. The outside world of commerce, industry, and male labor, it was believed, had harsh features. There unbridled competitiveness, corrupt business relationships, and an unsanitary work environment reigned. Families—except for male children when they reached the age of maturity—needed therefore to be isolated from the work environment. A rigid hierarchy of the social classes at work and home was upheld. Differences in social relations among the classes, it was believed, needed to be acknowledged, respected, and fostered, never disregarded. Individually, refinement, restraint, and privacy marked the personal behavior of good citizens in a civil society.

Homes along the main streets of the Old West End defined and nurtured these values with respect to class and gender. A family's shelter formed a visible haven from the gruelling, frenzied world of business affairs, and a private refuge of peace. Hard sometimes to acquire and maintain, a new house in a residential suburb nevertheless stood as reward for and evidence of middle-class diligence and thrift.

Rows of Old West End houses rarely went up as individually designed and built edifices. Rather, master builders, or savings and loan companies, acquired property from country estates. The latter leased lots to builders who set up whole blocks or sections of a block at a time, putting dozens of craftsmen to work on housing groups. Savings and loan companies often kept temporary headquarters near the developments. As houses went up they extended credit to builders and to home purchasers. They thereby performed a crucial service to both, as commercial banks were prohibited by law from providing credit for real estate.

Copying plans from one another, and from wholesale catalogues and magazines that circulated widely, builders put up simple, orderly Italianate row homes. The popular style may have derived from rural Italianate dwellings, inspired by the villas of Tuscany and noted for asymmetrical grouping of forms and ornamented gables. But plainness and regularity marked the style in an urban locale. Built sixteen- to twenty-two-feet wide, and thirty- to sixty-feet deep, houses harmonized with the brick of older city row edifices. Typically, they were plain enough to be set up by inexperienced builders whose brick work was the product of recent technological innovation. The irregular hand-made bricks of the old kilns in Baltimore, suppliers to Baltimore construction for a century, were now dispensed with, and new smooth, dry-pressed bricks, generally of a uniform color, were substituted.

In form, only a flat roof, a practical adaptation to prevent the streetward slide of snow and ice, departed from that of traditional city row houses with pitched roofs. Streetfront facades displayed innovation with second-floor dormers eliminated entirely, replaced by symmetrically aligned, modestly ornamented windows. They jutted like rectangular boxes across three stories. Decorative cornices distinguished otherwise identical rows from one another. The products of advances in power-driven shapers and scroll saws, the cornices were mass produced, lumberyards turning out great quantities and varieties which afforded home owners a wide choice. All but a few homes fronted on sidewalks without front yards. Many made liberal use of marble facing.

Row home interiors encouraged both privacy and separate space for the sexes and for adults and children. Eight to ten rooms allowed for distinct activities in each section. Typically, entry halls marked a transition from the outside world to the family sanctum. There alone people of different classes interacted. The parlor served as a place for formal entertainment and social interaction with one's own class, not for casual or informal recreation. The handiwork of women—crochet work and doilies which testified to female precision and creativity—was displayed. The parlor fireplace, one of four or five on all three floors, symbolized domesticity. Windowless dining rooms afforded scheduled togetherness without distraction; children's rooms were separate from the kitchen, a place in older houses where children played and slept. Bedrooms doubled as sitting rooms and settings for educational time for young children with their mothers. Rear parlors, centers of relaxed women's activities, housed sewing machines, pianos, and organs. Kitchens, often with coal stoves, were commodious spaces isolated to the rear with rear entrances.

Builders paved streets and designed parks that estate owners donated either to the City or to associations of home owners who maintained them privately. All of the familiar squares close to Baltimore Street kept the manicured look of a picturesque garden. They were built to afford a visual, aesthetic appeal rather than as recreation or play space for the young.

Communities of renters originated with racial segregation in housing and employment in Baltimore, and with periodic shortages of inexpensive housing for both races. From 1860 to 1950, forty to sixty percent of city African Americans worked as domestic or clean-up laborers—maids, laundresses, janitors, sweepers, and porters—holding something of a monopoly on such employment. Baltimore middle-class households were less inclined to rely on young white immigrant girls as domestics than those elsewhere.

Before the advent of trolley transport, African Americans and white working classes alike inhabited racially integrated back streets and alleys throughout the city. But as whites migrated into whole sections of East and South Baltimore, both new and old Westside alley housing moved toward solidly black inhabitation. Housing there remained in high demand until World War II, for builders ceased to erect alley homes behind new blocks put up after 1910, and the rules and mores of segregation discouraged African Americans from new housing generally. During World War I, the Supreme Court's decision to overturn housing segregation ordinances in 1917 briefly stirred optimism. ("The joy in Bunkville /sic/... when home run Casey came to the bat . . . is nothing compared with the rejoicing in Baltimore," exulted the *Afro American*.) But new devices perpetuated shortages of housing for blacks. Real-estate companies blacklisted, mortgage companies and credit unions "redlined," or denied credit for construction beyond the inner city, and restrictive covenants were attached to deeds. Federal housing statutes discouraged home improvements in old houses on the main streets, Depression-era FHA and VA programs of the 1930s and 1940s alike supporting new construction of single household dwellings in the suburbs while providing scant funds for home rehabilitation and repairs. Home demolition exacted a final price. While the city's African-American population soared from 142,000 to 329,000 between 1930 and 1960, expressway, school, and public housing construction, and slum clearance and urban renewal projects, demolished more housing for the less affluent than they created.

The shortage of living space city-wide over time accounts for the very populous pockets of settlement within neighborhoods along the Old West End. Oldest alleys, most of them demolished since World War II, curved behind the main streets as narrow stone or unpaved pathways. Hidden from the main streets, many dead-ended in back of adjacent main streets or other alleys. Frame and occasional brick one-story dwellings lined them, many dwellings unconnected to sewer lines and without indoor plumbing as late as the 1940s. Miniature Italianate houses, four rooms without ornamentation, were built on the wider-paved east-west alleys parallel to the main streets after 1880. With two or three steps to the alley front, they more often had brick and wood trim than the marble ornamentation of main-street housing.

On busy, commercial streets, floors over stores and shops were converted into rented rooms and flats for white inhabitants as early as 1860. East of Carey, whole houses were subdivided into African-American-rented, one-floor or one-room units after 1900. Houses throughout these neighborhoods were subdivided for Appalachian white renters during World War II and African-American renters thereafter.

The pockets of rented housing forged little urban communities distinct from home owners' neighborhoods. Among both white and black renters, the sharing of facilities, both within their living quarters and on the streets, tended to draw young and old alike into social contacts beyond the family circle. In the main-street flats, for example, one bathroom served two row apartments. Alley tenants rented rooms and even beds to outsiders. The very populous pockets of settlement, and the mix of shops and commercial establishments along alleys and Baltimore Street, forged a busy street life. Young people loitered next to stores, adults socialized outside as they minded the young, peddlers found a trade among streetcar patrons at busy intersections. The staid, well-cared-for park squares were transformed. In times of overcrowding, young and old found relief there from the cramped space of streets and houses. Like the streets and alleys, they busied sun up to sun down with children and adult loiterers.

African-American women and men in the rented housing found work in their own streets and blocks and in the middle class households built north and west to North and Fulton by 1900. Women with minimum equipment—tubs, irons, and soap, for example—took in outside work at home, especially laundry. Nineteenth-century home washing was often done in forty- to fifty-pound tubs, with cleaning a day-long sequence of sorting, soaking, draining water, and boiling garments, and rubbing, wringing, hanging, and folding them. It ended with the use of heavy irons kept over fireplaces winter and summer. On main-street blocks, middle-class affluence created a great demand for delivery work. Ice, meats, groceries, and coal were brought in over back alleys and streets by African-American delivery men. In an era before appliances, women fanned out by foot and trolley to nearby middle-class households, working as maids or day workers. Victorian homes abounded in accouterments requiring great care: bric-a-brac house trim, china ware, table coverings of linen and lace, and formal clothing. Spring and fall housecleaning rituals required extra hands and male labor. Men carried furniture from room to room, and conducted the semi-annual carpet beating, carrying rugs to vacant land where they were flogged for hours.

Older alley blocks with a single entryway fostered close contact and neighborhood intimacy. Often hidden from main streets, alley space blended with tiny yards as a patch of ground for shared activity. Children romped, women shared child care, and men idled over checkers and cards, all on an isolated unpaved or cobblestone stretch which formed a neighborhood commons. Outsiders there were easily identified. All but the very old or young rendered a support function. Boarders supplemented household income, and aunts, cousins, and the elderly took care of children. Adult men and the young of both sexes used space around the houses to "junk" or make money by scavenging. They piled rusted objects or appliance parts and stacks of old wood for stove-burning, eventually to be peddled, against the houses or in back yards.

Alleys and alley life among African Americans forged a communal culture of interdependence and mutual support. Newcomers from the upper South met cousins and neighbors from the countryside. Networks of residents with a few months or more in the city spread news about employment—where jobs were available, which bosses paid well, and where workers had been laid off. Churches flourished either as modest frame buildings or in the front rooms of preachers' homes. Extended and augmented families, so vital in the rural South, took on a new life. New arrivals from the country clustered in the same alley block, neighbors from the countryside or kinfolk living very near by. Rituals of birth and death were celebrated and observed with humble fanfare, as country relatives visited and city folk entertained. Neighborhood collections funded funerals.

Public housing built in the 1940s replaced alleys in eastern sections and tended to be sturdy, austere, and functional. Two-to three-story dwellings were put up with a minimum of storage space, government regulations prohibiting costs exceeding the average of private housing. Federally subsidized renovation programs and so-called Section 8 housing, whereby the government subsidized the rent payment of low-income families, intermixed with nineteenth-century row houses during the 1960s and 1970s.

Poe Homes

Bounded by Fremont, Lexington, Saratoga, and Amity, Poe Homes spreads over flat land on eight acres. It contains a public housing project of the same name, one church and church buildings, and a city museum.

Tiny workers' suburbs typically dotted the rural countryside just outside the borders of United States cities in the early nineteenth century. Baltimore was no exception. Once a small section of estate land owned variously by John Eager Howard, Charles Ridgely, and James McHenry, the Homes made up part of a sparsely populated industrial suburb. It spread northwest from Baltimore and Cove (Fremont) from about 1830 to 1850. Craftsmen who lived west of Cove beyond the built-up portion of the city worked at neighborhood plants or walked to jobs in the city. A four-story cotton plant (the Knox factory) sat at Lexington and Cove until 1848 when fire destroyed it and frame buildings nearby.

Typical small thirteen-foot brick rows, with dormers, slant roofs, and frame back buildings, replaced burned-out houses. They lined main streets and eight curved alleys three to eight feet wide. The narrow alleys, not demolished until 1940, quartered generations of immigrant workers in Mount Clare, especially the Irish, and African-American domestic workers, drivers, and peddlers. Some blocks were racially integrated as late as 1900. The main streets housed whites until the 1900s, African Americans thereafter.

The Irish blocks inspired neighborhood lore. In 1901 seventeen-year-old amateur boxer Joe Tipman, the "Pride of Rock Street," brought the neighborhood fame, when he delivered a knockout blow to Terrible Terry

McGovern, Featherweight Champion of the World. The two squared off in the famed Holliday Theatre, downtown. Customarily, local theatres featured hometown pugilists and well-known professionals on the last night of a successful dramatic performance in order to swell attendance and draw public attention. Newspaper delivery boy Tipman, reared over a saloon on Rock (since leveled by the Homes project), had "trained" for two days at a neighborhood gym. As he entered the ring, Terrible allegedly told him, "Don't Worry, Kid, it's just an exhibition and I won't hurt you." But after being knocked to the floor, the "Pride" arose and leveled McGovern in the second round. He then fled the theatre in a fit of nervous fright. Tipman was still a celebrity at his death, age eighty-two, in 1966.

In 1939, Mayor Howard Jackson, assisted by Tipman, turned over a spadeful of dirt for the first African-American public housing project in the city. Demolition of 280 homes with alley buildings touched off a massive exodus into surrounding blocks in the midst of wartime housing shortages. Priority renting drew many back when the project opened one-half year later. In a single week, 25,000 prospective tenants visited a model apartment for what was the first new, main-street housing open to African Americans in a century. Federal regulations encouraged a certain homogeneity of the Homes and insured that the displacement of many tenants from older housing was permanent. The unmarried and unemployed, large families, and former residents who had located acceptable housing elsewhere, were all permanently scattered, barred from the Homes by regulations. An improved income status required new tenants to move, as the Homes housed eighteen percent fewer people than the nineteenth-century housing. Rules were amended in 1956 to allow the tenancy of the single and elderly.

Designed by commissioned architect G. Cormer Fenhagen, the cellarless, two- to three-story flats of the Homes number 298 units with 1090 rooms, one to three rooms per apartment. The project reflected New Deal era views that public housing needed to provide for families and blend in with existing structures. Yard and play space for children was allowed for (seventy-two percent of acreage), an unadorned dark brick exterior resembled older adjacent houses, and interior courts effected a sense of isolation from the streets. The Projects were built with concrete floors and flat concrete slab roofs; renovation was undertaken in 1988.

A few nineteenth-century structures sit close to Poe Homes. Built on Amity in the 1820s, the Poe House was occupied by Edgar Allen Poe and his aunts and a cousin from 1832 to 1835, a particularly productive period in the poet's life. Its third-floor garret may have served as a writing chamber. At the urging of the city Edgar Allen Poe Society, which sponsors public readings and preserves memorabilia, it was spared from demolition in 1939. It opened in 1949 as a city- and Society-sponsored museum.

Mount Olive Free Will Baptist Church, Fremont and Saratoga, was built in 1867 as St. Paul's German Evangelical Lutheran, a narrow, tall German Gothic structure with ornate ceiling arabesques, foliation along Gothic arches, and a vaulted ceiling. Known for its

190-foot tower, one of the city's largest, and for large resonant bells and carved wooden figures of the four evangelists and Jesus (imported from Germany), it served a German community to the south and east. The church was popularly known as the "Boxers' Church," for its congregation of craftsmen box-makers. A school opened in 1869 and a parish house in 1897. The growing Mt. Olive congregation, of Bond and Lombard in East Baltimore, acquired it in 1956 and remodeled the parsonage and old school.

Poppleton

Poppleton takes its name from the north-south street designated for the city artist and author of the grid street survey of the 1816 annex. Its borders zigzag clockwise from Mulberry and Fremont along Fremont, Saratoga, Amity, Lexington, Fremont, Pine, Baltimore, Carey, and Mulberry. School 161 (1950) and adjacent recreation center (1975), with the park at their western and southern edges, form a centerpiece. It numbers five blocks of mixed shops and row homes (Baltimore Street), thirteen churches—four nineteenth-century, two contemporary, seven streetfront—and no industry. Street names designated in the 1816 grid recall the Revolutionary Era and patriotism of the city fathers. Lexington, a name chosen by John Eager Howard, and Saratoga denote sites of famed battles; Fayette, the French hero Marquis de Lafayette who visited Baltimore with great ceremony in 1824. Mulberry likely derives from an eighteenth-century city estate of the same name; Schroeder, from Henry Schroeder, a merchant of German descent, a civic leader, and member of the Committee of Vigilance and Safety during the War of 1812. Carey was named for James Carey, a member of the City Council.

Poppleton formed part of two Colonial estates, Welshes Adventure and Ridgely's Delight, the latter patented in 1667 to John Howard, Jr. and known as Timber Neck. It was eventually acquired and designated "Delight" by Revolutionary war officer and Maryland governor, Charles Ridgely. James McHenry, a surgeon of the War era, a delegate to the Constitutional Convention, and Secretary of War under George Washington, obtained part of it in 1799. He resided in an estate house, "Fayetteville," named for Lafayette, near Baltimore and Cove.

The city encouraged development at eastern and western ends with the street openings of Cove, between 1800 and 1820, Poppleton and Lexington, 1821 to 1835, and Carey, 1846. Elegant housing was built near Franklin Square before the Civil War; desirable middle-class houses for individual home owners eventually also lined the western ends of Baltimore and Fayette. The western blocks were home to very prestigious, private institutions: St. Luke's Episcopal School for boys on Carey operated from 1853 to World War I, St. Luke's Hall for "young ladies" after 1870, the Isaac Newton Academy in country-like mansion quarters on Baltimore near Carrollton from 1853 to 1893, and the Moore Institute lecture hall at Baltimore and Carey from 1894 to 1919. In mid- and eastern Poppleton, the housing reflected city statutes which forbade new frame houses, as pre- and post-Civil War homes alike were built of brick. Stables, neighborhood coal yards, and old industries nestled on main and alley blocks, an extension of the Mt. Clare and Hollins Park districts. A saw and grist mill on Baltimore between Schroeder and Carrollton, built on a since-covered stream, dated from the 1820s. Steam engine and sash factories dotted Baltimore; a slaughterhouse space was behind the 1000 blocks of Saratoga and Lexington.

New suburbs to the west and north after 1890 prompted conversion of Baltimore and Lexington Street individual row homes to flats and stores, and brought new industry—coal and lumber yards and ice houses—to serve the solidly residential build-up beyond. Elite, private institutions moved or closed their doors. Moore Institute buildings were converted to the West End YMCA, Newton, to a forerunner of Franklin Square Hospital, The National Temperance Hospital (used by physicians who opposed medicinal uses of alcohol) and a small medical college (Maryland Medical). Predominantly white main-street settlement yielded gradually to African-American settlement, blacks inhabiting Rayborg, Vine, Acorn, Harmony, Stockton, Amity, and Carlton before 1900, the main streets east of Schroeder from 1900 to 1930, and Schroeder to Carey by 1940.

As a racially integrated neighborhood, these blocks were home to notorious political boss John S. (Frank) Kelly in the early twentieth century. A gamin reared by a foster mother on the West End, the illiterate and orphaned Kelly controlled the Democratic clubs of the Eighteenth Ward and bossed the city Democratic machine in the early twentieth century. On 1100 Saratoga—a block dubbed Pigeon's Row and known for its ancient bricks—mayors, governors, and presidential aspirants all made pilgrimages to a humble row house basement office, seeking "The Kelly's" blessing. The "Czar," also known as "Slot Machine" Kelly, was as famous for charity as for political favors. Christmas baskets and coal—to keep white Irish loyal and black Republicans at home away from the polls--made their way to hundreds of Poppleton flats until his death in 1936.

During the Depression years, vacated buildings drew many homeless and hoboes. A Fayette health care facility, Lincoln Convalescent, was the setting for a novel labor

The Newton Academy, or University, also used briefly as a hospital, was an elite, private academy on West Baltimore Street east of Carrollton between 1853 and 1893.

union experiment in the 1960s, the formation of the Maryland Freedom Union Local #1, an influential female-led "freedom" union. Large international labor unions affiliated with the AFL-CIO had rarely organized women, minorities, or low-paid service workers anywhere in the United States before 1960, let alone in Baltimore, a city with a traditionally weak labor movement. But at what was then the Lincoln Nursing Home, nurses aides, housekeepers, and kitchen staff set up the Maryland Freedom Union Local #1, in February 1966. Female leadership headed the ninety percent female organization, one of the earliest gender-integrated labor organizations with entirely female officers. It struck Lincoln in protest of sub-minimum wages and unsanitary conditions for patients and workers alike, with tactics that bridged the gap between the then flourishing civil rights movement and organized labor. Officers enlisted the support of civil rights organizers, secured newspaper publicity from the black press, sponsored study groups on labor and black history, and traveled to Washington to demonstrate against the VietNam War. Short lived, the union nevertheless spurred efforts to move civil rights activism beyond concern for desegregation of middle-class accommodations, restaurants, and housing, to militant efforts for workers and the poor. CORE, the Congress of Racial Equality, designated Baltimore a "target city"; in the late 1960s, picket lines and boycotts were employed to draw attention to economic discrimination. Black steel workers formed a caucus at Bethlehem Steel Sparrows Point plants, and minority caucuses spread rapidly throughout the industry in the late 1960s and early 1970s.

Condemnation, demolition, and the construction of Expressway I-170 between 1966 and 1979 greatly affected Poppleton. To eliminate the so-called "worst bottleneck on the east coast"—commercial roads through Baltimore—city planners had projected an expressway along the Franklin-Mulberry corridor, path of Route 40, as early as 1942. The Federal Aid Highway Act of 1956, designed to encourage suburban commuting by automobile and bus, gave impetus to the project providing ninety percent of the funds. But it touched off a controversy over proposed routes that lasted a decade. The eighty-million-dollar highway, one of the few city expressways actually completed, displaced a school, 62 businesses, and residents of 971 homes, many of whom re-located in northwest Baltimore. A 20-feet depressed highway, I-170, was built with new storm drains and over-roads.

Both renovation and new home construction within Poppleton afford it one of the richest arrays of residential housing within Baltimore. Extant architecture went up over one and one half centuries. The variety is visible within a single block, such as 900 Saratoga and 100 Amity and Carleton, and from a single intersection, such as Fayette and Schroeder. Pre-Civil War era construction includes two-story rows with shallow gables and dormers (1830-1860); the highly popular two-story rows with four-foot attics; brick rows with rear promenades and frame attachments widely used as pantries and kitchens; and forerunners to the Italianates, flat-roofed houses built with carefully done brick work and detailed ornamentation (as on 100 Fremont and 1000 Lexington). Except for modest dwellings, elaborate iron work in pre-1860 housing abounds, especially on front facades, fences, rails, lintels, and footway balustrades. (The Bartlett-Hayward ironworks in nearby Mount Clare encouraged its liberal use.) Late nineteenth-century Italianates, elaborately corniced and some with very ornate modillions, line a few blocks; turn-of-the-century swell-front houses are found in the 1200 block of Mulberry; and extant and restored brick alley homes grace Sarah Anne Alley.

Rehab and new houses, perhaps a sixth of the residences, originate from diverse Federal and city programs and, like old houses, display a range of interior and exterior design. Owner-rehabilitated home- and shop-stead edifices are on 800 Baltimore, and owner-refurbished apartments formed from renovated row houses on Poppleton, Amity, and Vine. Streetfronts with rear mews are at 800 Fayette and Lexington; plain-corniced contemporary brick rows with concrete steps and symmetrically placed windows at 1000 Lexington. Rental property includes extensive so-called Section 8 housing, with Federal subsidies comprising the difference between one quarter of tenants' income and rental rates.

Waverly Terrace, brownstone row house mansions with stucco facades on Carey, dates from the 1850s. Noted for the elaborate wrought iron of second-floor balconies and vast second-floor parlors and spiral staircases, the Italian Renaissance-revival mansions overlook Franklin Square. Fifty-one resident-owned co-op apartments were formed from eleven houses with brick additions in 1978.

Churches house venerable city congregations. Georgian ecclesiastical architecture is represented in St. Paul's United Methodist, Schroeder and Saratoga, built in 1847, and at Allen African Methodist Episcopal, formerly Bethany M. E., Lexington and Carrollton. Gothic is represented with St. Luke's Episcopal, Carey, and Morning Star

Small row houses built with slant roof and single gables, such as these on the south side of Saratoga between Fremont and Amity, were built before the Civil War, often by carpenter entrepreneurs. These were razed by the Baltimore Housing Authority in 1939, but many extant ones blend with later and larger nineteenth century row houses in West End neighborhoods. (Courtesy Enoch Pratt Free Library)

This house at 233 North Shroeder Street in 1939, razed by the Baltimore Housing Authority's slum clearance project, illustrates use of latticed iron trim in residential construction. It abounded in fences, railings, window baskets, and foot balustrades in Poe Homes and Poppleton, greatly encouraged by the location of the Bartlett and Hayward Company in east of Mount Clare nearby. (Courtesy Enoch Pratt Free Library)

Baptist, Fayette near Carrollton. Organized near Hollins and Oregon (Arlington), St. Luke's was built as Franklin Square was landscaped in 1851. The nave and main aisles were designed by local architects Niernsee and Nielson, transepts and chancel added after 1858 by New York architects J. W. Priest and H. M. Congdon. Fourteen stone columns in a cruciform of gray stone stand for eleven disciples and Saints Barnabas, Matthias, and Paul. The capitals are individualized to represent the distinctiveness of each saint. Rich in stained glass, St. Luke's has an altar window possibly designed by famed architect William Butterfield. The church was the setting for the American premier of "The Crucifixion," the renowned composition of British composer and St. Paul's Cathedral organist John Stainer.

Morning Star Baptist, organized in 1890 by rural Virginians recently moved to Baltimore, served for decades as both worship place and community gathering spot for generations of city newcomers with strong ties to the countryside. Choirs, women's groups, church schools, and the deaconry assuaged the loneliness of urban life and served social needs. Organized around the leadership of Rev. Robert T. Winn by members of Leadenhall Baptist, it first met on Pierce Street; it owned two facilities on 800 and 900 Saratoga before acquiring the present facility in 1925. As late as 1940, a majority of adult members were still native Virginians.

Franklin Square

Its name taken from the park on Carey, Franklin Square's twenty-two blocks spread westward uphill to a peak near Fulton, and beyond to the beginning of a descent along Monroe. Carey, Mulberry, and Monroe form east, north, and west boundaries; Booth, Gilmore, Frederick, Fulton, and Booth a zigzag south boundary. Nineteenth-century row houses and property extend over eighty percent of the acreage. Commercial establishments traditionally serving a pedestrian patronage line the 1300 to 1700 blocks of Baltimore and dot the street corners of squares four to six blocks north of Pratt and Baltimore Street commercial stretches. Old Ma and Pa groceries, many converted to taverns, delicatessens, and craft, shoe repair, auto repair, and hair shops, relieve dependence on distant commercial sections. Churches also serve pedestrian congregations, thirteen of twenty-one in streetfront rooms. The seven Baptist and three Church of God congregations among them draw from different sections of the neighborhood. With no industry, Franklin Square has five social services agencies including two health care facilities.

The first urban development spread over speculative lands and estates owned by prominent nineteenth-century Baltimoreans. John W. Garrett, 1824-1884, president of the B and O railroad from 1858 to 1884, resided at the estate of Montebello north east of Baltimore but also owned Westside real estate west of Fulton between Saratoga and Lexington. Steuart Hill, the property of George Hume Steuart, West Point-educated, Baltimore-born (1828) general of the Confederate Army, stretched south and west from Baltimore and Fulton. Steuart once

Old West End

figured prominently in neighborhood lore. Crossing the Potomac during the northern thrust of the Confederacy (1862), he allegedly dropped to the ground to kiss Maryland soil before combat in the Battle of Sharpsburg. He fought at Culp's Hill (Gettysburg), and was eventually wounded and taken prisoner of war at the Battle of the Wilderness. Thirty years later he regaled neighborhood children of the new suburbs with war stories, venturing into the streets from his mansion dressed in Confederate grays.

Blocks developed slowly west and north from the Square and on Baltimore and Frederick between 1850 and 1910. In the era of horse-drawn trolleys, the Baltimore and Catonsville Passenger Railway, incorporated in 1860, ran a line from 1700 Frederick, the edge of build-up, to Catonsville. The ascent on Baltimore beyond Stricker required a change of horses. Settlement beyond the Fulton hilltop awaited the electric trolleys laid out in the 1890s.

Brick edifices began to replace old frame dwellings along Baltimore in the 1850s; the Malachi Mills house at 1504 is representative of the pre-development structures of the early nineteenth century. Most of its type were inhabited by families of craftsmen. Twelve-feet-wide and set back from the street, it may have been built in 1827 by a Baltimore carpenter.

Row house mansions around the Square set the standard for the rest of the neighborhood. Delaware real-estate developers James and William Canby purchased thirty acres of the Ramsey-McHenry estate in 1839, on a slope considered ideal for its access to Baltimore Street (one block) and to the city (one third mile). Fayette Street brownstones with ornate door lintels and iron balconies, called Canby Row, contrasted agreeably with Waverly Terrace stucco on Carey (in Poppleton). Ivanhoe Terrace, on Lexington, was distinguished by exterior entryways with highly decorative columns and cornices, the latter not mass produced for Italianate homes until several decades later. Large homes on Delaware Row (Calhoun) eventually housed Franklin Square Hospital. It spread from two houses in 1901 over the entire block before it moved to Baltimore County in the mid-1960s. Tiny front yards all around the Square, a rarity for streetfront Italianates as late as 1900, extended the open space of the Square, heightening a sense of grandeur. Linden Terrace just off the Square on Carey, also with yards, was noted for its elaborate entryways and stylish mansard roofs. Wealthy bankers, merchants, judges, one governor (Augustus Bradford), and a congressman (Henry Stockbridge) lived along the Square in the mid- and late nineteenth century. Public officials were prominent in the Concord Club, a Democratic Party club at 12 Carey.

Plain-faced Italianates built between 1870 and 1904 in northern and western blocks displayed similarly distinctive if less elegant exteriors. A block known as "The Row," 1800 Lexington, with unusual front porches, was constructed by Baltimore builder Jeremiah Blanch. Southerners, once antebellum planters, acquired its houses, perhaps with the encouragement of George Steuart. The alternate square- and swell-front houses of 1800 Baltimore were also built back from the street. For many years western blocks all sat close to farm land beyond Monroe and to a private park, Garrett Park, on a city square west of Fulton, between Fayette and Lexington. A homeowners association maintained a fenced and gated park locked to outsiders until about 1900.

As a largely African-American neighborhood (east of Fulton after 1910, west after 1950), the area housed institutions with a city-wide patronage. The Douglass Theatre, forerunner to the Royal, was located on Gilmore near Saratoga. In 1918 it advertised itself as "the only Vaudeville and Motion Picture Parlor owned and managed exclusively by colored people." The career of Bessie Smith, famed empress of the blues, was launched from the Douglass. Macedonia Baptist, a neighborhood congregation at Saratoga and Gilmore until 1925, Sharon Baptist, and three other city African-American congregations opened the Baptist Aged Folks Home at 1620 Lexington in 1920. With little new housing, Franklin Square's population was halved during the years in which I-170 was constructed.

The oldest of six mid-nineteenth century hilltop squares in the city, Franklin Square park retains its Civil War era grandeur. Carved from a three-acre plot sold to the city by Canby in 1845, it was built with diagonal walkways, iron railings, marble fountains, and gas lighting. Water from four wells, allegedly with medicinal qualities, was carried away for a few years until the wells were covered over. H. L. Mencken spoke of the Square as Baltimore's loveliest and most "dignified."

St. Martin's is the neighborhood's oldest continuous church congregation. Initiated by a priest at St. Peter's, Hollins Park, John S. Foley, it was built on an encampment site of Civil War soldiers during the Civil War and dedicated in 1867. The 150-foot church tower was subsequently added to the handsome Romanesque structure. The complex around the church, including school and gymnasium, was built between 1888 and 1915; new bells and a clock tower were installed in 1923. St. Luke's United Church of Christ, Carey and Fayette, was built in 1861 as Franklin Square Presbyterian with funds contributed by a member of First Presbyterian. Formerly St. Luke's German Evangelical Lutheran, organized in south Baltimore in 1864, it acquired the graystone in 1923.

The sixty-five unit apartment house at Saratoga and Mount, built as a school in 1888, was one of the West Baltimore homes of Coppin Normal School, today Coppin State. Coppin may have been the first black-staffed public school, the teacher training program dating from a training class established in connection with Douglass High School in 1900. A two-year curriculum was introduced in 1902, its first commencement conducted in 1914 at the Lyric Theatre; formal designation as Coppin Normal came in 1926. It was named for the slave-born Fannie Jackson Coppin, allegedly the first African-American woman to receive a college degree. Educated at Rhode Island State Normal and Oberlin, and married to an African Methodist Episcopal Bishop in Africa, Coppin introduced teacher training for African Americans into the Philadelphia school system and served as principal of a school which became Cheyney State.

Coppin School occupied the top floor of School 100, with training taking place within the school. In the 1920s and 1930s, men wore ties and coats, women, dresses, gloves, and hats. The Bachelor of Science degree was first conferred in 1938. The school was subsequently housed in Sandtown-Winchester at Mount and Riggs and, outgrowing its space, moved into the facility of the Lutheran Deaconess home (Greater Mondawmin) in 1952.

Union Square and West Pratt

Union Square and West Pratt spread along a gentle ascent to Monroe and a descent beyond. Ninety percent of their houses are brick rows, three-story on main streets, two on alleys, most of them post-Civil War Italianates. Carey and Payson have a few pre-War, two-story-with-attic row houses. Close to the commercial districts of Baltimore and Frederick, and with a stretch of shops, stores, chain markets, and pharmacies from 1700 to 2000 Pratt, solid residential blocks lack the Ma and Pa corner markets characteristic of row house neighborhoods. Seven of ten churches cluster about the Square.

Union Square's boundaries extend clockwise from Carey and Pratt along Pratt, Fulton, Frederick, Gilmore, Booth, and Carey. Named for the park, which, with Steuart Hill Elementary, abuts the neighborhood edges as a centerpiece, it encloses mostly residential blocks and alleys that span the five blocks west of Carey.

The area built up around a landmark estate razed in 1965, Willow Brook, on the site of Steuart Hill Elementary. Thorowgood Smith, a city merchant-shipper and mayor of Baltimore from 1800 to 1804, built a section of it in 1799, but, suffering hard times with French seizure of American ships in the Atlantic trade, sold it within a year. With twenty-six acres it passed to a nephew, merchant privateer John Donnell. Built in the style of the Palladian villa popular in mid-eighteenth-century England and the United States, it sat on a natural incline. A dry well or moat encircled it. Two balancing pavilions on two sides extended from a dominating center section.

The estate house was acquired in 1864 by Emily Caton McTavish, granddaughter of Charles Carroll. She in turn donated it to the Roman Catholic Church for a school for delinquent girls. Six sisters of the Congregation of the Good Shepherd started up a convent and home in 1865, three side buildings and a surrounding wall eventually being added. H. L. Mencken recollected Good Shepherd as a forbidding neighborhood institution, a "vast, mysterious compound" with "high stone wall shutting it in from the world." It closed when the property was sold and buildings dismantled in 1965. Willow Brook's interior oval drawing room had long enjoyed national acclaim, and, still intact, it was moved to the Baltimore Museum of Art for public and permanent display. Its cornices possessed a very delicate frieze, its raised plaster an unusual intricate design. A carved door was shaped to conform to a curved wall.

Middle-class housing on the Donnell property and the Ramsey-McHenry estate lined blocks around the Square before the Civil War, workers' housing the western blocks close to Frederick and Pratt after the War. Three sons of John Donnell leased grounds around the park, laid out specifications for houses, and graded and paved streets bordering the Square in the 1840s. Rivaling the terraces about Franklin Square for prestige, Stricker (on the Square), occasionally dubbed Millionaire's Row, was home to bankers, investors, and factory owners. But elsewhere in the eastern blocks plainer homes were put up in groups with identical features such as cornices, brownstone facing, marble steps, and iron work. Common brick was often used on side walls, hard surface English brick on the front. The largest rooms were typically the front parlors and master bedrooms; small rooms were placed to the rear. Ceiling medallions and fireplace designs were individualized features, chosen from home order catalogues.

The life of Victorian Era children in Old West End neighborhoods is charmingly captured in *Happy Days*, H. L. Mencken's widely read autobiography published in 1940. Reared on Hollins across from the Square in the 1880s and 1890s—the era of new homes, first home owners, and many children—Mencken humorously recalled life around the Square. Nearby yards and streets were the locale of high adventure and fantasy, especially for boys. Petty mischief and intrigue occupied youngsters free to roam long back yards, thoroughfares, and nearby woodland.

> "I spent . . . pre-school leisure in . . .\the backyard.\ a strange, wild land of endless discoveries and enchantments. . . . /W/e dug worms/ ,/. . . watched for robins/,/. . . chased butterflies, . . . stoned sparrows, and . . . made bonfires of falling leaves." "My brother and I used to begin on /the tree of/ cherries when they were still only pellets of hard green, and . . . got through three or four . . . belly aches before the earliest was ripe."

> Adolescents roamed farther. "Every Baltimore boy . . . had to be a partisan of some /fire/ engine company, . . . or, as the phrase ran, /had to/ go for it. . . . If the fire was nearby . . . all hands dropped whatever was afoot and set off for it at a gallop." And "every self-respecting boy . . . belong/ed/ to a gang. . . . There was /a/ difference between the proletariat and. . . the more tender bourgeoisie, . . . the former . . . devoted to stoning cops and . . . looting . . . freight cars of the Baltimore & Ohio Railroad. . . . The latter carried only clubs . . . and never got . . . further along the road to debauchery than reading dime-novels and smoking cigarettes."

A tall, stone wall surrounded the House of Good Shepherd at Mount and Hollins Street, today the location of Steuart Hill Elementary School. It was operated by the Sisters of the Congregation of the Good Shepherd from 1864 to 1965 for delinquent girls. Its buildings comprised part of the estate, "Willow Brook."

"The frontiers of the various gangs in West Baltimore were known to all the boys denizened, /and/ fights between adjoining gangs were relatively rare, for the cops kept watch along the borders.... Any boy in flight from a cop was sure of sanctuary anywhere."

"I was a larva of the comfortable and complacent bourgeoisie," he reminisced, "encapsulated in affection and kept fat, saucy, and contented. Thus I got through my nonage without . . . an inferiority complex."

Nineteenth Century workers' homes beyond Mount reflected the presence of industry in West Pratt. The trend to convert Italianate homes to flats and rooming houses was accelerated during World War II by a large influx of defense workers from Appalachia. Organization of the Union Square Association in 1967 prompted reconversion to single-family dwellings in blocks next to the Square. The Square was designated a preservation district by the City Council in 1978, enabling investors to take advantage of Federal legislation. The Tax Reform Act of 1978 permitted write-offs with accelerated depreciation in "historic" districts for rehabilitation work. A city "shopsteading" program, one of the nation's earliest, was established on West Baltimore in 1977.

Edged in cobblestone, the landscape of Union Square, with its walkways, pavilions, fountain and wrought iron lamps, recalls Victorian Era Baltimore. Built on two-and-one-half acres given the City by the Donnells, it covered a once exposed spring accessible by steps. The city sold the water rights to the B and O at Mount Clare to finance gas lighting and iron fencing since removed. Architect John F. Hoss designed the Greek-style pavilion with fluted columns in 1850. The name may reflect patriotic sentiment in the time of sectional unrest. Old iron urns were smelted

Old West End

Union Square in 1895. Victorian Era city squares, built often with decorative entryways, kept well-maintained and manicured looks, with a visual, aesthetic appeal, for nearby middle class residents. They were seldom made use of for recreation or sport.

down during World War II for the war effort; new lighting, shrubs, pink sidewalks, and cast iron benches were installed during the 1970s. Fog scenes of the Square, lights agleam over wet pavements and barren limbs, were often featured in local landscape artistry.

The tall-pillared, Greek Revival Union Square United Methodist, seating 900 at Calhoun and Lombard, opened in 1853 on land donated by the Donnells. It was built by the Fayette Street Station congregation, formed in 1839 on Carrollton near the Mount Clare yards. The twin-towered Romanesque New Mount Zion Cathedral, Mount near Lombard, was built as The Church of the Holy Martyrs (Roman Catholic) in 1902, replacing an earlier edifice put up in 1871. The first ethnic German church on the Westside, it was staffed by Redemptionist and Benedictine priests, and nuns of the Benedictine and Notre Dame orders, the latter staffing a parochial school for many years. An urban services agency also occupies an old, red-brick, Richardson Romanesque building, a former branch library built at Calhoun and Hollins in 1886.

Number 1524 Hollins, the lifetime home of Mencken, opened as a city museum with period furniture, his restored second-floor office, and backyard gazebo in 1983. The city's oldest soup kitchen, Viva House on Mount, affiliated with the Catholic Worker movement, has been the center of city-wide advocacy for both the poor and for tenants affected by restoration and gentrification programs.

West Pratt's boundaries extend clockwise from Fulton and Pratt clockwise on Pratt, Pulaski, Frederick Avenue, Monroe, Booth, and Fulton. Its architectural character reflects the presence of nineteenth-century neighborhood industries, as well as breweries and slaughterhouses along the Gwynns Falls close by. A cooperage sat on Goldsmith and a wagon works at Pratt and Pulaski. Workers' housing, never entirely replaced by middle class Italianates, spread over blocks next to Pratt. The commercial district on Pratt developed with theatres and auto service stations in the 1920s.

Acreage east of Monroe forms part of Union Square Preservation District. Miracle Temple Seventh Day Adventist Church, Fulton and Lombard, was erected in 1867 as a United Brethren in Christ church for a German ethnic worker population along Frederick and Pratt. It was redesignated the Third Church of the Evangelical United Brethren in 1946.

Booth-Boyd

Bounded by Monroe, Baltimore, Frederick Avenue, and Calverton Road, Booth-Boyd is named for two east-west alley streets. The former name derives from William Booth, operator of a five-acre nursery along Baltimore Street, who rented property from James McHenry between 1796 and 1818. The latter may come from Anna McHenry Boyd, daughter of James McHenry. Commercial establishments line the two blocks of Frederick, two- and three-story row homes, mostly streetfront Italianates with corner stores, every other block except Calverton. The streets edge the 1816 Annex boundary; the northwestern corner near Calverton and Baltimore was in Baltimore County until 1888.

Set on a downward western slope, blocks developed between 1890 and 1914 with the extension of electric trolley lines, pre-development institutions serving as links between city and country. The post-Civil War Baltimore, Calverton and Powhatan Railroad located a terminal near Baltimore and Smallwood, a transfer depot from horse trolley lines over rail to the northwestern villages of Baltimore County. Vacant hills of the Steuart estate (Monroe to Payson) drew city workers, sod-cutters who carved up and carted grassground to new middle-class houses, and carpet beaters who did their semi-annual "rug floggings" there.

Unusual four-story rows with double rear porches on the hilltop of the 1900 block of Baltimore afforded a rare panorama vista of the city. A 1902 fire engine house, 1908 Hollins, a two-story row brick Italianate structure with wrought iron fencing, blended with the residential housing. Central Baptist, organized in 1923, has occupied the Gothic graystone building at Baltimore and Pulaski Street since 1957, with a new educational building in 1979; the church reflects the largely African-American make-up of the neighborhood since the 1950s. The 13,500 squarefoot Hollins-Payson branch of Enoch Pratt, with auditorium, was built on the site of a nineteenth-century lumberyard in 1963, replacing Branch #2 of Union Square.

Lexington

Lexington's borders extend clockwise from Baltimore and Monroe Street on Baltimore, Warwick, the Amtrak railway, Mulberry, and Monroe. It straddles the city boundary of 1816. About half of it, on land west of Smallwood, lay outside the city until 1888. It slopes westward from Payson to just east of Warwick, a spot which until World War I formed the path of a narrow stream, Gwynns Run. It includes five churches, two elementary schools, and corner and streetfront shops on the eastern blocks. A warehouse-commercial district along Warwick and the western blocks of Edmondson and Mulberry are easily accessible to the Franklin-Mulberry corridor.

Western blocks formed a mid- and late nineteenth-century industrial section. Slaughterhouses which lay north of the Amtrak tracks (then the Baltimore and Potomac Railroad) were accessible to cattle pens of the Calverton stockyards on Baltimore. Lime kilns sat north of Baltimore. Waste was emptied into Gwynns Run. A workers' settlement lay close to the tracks in the area which is today School #150.

Eastern block development reflected the tendency of initial build-up to concentrate close to trolley lines, and newer row homes to be built without the servant quarters of alley housing. Built on the farmland of the Shipley, Garrett, Scribner, and Steuart estates, the first homes went up along the Baltimore streetcar route between 1890 to 1910. Houses northward, many done by prominent city builders James Keelty and Walter Westphal, were built bow-shaped with marble trim, those beyond the 2100 block connected to the city's new sewage system. Houses on

Sandtown

Harlem Park, named for the estate of Adrian Valck, about 1900.

City subdivisions typically take their names from old estates, wealthy land owners, or pastoral titles bestowed by real-estate developers. But "Sandtown" derives directly from the people who lived there. Sand-loaded wagons and trucks rumbled over cobblestone and paved streets bound for all parts of the city. They moved from a glass quarry, sand pits, and a sand-using asphalt company located along Monroe Street from at least the 1890s. Spilled grit covered the pavement everywhere, so thick at Mount and Riggs, neighborhood lore has it, that even horseshoes lay buried. Sandtown's two neighborhoods spread over the northwest quadrant of the old nineteenth-century city, blocks west of Pennsylvania and Fremont between Edmondson and North close to the city boundary of 1816.

Built as a white middle-class suburb from 1870 to 1900, the neighborhoods drew working-class African Americans after World War I. A fast-growing black population in the City (from 109,000 in 1920 to 329,000 in 1960), the residential stability of industrial sections of East and South Baltimore, and segregation and the exodus of the white middle classes all fed this transformation. After 1917, these blocks began to form a solidly African-American subdivision that by World War II was Baltimore's largest. Bordering Upton, its two neighborhoods included only a few families of professional people, businessmen, and civic leaders. But they drew many industrial and home workers, especially newcomers from the Upper South. For over two generations, from 1920 to 1960, workers labored in both traditional African-American trades—carrying and portering enterprises and domestic work—and in city industry and manufacturing.

Southern industrial production and employment lagged behind Northern in the twentieth century as it had in the nineteenth. Five Deep-South states actually offered fewer industrial jobs before World War II than they had prior to World War I, and the entire section experienced absolutely no industrial growth during the Depression decade of the 1930s. In Upper South states, the feeder area to cities of the Middle Atlantic states, industries such as cotton manufacture and saw mills and furniture manufacturing relied heavily on white labor. Programs to restrict agricultural production—reforms of Franklin D. Roosevelt's New Deal sometimes called the "American Enclosure Movement"—actually hastened the exodus of agricultural workers from farms during the Depression. In the 1940s, machines and mechanization accelerated it further. Southern farm population declined twenty-two percent during World War II. After the War, an underfunded segregated school system failed to offer African Americans industrial education adequate to the needs of modern industry.

Newcomers came north in search of work. In Baltimore, the door to industrial employment—barely unfastened in industrial production for African Americans before World War I—opened in bits and spurts thereafter. Under twin pressures—the agitation of black-enrolled labor unions and civil rights organizations, and periodic labor shortages—men secured a range of industrial jobs. They worked as common laborers in steel, shipbuilding, and chemicals, hod carriers in construction, and longshoremen and dock and bridge builders on the waterfront during the 1920s. Some secured jobs as auto assemblymen in the 1930s. During World War II, "Colored Defense Schools" trained skilled aircraft riveters, small parts assemblymen, and industrial sewers.

Women secured jobs as garment finishers in small plants along Pennsylvania and North between the wars. After 1940 they secured a major entry into the office, clerical, and waitressing trades.

Workers both within and outside of manufacturing enterprises faced obstacles. The city high-school system concentrated its vocational education programs in white schools. Unions tended to bar African Americans, or acquiesce in policies which reserved better paid, skilled slots for whites. Rank-and-file white assembly line workers resisted shop floor integration. (At the World War II Point Breeze plant of Westinghouse, whites struck when 1,700 blacks were hired, police and eventually the United States Army being called in to protect wartime integration. At Fairfield shipyards the military provided armed guards to protect black workers). Within Sandtown neighborhoods during these years work was often unavailable with local employers. The Schmidt Bakery and Capitol Cake Company, for example, both with large Sandtown-Winchester plants close to the North and Fulton Avenue thoroughfares, relied on white plant workers and drivers. Commercial places along Fulton, long a dividing line between black and white neighborhoods, similarly hired white clerks and workers from outside the neighborhoods.

Citywide, the "last hired, first fired" tradition exacted a toll. During the Depression, employers counted traditional African-American work (housekeeping, for example) a dispensable luxury or a favor to be bestowed on white relatives or friends suffering hard times. Ominously, the 1950s saw a more permanent threat to industrial work in Baltimore, as city industry relocated in the suburbs.

But jobs and employment were treasured all the more for their short supply. Aspiring carpenters, tailors, and shoe and auto repairmen packed the Evening vocational program which Douglass High School began to offer in the 1920s. (Chauffeurs, among others, jumped at the chance to learn repair of the new motorized vehicles.) Other workers signed on with garment workers unions and integrated CIO (Congress of Industrial Organizations) associations, including the powerful steel workers union in the late 1930s. Many joined the "Don't buy Where You Can't Work" campaign of the 1930s, a forerunner to the postwar civil rights agitation. Sandtown residents hoisted signs along the picket lines of white-owned Pennsylvania Avenue businesses. They promoted a citywide boycott until jobs were made available to blacks.

Sandtown blocks developed as a workers' suburb and as a consequence the electrified trolley, used more for recreation purposes elsewhere, became indispensable for commuters. The city *Afro-American* first listed streetcar directions to East Baltimore and Sparrows Point plants during the 1920s. The cars' modest fares—never more than ten cents with free transfers--and their relative speed, facilitated distant travel. Lines #1, #2, #13, and #19 extended over Gilmore, Carey, Pennsylvania, and North. Cars through Sandtown became busy especially at the two ends of the workday. In the mornings, workers congregated on opposite street corners, men, lunch pails in hand, catching cars bound downtown, east and south for plants, factories, and commercial districts. Women, empty-armed, awaited trolleys bound uptown to middle- and upper-class households. At day's end, workers stepped off at the opposite corners, men without packages but women often with arms loaded with hand-me-down goods, the traditional pay supplement of domestic labor.

Workers mostly rented flats in converted row houses, usually with one kitchen per floor, and with shared, cold-water-only bathrooms. Units were secured by word of mouth, advertisements in the *Afro*, and Pennsylvania Avenue rooming agencies. The search for amenities—a private bath or a pair of connecting rooms for a families—prompted considerable moving about, and many households uprooted and moved at least once every several years. (As late as 1950 forty percent of the housing units maintained shared baths.) Newcomers, often relatives from the South, doubled up in front rooms, while children in extended families doubled up with a grandparent. Weekly baths took place in the flat kitchen. Alley houses with four to six rooms tended to rent the least expensive; flats in corner homes, many with an interior "daylight" room with windows, the most.

Workers' organizations periodically took up the issue of housing shortages, protesting segregation and discrimination. During World War II, the Steel Workers Organizing Committee (CIO), with a large city African-American membership, exposed the condition of single lodgers, defense workers newly arrived in the city, being forced into overcrowded flats and individual homes throughout the city. Ties with the rural heritage nurtured community and family stability. Neighbors, and cousins, aunts, and uncles from the same county, or the same church congregation, in rural Maryland, Virginia, or North Carolina tended to cluster around the same blocks. Familiar faces soothed the loneliness and isolation. "When you came up here /from Virginia/, remembered one, "You had to report to a resident here, someone you knew. And they notified your family right away. And you stayed there, right there, until you got a job." A car on a block was often regarded as a community amenity, for trips to church and markets, and "down home" to the country.

Hard work by adults and children molded family and neighborhood life. Men held several outside jobs, women provided for boarders as well as working outside, and children worked as errand runners and delivery boys. Too busy often to shop away from the neighborhood, residents patronized busy Ma and Pa groceries, and the Lafayette Market at night. The area formed a pedestrian suburb to Avenue establishments which, with corner-located facilities in the two neighborhoods themselves, catered especially to the neighborhoods' many young. Cabarets and dance halls afforded escape from parents, and indulgence in a fantasy world apart from work. Theatres beckoned in the evenings; "Have to be Home Before Dark from the Royal" was often the rule at home. Neighborhood movie theatres—the Carey, at Carey and Presstman, and Lafayette, at Lafayette and Stricker—opened in the 1920s and advertised themselves as less expensive than Avenue establishments, and featured a daily change of fare. But severe hard times, work lay-offs and a shortage of jobs during the Depression, stimulated quite a different commerce and spurred the ingenuity of workers. Sandtown oldtimers remember austerity at home and a busy trade at pawnshops. "Now when we got married I told my wife, 'Now you're a lovely bride, but sweep up that rice they threw on you. That's our wedding supper,'" "Why men would walk all the way to the waterfront along Pratt Street, buy a suit for $3.00 and walk back up to Pennsylvania Avenue and pawn it for $6.00. This could happen three or four times a day until the pawn dealer caught on." "We used to go to the store and ask the man to sell us empty lard cans for our garbage. Then we'd take them back and put them on our stove and the heat would melt the lard remaining in it and sometimes we'd get a pound, pound and a half."

Nurtured by family and church, the country-ness of the Sandtown neighborhoods survived. Children moved back and forth throughout the year, city youngsters sent "home" for the summer months and "down home" youngsters brought north for winter-month schooling. Old rituals were acted out anew. Women brought their chickens live from Lafayette Market, and took them home for backyard killing and plucking. Baltimore's "sitting out" tradition was modified. In the evenings women brought chairs to the sidewalk, preferring them to stoops or steps for social time. Neighborhood clean-up campaigns, such as the *Afro-American* Clean Block awards program for flowers and window boxes, encouraged touches of the country. Regional accents—"Gee-chas's" of the Gulf states, and the hard sounds of Carolina and Virginia—could be heard in the streets and schools.

Churches, meeting religious and social needs, bridged rural and urban life. Larger congregations occasionally paid to bring downhome pastors to the city where they were expected to assume community leadership roles. Donors with no personal property of their own nevertheless possessed a share of community property. Members were known by name. Laypeople's activity—as office holders, deacons, superintendents—bestowed a sense of responsibility and recognition. Streetfront sanctuaries, opened in the front rooms of row houses, afforded a kind of urban equivalent to the crossroads country churches. Formed often by ministers who worked at full-time jobs, they especially attracted newcomers. Outsiders who felt out of place in the restrained services of the larger churches, or embarrassed by small contributions or humble attire, supported them. They served as familiar anchors for the rural-born in an unfamiliar setting.

(OVERLEAF - LEFT) Lafayette Market overlooking Pennsylvania Avenue in 1953 served a pedestrian trade in Upton, Druid Heights, and Sandtown-Winchester.

(OVERLEAF - RIGHT) Carey Theatre, Carey and Presstman Street, was a popular neighborhood institution in the 1920s. (Courtesy University of Maryland Baltimore County)

Harlem Park

Bounded by Lafayette, Fremont, I-170, Schroeder, Franklin, and Monroe, Harlem Park derives its name from the square at its center. Thirty-five blocks ascend gently east to west. Row houses, most three-story and built between 1870 and 1900, line main streets. It has three schools, no commercial streets or industry, and thirty-one parks. All but two of the last form "inner block" squares, built behind main streets on acreage once covered with alley homes and lots. Urban Renewal programs financed their construction during the 1960s.

Twenty-five streetfront shops, front rooms of converted row houses, include groceries, delicatessens, and hardware and beauty shops. Eighteen streetfront churches serve regular Baptist, free-will Baptist, Apostolic Holiness and non-denominational congregations. Five of six towering nineteenth-century church buildings anchor Lafayette Square and Harlem Park. A bisecting north-south thoroughfare, Gilmore, once a streetcar route with neighborhood commercial places, was named in the 1816 Poppleton Survey for Robert Gilmor, 1748-1822, and his son, Robert Gilmor, Jr., 1774-1848. The elder was a Scottish-born Baltimore shipper, City Councilman, and banker; his son a notable diarist, collector of national art, and sire to a family of prominent bankers and businessmen.

Before development, this acreage formed the speculative and estate lands of Baltimore shippers and merchants. Adrian Valck, Netherlands-born merchant and Pratt Street town dweller, secured a leasehold of thirty-one acres in the western section in 1789. Valck eventually built a large brick home, called

"Harlem," with workers' buildings, stables, and a dairy fronting on a pathway to the Frederick turnpike near present-day Fulton. Valck's gardens won national renown, with walks, squares, and espaliers, stocked with vegetables and fruits from European nurseries. The groves of trees and a six-acre orchard on a hill with a commanding view of the city soon passed into the hands of city merchant and speculator William Lorman, who sold at least part of it to merchant, shipmaster, and Mayor of the city of Baltimore (1815 and 1818) George Stiles. Merchant Thomas Edmondson acquired the leasehold in 1815 and an additional freehold in 1822 to comprise an estate of fifty-six acres. A son, physician Thomas Edmondson, Jr., maintained it with gardens of exotic plants until 1856. On Harlem Park's eastern edge, French-born Henry Didier, a fleet owner and town inhabitant, owned an estate near Fremont at the beginning of the nineteenth century.

During the 1860s, the city graded streets, and the estates passed into the hands of developers, the wideness of the thoroughfares and the high elevation affording excellent ventilation and drainage. Builders erected Italianate houses in the western section, five and six at a time, with identical exteriors. Builder Joseph Cone, active in the city since 1860, built fifty-nine around Harlem Square. While few homes had marks of exceptional affluence—distinctive individual styling, front yards, extra width, decorative iron trim—all possessed the amenities of middle-class style and comfort. Carved moldings, high ceilings, and basements distinguished interiors. Some incorporated stained glass, marble fireplaces, ornate plaster work, and gracious staircases. Rear yards afforded space for out-buildings and play area for children.

The horse-drawn North Baltimore Passenger Railway, called the Frick Line, which traveled along Edmondson to City Hall, stimulated further construction along western blocks, the car barn being located on the incline between Mount and Fulton. New houses drew families of businessmen and entrepreneurs, professional people and civil servants, and the institutions which they patronized. The Archdiocese of Baltimore maintained a school to train female teachers, St. Catherine's, at Harlem and Arlington. Run by the Sisters of the Holy Cross, and located two blocks from the public ("Maryland") Normal School (Sandtown-Winchester), it was the country's only Roman Catholic Normal School. Protestant congregations bound eventually for distant city or Baltimore County suburbs built churches, Grace Methodist a towering graystone at Lafayette and Carrollton, and Lafayette Square Presbyterian, later Hunting Ridge Presbyterian, on Carrollton. Memorial Methodist Protestant, later West Baltimore Methodist, built at Lafayette and Gilmore, Brantly Baptist at Schroeder and Edmondson.

Novelist Henry James once described the stately, prim row houses of Harlem Park square as "virtuous dames."

Set about a "large green table," they had "no more riotous end than that each should sit before.../an/individual game of patience." The dignified rows throughout the neighborhood indeed possessed a refined manicured look, and their first and second generation inhabitants a restrained, formal social life, which both befit-

ted middle-class status and required servant labor. "My grandfather's house . . . was one of the neatest . . . on Harlem," remembered one. "The yard was a showplace . . . . There was a lattice garden house, a prolific grape arbor, rose bushes and many other flower beds. . . . In the rear of the yard was the usual outhouse concealed by honeysuckle." "On summer evenings after supper the custom was for the whole family to sit out on the marble steps. But one could never sit directly on the marble. . . . The children were always detailed to bring out the straw mats which were stowed under the lift-up seat . . . in the front hall." "Illumination was by gas. . . . Every evening at dusk one of the adults would . . . light the strategic lamps . . . and then the great chandelier in the dining room. . . . Hung over the center of the table, . . . it was the most important lamp in the house. . . . When supper was cleared away, . . . /the dining room/ became the sitting room. . . . Sewing, reading, and the playing of dominoes and parchesi all took place."

A young German maid remembered,

"Ironing was a problem. /The mistress/ wore tight-fitting waist wrappers with high necks and trains, with ruffles all around the train and sleeves, neck and a crocheted watch pocket. . . . Ironing one of these was a long job, besides the ruffles on the petticoats and drawers. The children too had very fancy clothes and underwear." "Every Sunday Jessie /an African-American driver/ would bring the surrey . . . for a long ride through Druid Hill Park." "/He/ took care of the horses, yard work, the front marble steps and outside work."

African Americans had moved on main streets to Gilmore by the 1920s, Fulton during the 1940s, and Monroe the 1950s, main streets which were also a network of trolley lines. Throughout Harlem Park trolleys traveled seven of the eleven north-south streets, and three of the five east-west streets. A private college for African Americans, Morgan, to-day Morgan State University, was housed at Edmondson and Fulton between 1881 and 1918. At the request of black clergy in the Methodist Episcopal Church, the Washington Conference of the church formed the Centenary Biblical Institutes in 1867 to educate "divinely called" young men for the clergy. The first classes were held at Sharp Street Church, south Baltimore; the curriculum soon broadened to include the training of teachers. Rare for nineteenth-century colleges, women were admitted and black faculty hired. Prominent Baltimore clergyman John F. Goucher donated the Edmondson lot for a three-story edifice. It was renamed Morgan in 1890 as a tribute to clergyman and benefactor Lyttleton F. Morgan, a leading minister in the Baltimore Conference and one of the college's earliest benefactors. Morgan eventually sponsored two branches, Princess Anne Academy, now a branch of the University of Maryland, and Virginia Collegiate and Industrial Institute, since discontinued. The need for additional grounds prompted a move to northeast Baltimore.

Defense workers and their families crowded alley and main-street houses alike in the 1940s with basements, garages, hallways and even boiler rooms converted to makeshift bedrooms. Postwar demographic shifts brought in more children, with African-American churches and civic organizations taking the initiative for neighborhood betterment and converting old space to new uses, especially for the young. St. James Episcopal launched a settlement house with classes and athletics, the genesis of the Lafayette Square Community Center. The Northwest Improvement Center agitated for electric lighting along Edmondson, and tot space in

Morgan College at Edmondson Avenue and Fulton Street between 1881 and 1917. Once called Centenary Biblical Institute, it sat on property donated by Rev. John Goucher. (Courtesy Enoch Pratt Free Library)

staid Harlem Park. The Harlem Bears neighborhood football team won citywide fame during the 1950s.

Lafayette Square, three-and-one-half acres at the northeastern corner, and Harlem Park, nine-and-three-quarters acres at the center, form neighborhood touchstones. Every street intersection is within sight of one of them. The city acquired the former in 1857 from developers of the estate of William Lorman, naming it for the east-west street at its northern edge. But the city postponed landscaping during the Civil War, turning the Square over to the Third Regiment, Maryland Veteran Volunteers, which built barracks and recruited Maryland soldiers there throughout the War. Headed by William Louis Schley, the Maryland Volunteers were called the Public Guard Regiment, and the Square known as Camp Hoffman for a prominent Unionist, Henry W. Hoffman. Military units from New York also occupied the Square. Military occupation destroyed forest trees, but the barracks were dismantled and iron railings installed after the War. The Square was adorned with a bronze fountain and eight entrances flanked by urns, and with a flower garden and pond maintained by a city gardener.

Lafayette Square was acquired by the city in 1856 but used as the first camp of Public Guard Regiment in 1861, first year of the Civil War. It served as a recruiting center for other Maryland Unionist volunteer units throughout the War. The surrounding iron fence was erected prior to military use.

Sandtown

Twice the size of Franklin, Union, or Lafayette squares, Harlem Park, on a natural slope, was acquired by the city in 1868. Executors of the Edmondson estate donated it with the provision that green space be city erected and maintained. Dedicated in 1876, it was known for a variety of trees and twenty-seven beds of exotic flora, the latter a city attraction. The Odd Fellows fraternal order erected a monument in 1885 to James Lot Ridgely, a Lincoln-appointed collector of internal revenue in Baltimore and editor of a lodge magazine. Gold fish ponds were erected at the Calhoun edge in the 1890s, and along the Edmondson boundary in the 1930s.

Church congregations of African Americans which originated in older sections of the city acquired the graystones as members moved onto the main streets. St. John's AME, with an active relief program in East Africa, began as a mission on Tessier Street in the Bottom sections, acquiring Lafayette Presbyterian in 1929. The black-gray edifice of St. Pius V was built from 1878 to 1879 for a white congregation, seven years after the purchase of the land by the Archdiocese. It commemorated the twenty-fifth anniversary of the pontificate of Pope Pius IX and Pope Pius V. Priests of the Josephite Order, which served the African-American congregations, assumed control in 1931. The order had staffed St. Barnabas Church on Biddle (near "Murphy Homes") from 1907, acquiring a building of the same name from the Episcopal Diocese. St. Barnabas closed when its congregation transferred to St. Pius. The Oblate Sisters of Providence operated a parochial school there for many years. Reflecting the black consciousness movement of the 1970s, parish youth painted the statues black, and the parish subsequently sponsored tutoring services, prayer services at Murphy Homes, and a neighborhood housing sale and renovation program for low-income families. It hosted the city's oldest active Alcoholics Anonymous chapter, founded in 1953.

St. James Episcopal, formed as St. James African Episcopal, moved into the Lafayette Square facility of Ascension Protestant Episcopal in 1932. The congregation was organized on Park Avenue in 1824, by William Levington, a freeman ordained by William White, the first presiding bishop of the Episcopal Church. The congregation acquired a local reputation for unique congregational autonomy within the denomination and for its standard of equality between slave and free members. The third Episcopal congregation of African Americans in the United States, it was the first in the Southern states, and was Baltimore's only congregation affiliated with a white denomination but maintaining local control and with an African-American priest. All but one of the rectors since have been African Americans. It was housed variously in a former Baptist church and a synagogue at North and Saratoga, and at edifices at High and Lexington and Park and Preston before moving to Harlem Park. Civil rights leader and author George Freeman Bragg, Jr. served as rector from 1891 to 1940. The church organized a mission chapel in Atlantic City, a home for children, the "Maryland Home for Friendless Colored Children" located on Druid Hill Avenue until 1911 and thereafter in Catonsville. The sanctuary was remodeled in the 1940s and St. James Terrace Apartments next to the church completed in the 1960s.

Enon Baptist originated on Park near Dolphin and acquired Brantly Baptist in 1942. Among the city's largest Baptist congregations, it built the Arthur J. Payne Christian Center in 1968 with offices, and library, choir, usher, and classrooms, commemorating Payne's pastorate, 1923-1976. Harlem Park Community Baptist, once called the People's Community Mission, moved into the facility of the Harlem Theatre in 1975. Built as the Harlem Park Methodist Church (white), in 1924, it became a theatre, a mecca for big bands and screen stars soon thereafter.

Thirty-three acres of the neighborhood were designated an Urban Renewal Area in 1954, under provisions of the Federal Housing Act of 1954. They were among the country's first urban real estate set aside for restoration rather than demolition. But demolition in alleys touched off controversy, neighborhood organizations protesting the leveling of more neighborhood housing than the program created until 1957. Nevertheless, 900 trees were planted; 22 acres of park land, each park individually designed, spread behind nearly every main street. Two thousand living units were refurbished with Federal monies. Spreading, low-rise school facilities—the 2,160 student-capacity Harlem Junior High and the 750-capacity Harlem Elementary—were completed in 1963, on the site of 169 nineteenth-century residential properties. Harriet Tubman Elementary (1976, Harlem Avenue) replaced an 1893 school, with portable additions, at Harlem and Monroe. Displacement and other out-migration diminished neighborhood population fifty percent between 1950 and 1970.

Sandtown-Winchester

The sixty-two urban blocks of Sandtown-Winchester constitute Westside Baltimore's largest urban neighborhood formed within the 1816 annex. Clockwise, boundaries extend from Monroe and North along North, Carey, Cumberland, Pennsylvania, Fremont, Lafayette, and Monroe. Situated on a gradual topographical ascent, south to north, they form the highest elevation of the city until 1888. The name Winchester derives from a street, once a winding east-west road, through the central part of the neighborhood, named for George Winchester, a president of the Baltimore and Susquehanna Railroad and a director of the nineteenth-century Canton Company. A community association chose the neighborhood name over appellations offered by city planners. The area's residential population has varied widely over generations, from 20,000 before World War I, to 35,000 during World War II, 17,000 in 1970, and 12,000 in 1980. Ninety percent of the structures are residences. With little industry, it has one commercial section, made up of professional offices, a funeral home and auto repair shops, on North, serving a largely neighborhood, pedestrian patronage. A stationery company and large bakery operated large plants at Laurens and Fulton, and Laurens and Carey Streets respectively, for many years.

Situated between two streams, Gwynns and Chatsworth, but not on either, Sandtown-Winchester remained entirely uninhabited, the speculative real estate of Southern Maryland planters before 1800. Reisterstown Turnpike and Cove (Fremont), and a path cut south to Franklin near present-day Fulton, opened it up to owner-occupied estates soon thereafter. Harlem extended into its southern parts near present-day Gilmore Street. The property of Charles Ghequiere, city antislavery agitator and member of the Baltimore Society to Protect Free Negroes, spread along Mount and Riggs. Arteries into the country lured city institutions with the need for an expanse of inexpensive acreage. The Baltimore Archdiocese opened Cathedral Cemetery, twelve acres along Carey between Tenant (Riggs) and Winchester in 1815, six or seven acres added in 1849. Eighteen hundred lots were used by 1869 at which time trustees closed the cemetery, remains of all the buried being transferred to New Cathedral Cemetery near the Gwynns Falls (see "Greater Edmondson," Chapter Seven). New row house development soon spread over "Old" Cathedral.

Roads and railroads from Sandtown-Winchester into the country also spurred urban development after 1870. Liberty Road wound through the neighborhood from Fremont near Presstman seven miles northwest to Randallstown. A stagecoach line operated along Fulton into the city, and a horse railway, the Baltimore and Randallstown, a line to the city during the 1870s.

The Baltimore and Potomac Railroad secured a state charter in 1853 to join Pennsylvania and Maryland railroad lines with Virginia by a road along Maryland's Western Shore to the lower Potomac. Delayed by the Civil War, it built a section from Baltimore to Washington, today an Amtrak line, between 1868 and 1872, which joined the Pennsylvania Railroad to Southern lines. A tunnel extended underneath Sandtown-Winchester from below North Avenue west of Pennsylvania Station to Gilmore and Winchester. Designed by Thomas Rutter, son of the engineer of New York's Harlem Railway tunnel, and built by 700 craftsmen—stone cutters, masons, miners, rock men, blacksmiths, machinists, carpenters, and common laborers—it used 13 million bricks. Steam pumps pumped out subterranean springs. With the Union tunnel in East Baltimore, it allowed northern freight traffic, including anthracite coal from Pennsylvania, to pass under the city without a break.

Chartered in 1852, the Western Maryland built a twelve-mile so-called short line from Owings Mills to Fulton Street between Winchester and Laurens in 1873. There it joined the B and P line and tunnel into the city. The Western Maryland carried a heavy volume of coal, livestock, and grain. The B and P and Western Maryland both used a station and freight depot on Fulton.

These roads and railways afforded opportunities for neighborhood employment, especially industrial work, unusual for new suburban communities. The suburban location of the rail depot itself necessitated extensive wagon hauling of freight, giving jobs to haulers, drivers and blacksmiths. Farm workers in the county settled in northern and western blocks; lumber, marble, and coal yards operated next to new housing. Slaughter houses lined Butcher's Lane, a country road off Pennsylvania near Winchester. Hotels operated at Monroe and Patterson (Laurens) and McLean and Patterson.

Two- and three-story rows extended to Fulton and Baker and Cumberland by 1895 and beyond within a decade. Fulton was built as a broad thoroughfare with park land in the middle, and a grassy 240-foot diameter park circle, Baker Circle. A project of city planners, it was, with Broadway and Mount Royal Avenue, part of a plan to locate spaced boulevards with green space emanating from the central city but within the grids of regularly paved streets. With the introduction of the electric trolley, however, Fulton's green patches were removed for car tracks in the mid-1890s. Many streets, McKean, Lorman, and Baker for example, were named for developers or property owners. Stricker Street, named for General John Stricker of Frederick, hero of the Battle of North Point, wore an unusual street pavement for many years. John Purcell, the architect of City Hall (1875) and a home owner at Patterson (Laurens) and Stricker, secured small stones from marble blocks cut for City Hall. He saw to it that the block was paved with them, its whiteness glistening after a heavy shower.

The heterogenous mix of residents during the era of development attracted a mix of public and private institutions. Churches included Bethany German Reformed at Pennsylvania and Cumberland for the settlement around the nearby slaughter houses. The city's first athletic park for a professional baseball team went up on Pennsylvania below Baker. Billboard makers A. T. Houck and Brother put up Newington Park on the site of an open athletic field (the Peabody Grounds) in 1872 and purchased a franchise dubbed the Lord Baltimores. League and non-league teams played intermittently at the site before it was demolished in the late 1880s for a housing development.

The Maryland State Normal School, the oldest normal institution in the state and now Towson State University, secured its first permanent home at Carrollton and Lafayette in 1876. Formed ten years earlier, it had occupied rented rooms downtown, until the state erected a neighborhood landmark, a facility for 200 students with a 125-foot tower, broad granite steps and an iron railing. At Carrollton it expanded from a two- to a three-year institution with a largely female enrollment of commuters. The need for larger student facilities prompted a move to Towson in 1916. A model school for teachers, Carver High School and a city junior high school subsequently occupied the building.

The strict mores of residential segregation in Baltimore notwithstanding, African-American institutions broke down the rigid isolation of the races. Close to African-American blocks to the east and southeast, black schools, churches, and businesses acquired main-street Sandtown-Winchester facilities even as the neighborhood was developed as a white suburb. The neighborhood housed four Baptist and two AME churches, one funeral home, and the offices of a real-estate contractor before World War I. A pattern of mobility east to west within the neighborhood recurred: African-American institutions acquired facilities on main streets, followed by black migration onto smaller streets and then larger ones. Neighborhood civil rights committees occasionally formed to protect residential rights. With complaints that police behaved like "dog-catchers," not patrolmen—they had arrested teen-age roller skaters at Riggs and Mount—an NAACP neighborhood watch-dog club formed in the 1950's and the citywide NAACP began to compile records of "unjust arrests" of African Americans who lived at the edges of white neighborhoods.

Sandtown-Winchester's institutional buildings form a mix of structures built during the era of development which have been put to new uses, and pre- and post-World War II construction. Churches and old Douglass High School hug the Pennsylvania Avenue corridor. Laypeople in Macedonia Baptist formed Whatcoat Mission, subsequently Sharon Baptist, in a stable on Whatcoat, a small street near Stricker, in 1882. Housed variously on Patterson (Laurens), when it was known as Patterson Avenue chapel, and at Presstman and Carey, it acquired the facilities of Whatcoat Methodist, Stricker and Presstman, in 1914. Its history intertwines with that of civic and civil rights enterprises. A pastor, William M. Alexander, for whom a neighborhood school is named, published the *Afro-American*, perhaps from the church itself in the 1880s, to advertise black community institutions and the church. Alexander organized the People's Fraternal and Beneficial society, later the Southern Life Insurance Association, at the church, and served in the Brotherhood of Liberty, which challenged segregation statutes. A hurricane toppled the sanctuary steeple in the 1960s; a new fifty-foot steeple with an antique white cupola was added in 1981.

The oldest Westside Roman Catholic congregation of African Americans, St. Peter Claver, opened in 1888 at Fremont and Pennsylvania. Formed by descendants of Santo Domingo slaves brought to the Paca Street area (near St. Mary's Seminary), the congregation used a chapel within St. Ignatius from 1857 to 1888. It took the name of "Blessed Peter Claver"—known as the "Slave of Slaves"—a fifteenth-century Spaniard active among slaves in South America and canonized in 1888. Priests of an English order, the St. Joseph's Society, opened a seminary on Pennsylvania near St. Mary's Street in 1888 to train clergymen for service among African Americans. The same year they acquired the small frame Whatcoat Methodist Episcopal Church, subsequently erecting a church and school. Franciscan sisters staffed the school.

The soaring, massive stone structure of St. Gregory the Great opened in 1885 at Gilmore and Baker, its size and massive Gothic arches prompting comparisons to a cathedral. The complex included a school and a twenty-one-room rectory, but in 1973 a contemporary style sanctuary for the neighborhood African-American congregation was established on the second floor of the educational building as the main sanctuary closed. A choir was robed in African dashikis, and stations of the cross depicting the passion of a black Jesus were painted by local artist John Fayson. The Black Panthers, a civil rights group of youthful men, operated a breakfast program in the basement during the 1960s. Its sizeable facilities have been used variously as an alcoholism rehabilitation center, and neighborhood recreation and tutoring centers.

Old Douglass High, today a planned rehabilitated residential complex at Carey, Baker, and Calhoun, housed Douglass High School between 1925 and 1954, providing a college preparatory, academic curriculum for African Americans from throughout the city. Known as the "Colored High School" until it was named for Frederick Douglass in 1923,

Eleanor Roosevelt, wife of the President, was received with a floral bouquet at Frederick Douglass High School in 1935. Named for the Maryland slave-born abolitionist, writer, and ambassador in 1923, Douglass's facility at Carey and Baker was the first city high school structure built for African-American students. (Courtesy Enoch Pratt Free Library)

it once occupied facilities at Old City Hall—today the Peale museum—and at Dolphin and Pennsylvania. A complex of forty rooms, five science laboratories, and two gymnasiums and swimming pool costing $1,500,000 in Sandtown-Winchester, it reflected black aspirations to broaden vocational opportunities, both academic and vocational curricula having high enrollments. In the late 1920s one-quarter of its students were children of workers in city industry. A prestigious faculty in the 1920s and 1930s, graduates of Ivy League universities and private African-American colleges, prepared students for out-of-city universities, especially the University of Pennsylvania to which Baltimore youth often commuted. Eleanor Roosevelt visited Douglass in the mid-1930s.

Gilmor Homes, the last city housing project built under the provisions of the Public Housing Act of 1937, opened as public housing for East Baltimore defense workers on Gilmore Street in 1941. With a school next door and row houses on three sides, the Homes had a residential setting unusual for World War II era public housing. Thirty-five three to four-story buildings, with 586 living units, were erected by Woodcrest Company and Rosoff Brothers of New York on eight-and-four-fifths acres, with a playground located on each block. The Department of Housing administered it, providing preferential assignment for the elderly to smaller units after the War. The childhood home of singer Ethel Ennis, it sponsored its own neighborhood athletic teams for many years.

The Lafayette Multi-Purpose Center, Lafayette and Gilmore, opened in 1973, the first community center housed in a new facility in the city. Originating with the community center founded at St. James Episcopal, it was funded under the Federal Model Cities program and the Department of Housing and Urban Development. The Sandtown-Winchester Community Association sponsored the Sandtown Winchester Co-op in the 1980s, a project on 900 Fulton to convert three-story rows, with marble steps and trim, into forty-one living units, all tenant-owned. The $2,000,000 rehabilitation project was sold to residents for $250,000. Local artist Pontella Mason painted the eighteen-figured Wall of Pride at a playground near Carey and Baker in the 1970s.

Old Annex

Victorial Era country homes, such as this one at Baker and Poplar Grove in 1929, sat close to new row house developements in Old Annex blocks south of North Avenue.

Spreading out on all four sides, the terrain of Baltimore swelled sixfold with two annexations taking place within thirty years. Recalling the first, the Annexation of 1888, early twentieth century Baltimoreans often spoke of it as the "Old Annex," an addition to Baltimore they could remember. It brought in seventeen square miles to the north, northwest, and west of the old city and extended the Westside three square miles and beyond the Gwynns Falls. Rapidly built up between 1900 and 1930, especially east of the Falls, new Westside sections included what is today Mill Hill (see Chapter Three) and fourteen newer neighborhoods spread to the Falls.

Young families of middle- and working-class whites—salesmen and clerks, craftsmen and government workers, foremen and skilled factory workers—bought new housing in them. African Americans, also often young families, acquired houses in the era of greatest neighborhood change, the 1950s.

Speculation about a new annex first stimulated modest suburban development on all four sides of the city after the Civil War. The City Council voted to add a suburban belt in 1868, but the measure failed to win the approval of the General Assembly. County voters turned down a measure for incorporation in 1874 out of fear of higher (city) taxes and threats to its so-called noxious industries, the breweries, slaughterhouses, and refineries, barred or severely restricted by statute in the city, and built up in Baltimore County along the city-county boundary.

Annexation nevertheless appealed to landowners in the hilly, sparsely inhabited stretch west of the city. And it began to seem inevitable in the 1880s with the lure of superior city services—street pavement and lighting, water lines, schools, and the fire department—and with them rapid development and higher property values. With a provision to phase in higher real-estate taxes gradually, and to exclude built-up sections east of Baltimore (Highlandtown), the measure of 1888 was approved by referendum in Baltimore County handily. West of Baltimore, the annex was formed from the eastern section of the First and the southern parts of the Third Districts of Baltimore County.

The city provided both assistance to and careful regulation of developments in the neighborhoods. Street plans as early as 1877 had extended old east-west streets with the same names and designated north-south streets to be numbered sequentially east to west. The latter arrangement was scrapped and the streets were re-designated after the Annexation of 1918 incorporated already numbered streets in south Baltimore. A conventional rectangular grid plan was formally approved in 1898, new byways to be stitched to existing turnpikes and roads. Beginning in 1902 developers were expected to submit plats of planned subdivisions, and six years later were required to do street grading which would take into consideration the rolling hills and steep valleys adjacent to Gwynns Falls and Gwynns Run. The latter, also called Peck Branch, ran parallel to the Falls five or more blocks east of it (along Braddish in Ashburton-Presbury, Winchester, and Bridgeview-Greenlawn) until 1928. Covered over and diverted by tunnel to the Falls then, terrain along it is today the site of the most recent residential development.

The City initiated measures to finance improvements for the annex not previously undertaken for development in the old city. Traditionally, property holders paid for street development through "special assessment," an arrangement that inflated land prices beyond the reach of modest income-earners. But in 1906 the State Legislature authorized the city to use its credit for new construction. Long-term bond issues, which avoided tax increases and spread the cost of improvements over decades, won voter approval by referendum. They authorized loans for a new sewage system throughout the city (com-

Gwynns Falls below Edmondson Avenue, dubbed Baltimore's Niagara Falls, about 1900. (Courtesy Enoch Pratt Free Library)

pleted in 1914), and new streets, schools, fire halls, and park land. A street pavement commission was chartered in 1908 and appointed in 1911. The city's first storm and sanitary sewers went down in East Baltimore, but those put up in the early 1900s on the Westside encouraged rapid development. The system alleviated the need for alleys, which in the old city had carried off refuse, and thereby allowed street builders along the Westside to concentrate on main-street thoroughfares where homes were put up. Alleys for vehicular traffic only were a later addition to the street networks. Pavements of asphalt were substituted for the uneven cobblestones of the old city as contractors undertook to re-learn the ancient Roman system of placing crushed rock foundations on solid well-drained underpinnings beneath the asphalt.

Park land in the valley of the Gwynns Falls, acquired by the city from 1906 to 1911, encouraged western annex development. Named probably for the Gwinn, or Gwynn, family of seventeenth-century mill operators, the Falls, actually a stream, curves eighteen miles through the county and city. It extends from a source near Reisterstown through west Baltimore into the Middle Branch. Genuine falls did cascade along its winding route; the largest, below Edmondson, fell twenty to seventy feet, and was, before 1900, dubbed Baltimore's "Niagara Falls." A millrace south followed the contours of the valley to Frederick Road for many years and was visited and studied by engineers of the Erie Canal early in the nineteenth century.

Long an outlet for sewage and industrial waste (with ten legal outlets for discharge by World War II), the stream and its valley was nevertheless noted for its natural beauty. Famed landscape architect Frederick Law Olmsted, Jr., hired by Baltimore to design a system of planned parks, persuaded the city to acquire over 400 acres of land on either side between 1906 and 1911. Olmsted's master plan for the city called for a series of linking "natural," unlandscaped parks on three sides. "The valley of the Falls has the character of a wooded gorge," the Olmsted Report observed, "the scenery . . . remarkably beautiful, of a picturesque and sylvan sort seldom possible to retain so near a great city." It afforded a "sense of seclusion without loss of spaciousness." Persuaded that the steep land was difficult to grade anyway, the city used streetcar receipts to fund the purchase of the park land. City-owned wooded space extended from Dickeyville to Columbia Avenue. So that its natural beauty could be appreciated, the city built a winding road, Ellicott's Driveway, opened with public ceremony, from Frederick to the Edmondson Avenue bridge and eventually to Poplar Grove Avenue. Extant cement placards mark the road at both termini. The park land itself has been compared to Philadelphia's Wissahickson Park.

The residential sprawl to the Gwynns Falls represented a middle phase of suburban development, after the era of horse-drawn trolleys but before widespread use of automobiles. Tracks for new, faster electric streetcars went down before development and facilitated a more exclusively residential build-up than that of older suburbs or later automobile ones. Comfortable but not affluent home owners, lacking the means to build and support neighborhood institutions—churches and private academies, etc.—soon relied heavily on the "cars" to patronize downtown institutions. Women shopped less in the neighborhood and instead formed the clientele of Baltimore's huge downtown department stores in the first decades to the twentieth century. High-school students commuted to centrally located schools; whole families took the cars to downtown churches. In good weather, the lines added open-air streetcars for beyond-the-neighborhood recreation at city parks and amusement grounds. Carfare remained low during the era of development at $.06 to $.10, city political clubs and labor unions actively resisting higher rates by a privately-owned utility. The number of rides in Baltimore tripled between the 1890s and 1920s, averaging over 200 million per year in the latter decade.

Small row houses, built of two stories and five rooms with kitchen and bath, went up in every Annex neighborhood. In Baltimore and elsewhere, an expanding job market and unions of male workers exerted pressure on employers to pay male workers a so-called family wage, one sufficient to provide for spouse and children. One-income families were able to acquire property, but not to purchase large houses and pay for servant upkeep. Upkeep depended heavily on stay-at-home female labor.

Many family homes were designed as miniaturized Italianates, but with an interior free of the elaborate ornamentation and specialization of space so characteristic of Victorian Era row houses. An archway between living room and dining room reflected the passing of concern for formality and decorum. Special-purpose rooms, library, pantry, and sewing room, were absent entirely. Plainness in the interiors attested to general acceptance of the germ theory of disease and discredited the dark corners and dusty objects and trim so difficult to clean in nineteenth-century houses. Houses were marketed as easy to maintain, with walls of white plaster or plain wallpaper without carved ornaments, and bathrooms were built with white porcelain fixtures reflective of the prevalent values of simplicity and cleanliness. Venetian blinds replaced curtains; linoleum replaced rugs of cloth. The kitchen was put close to the front door, separated by only a hall or door, enabling housewives to be near it. Wall outlets facilitated the use of electric appliances, the so-called "electric servants." Vacuum sweepers, irons, stoves, refrigerators, and fans were all widely used by the Twenties.

Inside and out, homes embodied a regard for nature, sunlight, and the outdoors. To highlight the difference between Old Annex row housing and that in the older city, developers chose street names to emphasize a country-like, outdoors environment. Suffixes of "dale," "mont" and "wood" recurred often on new street signs. Early homes introduced either the so-called swell-front exterior on the street side, a convex wall with as many as three windows, or bay windows to draw in more light. To relieve the monotony of a line of swell fronts, developers often alternated them with "square fronts" also with more windows. Eliminating interior rooms entirely, "daylight" homes located every room on at least one exterior wall, all with windows.

Tan, cream, and buff brick which picked up the sunlight often replaced the deeper reds of older houses on the streetfront exterior. More spectacularly, lawn space and outside rooms (porches) spread out from the rows of housing. While Baltimore's size more than doubled with the 1888 annex, its population grew only seventy percent before the Annex of 1918, affording a far greater ratio of land space to resident. With indoor plumbing removing the need for outbuildings, and streetcars the need for backyard stables, more land could be devoted to patches of green space. Even small lawns in the city, little "carpets of green," had retained the association of status, a kind of barrier to the outside world. But with the street regarded more as an artery now than as a neighborhood commons or play space, yards afforded transition from public to private space. Front porches were popular. In an era before air-conditioning, these "open-air" rooms formed what historian Kenneth Jackson called a "physical expression of neighborliness and community." Part of, but also apart from, the street and green space it abutted, a front porch functioned as a seasonal place for "observing the world, . . . meeting friends, . . . talking, . . . knitting, . . . shelling peas, . . . courting, and . . . a half hundred other human activities." Young people, more confined to home than they were to be after the automobile, used the porch to escape the watchful eye of elders. The general absence of houses on side streets also enhanced the spaciousness of the blocks of main-street housing.

Second to fourth generation home owners moved beyond the Old Annex even faster during the 1950s than the first residents had settled it. The migration of African Americans soon stamped the neighborhoods, bringing both new and re-converted architecture and new civic organizations to serve the needs of young people.

Mobility into what was a suburb of the inner city grew out of the increasing African-American challenge to racial segregation in Baltimore, even before residential discrimination was outlawed by the Civil Rights Act of 1968. The Baltimore Urban League and the National Association of Colored People kept up a torrent of protest to courts, city agencies, and the press over legal segregation in the 1940s and 1950s. They sued the city over segregated park and recreational facilities, agitated against department store and theatre segregation, petitioned for the hiring of black police officers and taxi-cab drivers, and publicized overcrowding in housing and schools. *Shelley v. Kraemer*, a Supreme Court decision of 1948, finally decreed racially restrictive residential covenants unconstitutional. Encouraged by the favorable climate, home buyers, many of them veterans and workers in east Baltimore industry, sought out real-estate dealers, who, eager for profits, would violate the embedded taboos that discriminated against blacks. Lured by the opportunity to buy "low" from exiting whites and sell "high" to blacks purchasing in a still very restricted housing market, speculators, credit agencies, and real-estate agents opened up housing throughout the Old Annex. With housing in such short supply, the over-priced dwellings of the Old Annex nevertheless were in high demand.

African Americans moved into old streetcar suburbs exactly as the trolley system was being dismantled and transit buses began to move employed men and women all over the city. Crowded busses and bus stops, street edges now lined with parked cars, many young children in the neighborhood, and changes to the exterior of row houses bestowed a new identity, that of a commuter suburb of hard-working young adults. Twice-removed from the developers of the row housing—strangers to builders and the first occupants alike—residents tended to add individualized detail to homes rather than restore them to their original appearance. Porches were enclosed, awnings went up over windows, and artificial turf spread over steps and walkways. Flower gardens interrupted the patches of green. Backyards became utilitarian, children's play areas and storage and tinkering space for cars. Both the density of added detail and the functional use of the exterior removed the staid look of the 1930s and 1940s, and conveyed the owners' prosperity and pride. They also satisfied a need for self-expression.

More institutions dotted hitherto solidly residential blocks, and these reflected both the residents' new suburban status and their older urban roots. Fraternal lodges set up headquarters (see Easterwood), garages and gasoline stations nestled among row houses, and churches put up sanctuaries in the low-lying, ranch style very popular nationwide after World War II (see Ashburton-Presbury). The older streetfront church made its appearance in row homes with porches and lawns (see Rosemont). Institutions teemed with new civic leagues, associations and parent-teacher organizations agitating for city services and for new schools. Nearly a dozen new elementary schools went up in the 1960s and 1970s. Collectively, the modified architectural environment, new and refurbished old built close together, conveyed a sense of considerable neighborhood vitality.

Industrial Hinterlands

Industries discouraged from nineteenth-century Baltimore built up before 1888 in eastern sections of the Old Annex. Their edifices went up near the 1816 city-county boundary and along old turnpikes and roads. There they stamped the neighborhoods permanently, as zoning restrictions, taking account of old industry, eventually designated land as industrial, or as mixed residential-industrial or commercial.

Shaped like a tilted hourglass, Shipley Hill comprises two groups of rolling hills. They jut up next to two valleys, one the path of Gwynns Run along Warwick and Willard, the other east of the Gwynns Falls. Its name derives from Charles Shipley, estate owner and architect. Shipley built a mansion perhaps as early as 1802 and extant until 1980 at McHenry and Franklintown Road. Boundaries extend clockwise from Calverton and Frederick along Frederick, Ellicott's Driveway, the Amtrak lines, Warwick, Baltimore Street, and Calverton. It includes seven street stores, fifteen food, meat, and construction products warehouses and plants, intermixed with brick row houses. An unusual architectural blend of old industrial buildings and country and urban residences abounds: pre-Civil War slant-roof row houses (300 Franklintown and 2600 Frederick), detached stone houses with large yards (2700 Kinsey), and Italianate, daylight, and contemporary town houses. The last sit close to three- and four-story nineteenth-century brick factory buildings (south of Hollins) that still house industry and warehouses.

German-born entrepreneurs from Baltimore encouraged the earliest urban settlement with factories east of Gwynns Run close to

Frederick Road and the Calverton Turnpike. Instigated in 1816 by mill owners along the Falls, the turnpike extended on a southwest path from Edmondson. It was sold to Baltimore County in 1880. Narrow streets cut from Hollins to Frederick bear these entrepreneurs' names. Lipps derives from soap and glycerine manufacturer Christopher Lipps, Landwehr from feed merchant and builder John Landwehr, and Beck's Lane from brewery owner Thomas Beck, who operated a brewery between 1854 and 1894. The four-story and two-story buildings of Lipps and the towering red brick Eigenbrodt brewery, all extant, dominated an industrial district. The area held a machine shop, hide and leather works, and nine breweries by 1900.

West of Gwynns Run, the estate home and property of William Wilkens lay east of Catherine Street and the establishments of German butchers lined "Butcher's Lane," that is Garrison Lane or Franklintown Road south of Baltimore Street. Slaughterhouses were built west of the butchers' shops to the Gwynns Falls. As early as 1850 butchers from the city had met cattle drivers from the country at Frederick Road and Gwynns Falls. There they began the last leg of the drive into the city. But a burgeoning trade in salted beef and pork shipped to the West Indies prompted the opening of stockyards and slaughterhouses after the Civil War. The Baltimore and Potomac Railway operated Calverton Stock (or "Drove") Yards on Calverton south of the tracks (today Amtrak) until it was consolidated with the Union Yards in the 1890s (see "Bentalou-Smallwood and Mill Hill," Chapter Three). The Yards supplied neighborhood slaughterhouses for a half century, cattle being driven to slaughterhouses that had drainage into Gwynns Falls. Neighborhood legend holds that children were barred from wearing red in streets where animals were driven night and day.

Trucks replaced wagon traffic and street driving in the 1930s and refrigeration diminished the demand for locally butchered meat, but Butcher's Lane meat-processing plants thrived into the 1980s.

Main and side residential streets alike, especially south of Baltimore, built up as an extension of a large city German community that hugged the city line between Baltimore and Wilkens (see "Bentalou-Smallwood and Mill Hill," Chapter Three). Stylish two-story brick houses with balconies and yards lined Franklintown Road, the slaughterhouses hidden behind. New immigrants worked in the neighborhood as domestics. The German Bank of Baltimore City, chartered in 1881, operated on West Cemetery Lane, close to an ethnic casino, for many years.

African-American migration brought with it a new neighborhood school—named Jackie Robinson Elementary in 1974 and located in a new building in 1979—and new church congregations. Mason Memorial Church of God in Christ occupies a country stone church built near the Ellicott Mills in 1867 by a congregation established as a station or "circuit" of Summerfield Methodist Episcopal Church. With the sectional split of Methodism in the 1850s the chapel affiliated with Fayette Station of the Methodist Episcopal Church South in 1855. The building may have been a gift of Charles Shipley. The congregation of Shiloh Community, organized in 1944, ac-

Old Annex

Houses along Butcher's Lane (Shipley Hill), once named Garrison Boulevard, today Franklintown Road north of Frederick. Houses and shops fronted on the street with slaughterhouses to the rear next to the Gwynns Falls. Many establishments were German owned. (Courtesy Enoch Pratt Free Library)

quired St. John's Evangelical Lutheran Church (Lombard and Catherine, 1867) in 1987. Known as the "Butcher's Church," and identified by a gilded rooster weathervane, St. John's held services in German as late as World War II. A frame parochial school building was also used as a public school for many years. The Christian Community Church of God acquired Emmanuel Evangelical, at Baltimore and Franklintown, also a German ethnic congregation, in 1961.

Factory buildings between Hollins and Frederick reflect innovations in industrial architecture in the late nineteenth century. Conscious of fire hazards, insurance companies prompted builders to use brick without interior wooden ornamentation in a maximum of three to four stories. The requirement for wide rather than high structures encouraged an exodus from the high-priced industrial real estate districts of the city.

Western Cemetery and the commercial blocks of Franklin and Edmondson dominate the otherwise residential blocks of Western, bounded by Edmondson, Franklintown, Franklin, the Amtrak lines, and Ellicott's Driveway. Terrain within it formed part of the Abell estate along Edmondson, and the Charles Shipley estate, before development. West of Franklintown, it slopes south and east toward the old valley of Gwynns Run.

Western Cemetery opened in 1846 on land acquired in 1844 by Fayette and Bennett Methodist Episcopal Church in Baltimore. Early pathways to it extended from Franklintown Road and Baltimore Street. With two additions in 1887 and 1905 it comprises forty-five acres. Descendants of the buried mounted successful efforts in the 1960s to prevent construction of an expressway which would have removed a thousand graves.

Streetfront, two-story Italianate homes lined Lauretta Street before World War I; daylight houses with front porches and front yards filled four other residential blocks in the 1920s. The mural of artists James Voshell and Pontill Mann, "Men Playing Checkers as Boy Watches," spreads over a Lauretta Street building. With exposure to the Franklin Street thoroughfare, it is a familiar Westside landmark. Animal shelter facilities on Calverton Road date at least to 1932, operated variously by the Society for the Prevention of Cruelty to Animals and Baltimore City.

The name Rosemont Homeowners derives from community organizations that opposed an extension of Expressway I-170 west of Pulaski in the 1960s. Boundaries extend clockwise from Bentalou and Franklin on Franklin, Franklintown, Edmondson, Braddish, Arunah, and Bentalou. Sloping terrain forms a valley at Braddish, an old path of Gwynns Run, marking the beginning of a broad descent along the Westside to the Middle Branch of the Patapsco. The neighborhood has two churches, stores in a mixed commercial residential district on Edmondson, and row houses mostly built from 1910 to 1940.

The first urban development stretched along the high-elevation western blocks of Edmondson, the oldest east-west thoroughfare. Lined then with car tracks, and with a car barn at Calverton in the 1890s, Edmondson had opened to industrial traffic twenty years earlier. Freight from Franklintown Turnpike moved along it to the city and the stone of local quarries was passed over it to city and county.

Prominent Baltimore builder James Keelty put up streetfront Italianate homes on 2700 Edmondson Avenue between 1911 and 1913. The son of Irish immigrants, Keelty began building row houses in the old city in 1904. A stone mason by trade, he put carpenters to work on hundreds of nearly identical row houses in north and west Baltimore after 1910. Development extended west to east with tiny front porches or front yards along Edmondson. Bay-windowed daylight homes with larger porches and yards on Arunah and Lauretta went up between the world wars.

Plans for an expressway depressed home prices in the 1960s. Community associations protested the route and agitated for above-market prices, eventually persuading the city to resell its acquired property, some of it to the original occupants. Perkins Square Baptist, founded in "Murphy Homes" in 1881, occupies the facility of Emmanuel English Evangelical Church built in 1914, itself transplanted from an older building at Schroeder and Pierce.

Bounded by Monroe, Mulberry, the Amtrak lines, Bentalou, Lafayette, Payson and Riggs, Midtown Edmondson lies within the old city (Annex of 1816), except for acreage near the tracks south of Lafayette. Warehouses, a supermarket, and a small factory spread out in the old county sections next to the rails. Row houses intermixed with four streetfront churches and eleven shops, laundries, and service stations mark every other block. The graystone Union Baptist Church, once Franklin Street United Brethren, is at 510 Monroe, a city fire hall at Edmondson and Bentalou.

This acreage made up the western part of two nineteenth-century estates owned by prominent Baltimoreans Franklin Wilson and Thomas M. Keerl, and parts of the Scribner and Garrett estates. Baltimore-born, Brown University-educated Wilson, once pastor of Franklin Square Baptist Church, was a local writer, editor, and land speculator as well as pastor. His holdings included acreage in Peabody Heights (later Charles Village), but he lived on undeveloped estate land east of Monroe near Harlem. Descendent of a Hessian soldier brought to Baltimore as a prisoner after the Battle of Trenton during the Revolution, Keerl owned a vast estate that extended west of Amity in the city (Poe Homes).

Plants, lumber and supply companies, and a hotel (the Starlauf, at Lanvale and Payson) went up next to the rail line and close to the Fulton Street rail depot in the late nineteenth century. Its proximity to urban development notwithstanding, the steep east-to west ascent to Monroe delayed residential development during the era of horse trolleys. Houses along Edmondson show the tendency of initial build-up to concentrate close to trolley lines prior to 1910. Two-story streetfront houses beyond the lines went up between 1910 and 1917. Developers alternated swell fronts and square fronts, and plain cornices and peaked ones, to alleviate tedious uniformity on very plain streets with no green space. Close to the Pratt Street and Shipley Hill industrial districts, workers, many of them renters, both walked and rode streetcars to work. African Americans who moved in in the late 1940s tended more often to purchase rather than rent houses, their property generally blending with the similar older Italianates of city neighborhoods south and east. Four blocks of housing were demolished for the Franklin-Mulberry Expressway.

Along North Avenue

Urban build-up along North Avenue, together with a trolley line and a passenger station of the Western Maryland Railroad on North, gave impetus to the development of four northern Westside neighborhoods after 1890. Country roads from Baltimore County towns had wound through the area to Reisterstown Turnpike before development. Windsor Mill Road, known east of the Western Maryland Railroad as new Liberty Road, ribboned east northeast from Bloomingdale Turnpike. Dairy farms and speculative lands spread out on both sides. Among the latter was the property of James Carey Thomas, a city physician, medical school professor, Quaker minister, and president of the Young Men's Christian Association, and of his daughter, M. Carey Thomas. Martha Carey Thomas was an early female physician, educator, and feminist, and president of Bryn Mawr College from 1894 to 1922.

The boundaries to Easterwood, named for Eastwerwood Park, run clockwise from North and Monroe along Monroe, Presstman, Smallwood and North. Row houses, with five streetfront shops, spread over every block. Windsor Mill Road and two streams to Gwynns Run crisscrossed it before development. The earliest build-up spread out in the old city along North, and between Monroe and Payson close to Friendsbury Park, a since-covered-over landscaped plot that divided Monroe between Presbury and Baker.

The houses reflect the transition from streetfront Italianate to daylight homes, an intermediate stage of housing still built with interior windowless rooms but with daylight-catching swell-front exteriors and with marble steps. They were put up between 1896 and

1906. Daylight homes with bay windows, front porches and front yards went up in the World War I era and the 1920s around the Easter mansion. The latter, a Revolutionary War era landmark of French chateau-style architecture, sat close to acreage enclosed by Baker, Pulaski, Presbury, and Smallwood. Square blocks built with very narrow alleys enclosed large interior play space for children.

Jewish home buyers, many first and second generation Russians from East Baltimore, moved into much of the housing; the residents were thirty percent Russian-born as late as 1940. Many bought from builder Ephraim Macht, owner of the Welsh Construction Company and one of the first Jewish builders in Baltimore. Homes were marketed as near North Avenue, where many residents were employed, and near to the synagogues east of Druid Hill Avenue on both sides of North. Monroe, Route 1 out of the city, divided the neighborhood from the old City.

African Americans acquired housing to Pulaski in the late 1940s and throughout the neighborhood in the 1950s. Christian Memorial, occupies the building once held by North Avenue United Presbyterian on the site (Payson and North) of a Methodist Protestant country chapel. Omega Psi Phi Fraternity, 2003 Presbury, has lent support to Matthew A. Henson Elementary School, 1600 Payson.

Coppin and Ashburton-Presbury built up around Walbrook Station of the Western Maryland Railroad. Coppin's boundaries extend on North, Presstman, through Carver High School property east of the edifice, and the Western Maryland Railway. It sits opposite the main property of Coppin State College north of North Avenue. Row houses on irregularly sized blocks, two churches, one shop, one park, and one school and the athletic fields of Coppin State at the end of Whitmore, spread out on a gentle slope from North.

Regarded sometimes as the southern end of the community of Walbrook, Coppin's corner markets and North Avenue stores served a clientele to the north and west. Walbrook Station of the Western Maryland, close to Warwick and Baker, spurred the earliest development, commuters traveling to Hilton Station in the City. It closed in the 1920s. Old and new residential architecture incorporate thoroughgoing tendencies to embellish row houses with daylight and green space. Double bay windows and third-floor balconies jut out from hilltop rows on North, side porches from duplexes built with swell fronts along Thomas.

Carved from the estate of Hamilton Easter, a city merchant, Easterwood Park spreads over seven acres at Bentalou and Baker. The city purchased the property in 1909 and designed it as a landscaped park, at the recommendation of the Olmsted Commission and the Public Athletic League. The latter, a civic association headed by Robert Garrett, promoted outdoor recreation for city dwellers. North and Pennsylvania Avenue businessmen organized in the Northwest Businessmen's Association also promoted it to spur real-estate development. A field house for equipment and meetings, and walkways, baseball fields, tennis courts, and a children's playground were erected. The setting for organized athletics sponsored by the City Playground Athletic League, and later the Board of Recreation and Parks, it was redesignated from a "white" to a "Negro" facility in 1950, and made part of the integrated system of city parks in the early 1960s.

Organized in 1925 as the "Colored Vocational High School," Carver Vocational Technical sat on eight different Westside sites before the present structure at Bentalou and Presstman was completed in 1955. It was housed variously in an abandoned garage and little metal factory (Sandtown-Winchester, near Carey and Calhoun), and in buildings of Maryland Normal, at Carrollton and Lafayette. Named in 1944 for the renowned Missouri-born botanist and Tuskeegee professor George Washington Carver, it fielded a football team in 1933, and sponsored boxers with international fame in the 1940s. It won accreditation as a vocational-technical high school in 1963, the third such in the country. The red brick contemporary building with four concrete pillars houses twenty-two shops and stands next to Lloyd Sodie White Athletic Field to the east, named for a long-time school athletic director. It pioneered student work-study programs with carpentry at the Gilmor Homes (Sandtown-Winchester) in the 1940s, and has one of the oldest vocational-industrial student clubs in the country. Gender integrated within a year after it was founded, its curriculum broadened over the years from the traditional industrial trades and carpentry to auto, office, printing, machine and electrical work. It has a tradition of principals educated at Hampton Institute.

Mount Hebron Memorial Church took over a Spanish architecture edifice (2200 North) once occupied by Chatsworth Methodist Episcopal Church,

Dukeland, Baker, North, and the Western Maryland Railroad enclose Ashburton-Presbury, blocks of row houses with four stores, one church, and a schoolbus storage facility. They spread over the nineteenth-century estate of Carleton on property designated as "Boston Fear." It sat close to Gwynns Run and a stream extending northeast of it. The earliest houses went up on Braddish, alternating swell and square fronts, and on North with stylish three- and four-story homes with third-floor balconies. Duplexes surrounded by yards, porches that spread along the front and sides of houses, and green space between sidewalks and streets on other streets exude spaciousness. Mount Hebron Baptist, founded in 1927, built a brick structure with a stained-glass front on a hill at 2651 North Avenue.

Boundaries of the Northwest Community Action Group extend clockwise from Braddish and Baker along Braddish, the Western Maryland Railway, Bloomingdale, North, Dukeland, and Baker. On terrain which ascends from a valley at Dukeland, the area includes mixed commercial-residential stretches along North, Poplar Grove, and Bloomingdale, two schools, one church, an apartment house, offices of the city Department of Housing and Community Development, and row and detached houses. Bloomingdale derives from the Bloomingdale Turnpike, a macadamized road of one-foot layer of rock, chartered in 1852 along the path of Bloomingdale and Poplar Grove Lane. Named for a mid-nine-

Toll gate house for Bloomingdale Turnpike, chartered in 1852, along Bloomingdale just south of Windsor Mill Road. The horse line of the Baltimore, Calverton and Powhatan Railroad operated along the Pike in 1870s.

teenth-century estate close to Poplar Grove and Brighton, the pike was owned by the estate owners whose property bordered it. A toll gate stood at Baker and Bloomingdale. The Liberty Turnpike Company acquired it in 1866.

The Pike, and Windsor Mill Road built to the city, encouraged estate houses and detached Victorian country houses (see extant edifices on 1700 Bloomingdale and 1500 Braddish). They afforded an eventual blend of country and urban homes. Claremont, the estate of John B. Morris, spread out over the center of the neighborhood; Buena Vista, the family property of Jesse Slingluff who owned "Beech Hill," was located beyond North Avenue on Windsor Mill. Houses along Gertrude and Slingluff, cut in the 1880s from North to New Windsor, were interspersed among farms.

Streetcar lines along the high ground of Bloomingdale and North inspired the oldest row houses in the northwest corner—marble-stepped, streetfront rows on 1800 Rosedale, three-storied swell fronts on 3000 North, and alternate square- and swell-front housing on 3000 Westwood. Much of the rest of the real estate was built in the 1920s and marketed as part of Walbrook by the Walbrook Construction Company and builders Robinson and Slagel. The 3100 block of North developed as a solidly commercial block, with drug stores, markets and a movie house. Twenty-three modern two- and three-story public housing units opened along Gertrude in 1973.

The formstone-covered concrete sanctuary of Pentecostal Baptist was built in 1958 by a congregation founded in 1915. It exemplifies a tendency to surround institutional buildings as well as residences with functional green space. A broad front lawn serves the congregation as social space during warm weather. The School 63 Apartment Complex, Rosedale and Westwood, sits on the site of an old Baltimore County School, #15. The city replaced it in 1894 with a red brick edifice of twenty-two rooms and a library, Walbrook School. It closed in 1973 and was subsequently converted to apartments. Rosemont Elementary at 2777 Presstman opened as a neighborhood elementary school in 1973 for a new young population; Lillie Jackson Elementary opened in 1979 as a citywide school for a maximum of a hundred handicapped children. Named for a veteran Westside civil rights activist, the latter was equipped with a hydro-therapy pool and occupational, speech, and music therapy rooms.

Greater Rosemont

Neighborhoods from Payson to Franklintown Road took the name "Rosemont" in the 1960s from citizens' coalitions against expressway construction. Residential sections of the two newest neighborhoods, Bridge View and Evergreen Lawn, built up east of Gwynns Run as it was covered over in the 1920s. Distance from the east-west streetcar lines, the Edmondson and North Avenue lines, also delayed development on residential blocks set back from them.

Clockwise from Bentalou and Calverton Heights Avenue, boundaries of Bridgeview-Greenlawn run on Calverton Heights, Whitmore, Lafayette, Braddish and a line north of Braddish, southern and then northern lines of the Western Maryland Railroad, Monroe, Amtrak lines, Lafayette and Bentalou. Fuel, tire, and scrap metal companies, and private and government warehouses spread over a nineteenth-century railroad district from Monroe to Bentalou. Trackage for the Western Maryland railroad was completed by 1873. The Maryland Pavement Company, forerunner to Baltimore Asphalt, excavated the rolling rocky land west of Monroe and close to a plant of the Baltimore Car Wheel Company, as the gritty sand was in high demand for construction projects all over the City.

Blocks west of Bentalou, mostly residential, contain row houses built over a century, modern apartments, two churches, two schools, one armory, and one cemetery, but no stores, markets, or industry. Lafayette Avenue, opened in the county to Franklintown Road, and Riggs and Mosher Street built to Gwynns Run (along Braddish) by 1876, encouraged modest scattered nineteenth-century development. The eastern sections probably housed workers employed along Bentalou and eastward. Italianate houses built as duplexes with yard space front and side, such as those extant at 2300 Riggs and on Mosher near Whitmore, exemplify the adaptation of familiar city architecture to a setting of more ground space.

Webster Methodist Episcopal Chapel sat on Mosher near Whitmore in 1889. Goose-Hill (its named derived from the flocks of a nearby farm), an open-air baseball field, spread over land west of Bentalou and south of Winchester until the 1920s, forming a vacant land island in a sea of new development. Grandstands were built in the 1920s, semi-professional teams played there, and a traveling circus first tented along Edmondson made use of it until houses went up.

Car lines on Baker and the paving of Bentalou encouraged developers who built daylight row houses in the 1920s and 1930s. They featured lawns and porches, and automobile garages on side streets, the blocks marketed as a suburb from which one could "motor out or take the cars." Nineteenth-century housing on Riggs, Whitmore, and Warwick was eventually demolished for modern apartments and Calverton Junior High School.

A chapel for Holy Trinity Episcopal went up at Lafayette and Wheeler in 1875, but home owners put up a new church and parish hall, surrounded by the neighborhood's most spacious yard, in 1921. Its white congregation joined St. Bartholomew's (Ten Hills) in 1952 as African Americans formed a new congregation and parish of the same name. The two-story redbrick James Mosher Elementary went up in 1933 and was enlarged in 1955.

Eighteen acres of St. Peter's the Apostle's Cemetery, one of eleven Baltimore Roman Catholic graveyards, spread west of Bentalou. St. Peter's, Hollins Park, acquired a plot of thirty-three acres before the Civil War. The western end of the property was later transferred to the Cade Armory. Many among the 10,000 graves are of Irish born; St. Peter's first three rectors are buried there.

Melvin H. Cade Armory, built in 1960, quarters a descendant military unit of an old African-American national guard unit organized in 1879. Black Baltimoreans enrolled in the First Separate Company, a unit of the Monumental City Guard, Maryland State Militia, which met in armory rooms in the Richmond Market (near Bolton Hill). As Company I of the 372nd Infantry, it was the first Maryland guard unit sent to Europe in World War I. Its members won the coveted Croix de Guerre with palms, the highest French military honor. Re-organized variously as Company C, 58th Support Battalion, 243rd Engineer Company, and as the 229th Supply and Transportation Battalion, it served in every American War until the Vietnam War, and was the only Maryland Guard unit activated in the Korean War. Unit personnel donated bricks and money for a building twice enlarged since 1960 and used by full-time and week-end personnel of the 229th.

Boundaries of Evergreen Lawn extend clockwise from Calverton Heights and Bentalou along Bentalou, Harlem Avenue, Arunah, Braddish, Lafayette, Whitmore, and Calverton

Heights. It slopes gently to the west. Most of it was carved from the nineteenth-century estate of Arunah S. Abell, founder and proprietor of the *Sun* papers.

In housing put up by 1930, Baltimore builders H. M. Nichols, George Schoenhals and others introduced features to maximize the daylight brought into home interiors. They installed light-catching stained glass over doors and windows, and extra bay windows in corner houses. Early automobile garages, popularly associated with livery stables, were feared as unsafe; gasoline stored next to cars, it was believed, could catch fire easily. Garages therefore were put on side streets.

Developers introduced the English Tudor-style row houses on Wilborn and Harlem off Braddish in the World War II Era. With distinctive pitched roofs, they afforded a sense of harmony and uniformity within a group, and suggested isolation from surrounding blocks. First Abyssinia Baptist, organized in 1929, moved into an edifice at Warwick and Arunah in 1965; Union Memorial United Methodist was organized in the church of Harlem Park Methodist Episcopal at Harlem and Warwick. Opened in 1963, Lafayette Elementary at 850 Braddish Avenue was enlarged in 1968.

Bounded by Edmondson, Poplar Grove, Riggs, and Braddish, Mosher slopes up and west from the path of Gwynns Run to a hill-top peak along Poplar Grove. It is named for the street in the Poppleton Survey designated for James Mosher, the Revolutionary War soldier, city councilman, and contractor of city buildings in the early nineteenth century. Poplar Grove once formed a southern extension of the Bloomingdale Turnpike, and the beginning of a slope to Gwynns Falls. Mostly residential with no industry or schools, Mosher includes a mixed residential-commercial section on Poplar Grove south of Lafayette, the Lutheran Hospital and social services building complex on Rayner, and row houses built over a century. It spreads over the nineteenth-century estates of William S. Rayner, H. Broumel, A. S. Abell, and John Summerfield Berry. Drygoods merchant Berry, president of the Bloomingdale Turnpike Company and owner and organizer of the Maryland National Guard, owned "Dukeland," a dairy farm which spread beyond Riggs. The acreage south of Harlem was often regarded as an eastern part of Calverton Heights.

Four nineteenth-century roads, Franklintown and Bloomingdale turnpikes and Edmondson and Lafayette, prompted the earliest development at the western edge, houses built in Baltimore County but of city-like architecture. Brick Italianates, some duplexes, went up on Poplar Grove, Rayner, and Lanvale, close to country frame dwellings and housing for workers in a nearby grist mill. (Extant double mill houses at 2812 to 2818 Lafayette typify workers' housing.) Marble-trimmed row houses with bay windows went up on Edmondson and Harlem, and alternate swell- and square-front homes on Rayner were built before World War I. Daylight homes were built on the Berry estate in the 1920s. Post-World War II and contemporary rows at the eastern edge, especially on Braddish and Claymount, exhibit the modern tendency toward smaller daylight homes and alternation of exterior color house to house.

The deep red Romanesque structure of the Lutheran Health Care facility, at Rayner and Dukeland, was erected in 1876. William Rayner, a prominent Bavarian-born merchant, banker, and religious leader from Baltimore, and father of a United States Senator (Isador Rayner), donated the land in 1873 for the Baltimore Hebrew Orphan Asylum, chartered in the city in 1872. An active Hebrew scholar and translator, and warm advocate of reform Judaism, as well as a businessman, the elder Rayner presided over a range of city charitable institutions. Designed by architects Lupus and Roby for 125 students, the Asylum building featured octagonal towers that provided lighting and ventilation over a main stairway. Front and sides were built of pressed brick and Ohio sandstone trim. Well-known city rabbis directed the Asylum, and banquets, fairs, and charitable functions sponsored by German Jews supported it. Children solicited contributions with public recitations in the city. Trained as domestic servants, the orphans were placed as servants in mansions along Eutaw Place and Madison and in downtown department stores.

When the Asylum moved to Mount Washington in 1923, West Baltimore General Hospital, newly organized and underwritten by doctors and neighborhood businessmen while subsidized by the city, acquired it. The hospital added a nurses quarters, a maternity wing, and a power plant in the 1920s. The Lutheran Home and Hospital Association representing several denominational synods acquired it in 1949, redesignated it as a "general" and "chronic illness" hospital, and added new buildings. Community representation of African Americans in the 1970s secured redirection again toward clinical and emergency care for a largely neighborhood clientele. The original orphans asylum building has housed city social services agencies since 1977.

St. Edward's Church, built in 1941, is the third edifice of a parish formed as a mission to St. Peter's, Hollins Park, in 1878. A school, convent, and rectory opened in 1923. The Romanesque-style sanctuary, seating 1,000, has simple lines with granite exterior walls trimmed in Indiana limestone, and extensive marble wainscoting on interior walls and floors. The statuary, altar, and exterior twenty-five foot grotto built in 1947 all recall World War II. White marble statues replaced figures sculpted by Italian artist Angelo Lauldi of Florence for the church, but destroyed by a German air attack that devestated his Tuscany, Italy studios. The granite grotto which enshrines a ten foot figure of Christ was dedicated to parish "boys and girls" who served in World War II.

Maryland Aged Baptist Home on 2800 Rayner went up in the 1970s on the site of the nineteenth-century Henshaw Baptist Chapel.

Bounded by Edmondson Avenue, Ellicott's Driveway, Lyttleton, Rosedale, Mosher, and Poplar Grove, Franklintown Road sits on the slope to the Gwynns Fall. It built up around the Road (originally Franklintown Turnpike) which bisects it diagonally, a link between Reisterstown Pike and Frederick Road opened between 1827 and 1831. The city acquired Franklintown Turnpike in 1909.

The blocks spread over the nineteenth century estates of Charles Shipley, George R. Vickers, and J. Thomas Scharf. Vickers, an amateur etymologist and director of the Bloomingdale and Calverton turnpikes, operated a grist mill close by Bloomingdale near Lafayette. Scharf, a Confederate veteran, acquired fame as a local historian, employing a virtual army of helpers to compile and publish multi-volume chronicles of Baltimore, the state of Maryland, and other East Coast states. Earliest settlement took place on the Pike near Mosher and included road-related businesses such as a wagon wheel company. Streetfront Italianate homes went up on the rest of the Road before World War I, daylight homes with front porches and yards in the 1920s. Developers advertised them as set in the idyllic valley of Gwynns Falls. Contemporary row houses filled in open space along Ellicott's Driveway and Franklintown in the 1960s.

The three-story, 600-student-capacity Alexander Hamilton Elementary opened in 1982 on the site of an old county school and an annex city school building built in 1890. Delays in construction of the building approved in 1977 prompted demonstrations by parents and students in the young African-American neighborhood in the 1970s. Jesus Saves Rehobeth Church uses a facility built by Summerfield Methodist Episcopal on the site, at Borchers and Poplar Grove, of a Methodist chapel dating from as early as 1850.

Bisected by Poplar Grove, the entirely residential section of Winchester descends on both sides toward Gwynns Falls and the path of Gwynns Run. Its boundaries zigzag clockwise from Poplar Grove and Mosher on Mosher, Rosedale, Lyttleton, Ellicott's Driveway, Mosher, the Western Maryland Rail Line, the path of Braddish, Riggs, Poplar Grove, and Mosher. Park land, wooded patches, and vacant fields at the northern and western borders and the steeply sloped western edge, provide a distinctly rural environment. "Dukeland," spread over the eastern sections; "Poplar Grove," the estate of John Hurst and the wife of S. B. Morgan, along Poplar Grove and Winchester; and the southern part of the "Rosedale" estate and the Vickers and Purnell property were located west of Poplar Grove Avenue. Western sections were occasionally known as Woodland Grove.

Daylight homes with lots covered eighty percent of the acreage by 1930, houses on Poplar Grove, Riggs, and Mosher put up by James Keelty. Braddish and parts of Ellicott's Driveway are lined with more contemporary rows.

Twenty-eight square blocks of Rosemont, with park land along the Gwynns Falls and Franklintown, are bounded by North, Bloomingdale, Western Maryland Railroad, Gwynns Falls, and the Hilton Parkway. They contain four churches, one library, one school and no industry. The Baltimore, Calverton and Powhatan Railroad ran a horse line on Bloomingdale Pike through to the Baltimore County towns of Wetheredsville, Franklintown, and Powhatan in the 1870s. Mill owners made use of a millrace built close to Ellamont and Presstman. A graveyard sat near present-day Rosedale and Presstman before development. Streetcar lines along Bloomingdale and North, and the development of Walbrook to the north, stimulated early development in the 1890s. Detached houses of brown shingle built on hills, as on 1500 and 1600 Rosedale and 3100 Westwood, resembled Walbrook housing. Row and duplex houses north of Presstman, put up in the 1920s and 1930s, featured second-floor porches and built-in sun porches (as at 2900 Baker and 3100 Brighton). Many were built with garages. Houses along Belmont, Normount, and Elmont, built by the Welsh Construction Company in 1929, were advertised as overlooking the park. Contemporary apartments extend even closer to Falls parkland.

One of four streetfront churches, St. Mark's Spiritual Baptist at 1025 North Hilton, is representative of the sanctuaries adapted to a row house, but with front porch and yard and the setting of a park. The African-American congregation of Whitestone Baptist Church, organized in 1941 at Franklin and Arlington (Poppleton), acquired the graystone church at Baker and Longwood in 1957, as many members moved into the neighborhood. St. Paul's Evangelical Lutheran, which had moved from Upton (the edifice of Trinity Baptist, Druid Hill and McMechen) in 1919 and merged with the Evangelical Lutheran Church of the Covenant in Winchester, built its present edifice in 1923. Housed earlier at Clifton and Hilton, the red brick Walbrook Branch of Enoch Pratt was erected in 1952.

Beyond the Gwynns Falls

Entrance to Loudon Park Cemetery named for the estate of James Carey, Baltimore merchant, banker and city councilman.

Seventeen residential neighborhoods spread west of the Gwynns Falls along Frederick and Edmondson Avenues to the west and southwest boundaries of the city. Developed as streetcar and automobile and transit bus suburbs, they extend through the western one-third of the Annex of 1888 and throughout the 1918 annex. The stone and frame houses of Baltimore County, less often demolished by developers here than in older suburbs, jut up next to blocks of traditional city daylight row homes and next to houses built in post-World War II construction styles. They make up the Westside's most spacious neighborhoods.

Wide concrete bridges went up along Edmondson, Baltimore, and Wilkens Avenues before World War I, replacing the traditional wooden trestle spans and thereby removing a major obstacle to residential neighborhood development in the acreage to the west. The city erected the largest in 1908, a four-arched, 540-foot overpass, on Edmondson Avenue. Allegedly the longest intra-city concrete bridge in the South, 63 feet above water level, it used concrete equal to three 30-foot-square Washington Monuments. Builders completed it by bush-hammering, a process of knocking the surface from the concrete to show the stone underneath.

The new annexation and the automobile both stirred growth. Eager to introduce heavy industry to the city, the Merchants and Manufacturers Association of Baltimore spearheaded an expansion on all four sides during World War I. Development at the city's edges was expected to locate city industrial workers close to streetcar lines, and to permit modest de-centralization of industry itself. Approved by the state legislature, annexation in 1918 added fifty-two square miles of Anne Arundel and Baltimore County to the city. The western boundary shifted one-and-one-half-mile west from a parallel along Woodington (Rognel Heights) and Augusta (Irvington) to the present city boundary.

Cars became a common American conveyance in the 1920s when the price of the Model T Ford developed by Henry Ford in Detroit dropped by one-third. The United States numbered one motor vehicle for every five persons in the 1920s, ownership doubling during World War II, and again from 1950 to 1980. Beltways and expressways built around and into Baltimore attached esteem to West Baltimore neighborhoods that were entirely accessible to highways but remote enough from them to escape noise and traffic. Residents commuted both to suburban counties and to the city, as automobile bridges and highways built within neighborhoods facilitated egress and ingress. The West Baltimore Street bridge opened over the Gwynns Falls in 1932, and grading for the Hilton Street parkway, a Civil Works Administration project later carried out under the works division of the Baltimore Emergency Relief Commission, was begun one year later. The latter eventually linked North Avenue and the southwestern arteries out of the city. Cloverleaf access was added in the 1950s, and a bridge over the Pennsylvania Railroad at Hilton, Caton, and Frederick, in 1957. The bridge and parkway both eliminated automobile bottlenecks, and, with other road projects, provided a network of new roads and bridges beyond the Falls. They formed sinuous parkways with a minimum of stoplights and intersections.

Commuting from home to work became feasible over greater distances throughout metropolitan Baltimore. Consequently, developers could maintain a greater ratio of green space to population within new residential neighborhoods including those west of Gwynns Falls. They were more willing to leave old country settlements standing, rather than demolish them for denser, newer housing. Consequently, edifices built as groups in the style of city row homes but sometimes surrounded by extensive greenspace, frequently blended with the old. Motored transit facilitated residency apart from streetcar lines, reversing the previous priority which homeowners attached to living on the car lines. The hills and valleys between Edmondson and Frederick Avenue became treasured real estate, while throughout the neighborhoods more green space extended between homes and streets. In contrast to older sections, extensive lawn, park, and wooded space also stayed up between developments and between individual residences.

Automobile companies hastened the demise of the streetcar. A subsidiary of General Motors acquired an interest in the city transit system in the 1950s, instigating the substitution of rubber-tire vehicles within a few years. Trucks facilitated the suburbanization of industry and warehouses, as even early models carried several times the volume of horse-drawn wagons and alleviated the dependence on rail traffic. The drive-in culture associated with automobiles similarly left a mark. Gas stations marketing gasoline and repairing vehicles opened on commercial and residential streets alike. Shopping centers, an assortment of businesses under unified management with abundant free parking, made an early appearance.

Home architecture beyond Gwynns Falls reflects distinct eras of in-migration. Affluent home buyers moved into planned suburban communities in the rural settings in the early part of the century. Young, mostly white families, taking advantage of the boom in housing construction, formed a second wave of in-migration after World War II. City African Americans, part of the great out-migration of the 1950s, acquired both old and new houses thereafter.

Country houses built of stone, frame, or brick, and still extant beyond the Falls as nowhere else in West Baltimore, initially went up next to farm land. Many nevertheless reflected the influence of nearby urban construction, with styles adapted to a rural setting. Row house Italianates were built as duplexes with yards, some with frame construction (see Gwynns Falls). Many were put up by builders from the city. Like Baltimore Italianate row houses, detached Victorian Era frame homes were bedecked with exterior ornamentation. Porches or an open veranda wrapped around on several sides. Cultivated lawns on four sides emphasized the natural environment and exuded spaciousness; interiors placed kitchens and pantries to the rear and allowed different zones for different home activities. (See Irvington, St. Joseph's, and Beechfield.) The houses in planned suburban communities emphasized a wooded environment with spacious "shoulder" homes fronting perpendicular to the streets (see Ten Hills). They afforded maximum privacy. Winding, curvilinear roads and lanes, a departure from the grid pattern of street development in earlier annexes, suggested a bucolic, pastoral escape from the city. Gentle turns emphasized the natural landscape. Popular frame bungalows, put up in the 1920s and 1930s, blended with a natural environment. (See Rognel Heights and Westgate.) A low pitched roof over one- to one-and-one-half stories lowered the structural silhouette. Often brown shingle, most houses were built with front porches. English Tudor houses with steeply pitched roofs, when built in a group, suggested the unity and distinctiveness of a subdivision, and, if made with stone facing, afforded a reminder of the country environment (see Edmondson).

Throughout the nation, depression- and wartime-era postponement of new construction, and a soaring birthrate after World War II, instigated massive home and apartment building programs in the 1940s and 1950s. The American birthrate climbed from 2.2 to 3.5 births per woman from the 1930s to 1950s. After the War, two-and-one-half million reunited and recently married families throughout the country doubled up with relatives. In these years, veterans and their familes inhabited garages, barns, and even chicken houses.

Federal programs encouraged new construction gradually. Traditionally, home loans extended a maximum of twenty years, with a mortgage not fully paid at the time of final settlement and home mortgages difficult to renew during a period of tight money. But the Depression Era Home Owners Loan Corporation had introduced long-term self-amortizing mortgages. They provided for uniform payments spread over the whole term of the debt. The FHA (Federal Housing Authority) program began the practice of insuring loans on new construction. The VA (Veterans Administration) program of 1944 allowed servicemen to borrow the entire appraised value of a house without down payment, and the Federal Housing Act of 1949 allowed apartment construction by builders without risk of investment capital.

Collectively, these programs prompted unprecedented home construction after World War II. Three-quarters of the nation's housing in the 1980s had been built after World War II, much of it in the late 1940s and 1950s. Establishing a priority for new construction, rather than rehabilitation, and allowing lower standards for loans and loan guarantees in new areas than in built-up ones, Federal programs all encouraged highly homogenous settlements at the fringe of cities. The exodus into outlying areas of cities was largely that of white, two-parent households.

Baltimore's population swelled from 805,000 to 950,000 between 1930 and 1950, and young, white, two-parent families predominated among the new arrivals into communities beyond the Falls. Churches, some making a third move westward from the center city, accompanied the young families. More space encouraged experimentation and innovation in home architecture. But while Federal regulations, such as an FHA mortgage ban on flat-roofed homes, distinctly discouraged traditional city row houses, a century of row-house construction in Baltimore guaranteed a large local market for what was now marketed as a "town house." Builders adapted row styles to the new setting. For marble ornamentation, they substituted plain concrete trim. They put up houses in groups of five or six within a block, and built them away from the streets on grassy plots and sidewalks perpendicular to traffic lanes. (See Tremont, Uplands, West Hills, and Yale Heights.)

Popular low, rambling, ranch houses, and "split-levels" are represented in construction in Ten Hills (Drury Street) and Yale Heights. Planned to be efficient and functional, they were designed for households where women spent extensive time at home. Carports and picture windows allowed women to shop by car and watch children at home. Like Victorian Era houses, they incorporated separate zones of household activity for the sexes. After the fashion of what has been called the "crab grass frontier," patios and backyards celebrated family activity. But, like most post-World War II housing, they were built with a minimum concern for energy consumption. And, requiring extensive yard maintenance, they were less suited to the needs of residents with heavy demands on their time, such as women with full time outside employment.

Along Frederick Avenue

The first settlement along Frederick Avenue and Old Frederick Road dates from the eighteenth century. It went up along rural roads which eventually formed the path of the Frederick Turnpike beyond the Gwynns Falls. The traffic of stage coaches and Conestoga wagons on the pike encouraged construction of stone houses, inns, and shops. A little village, Carrollton, formed near the present-day intersection of Frederick and Hilton in the late nineteenth century, constituted a town of 900, with post office and fire hall.

Frederick and the Falls led to more permanent development to the east. Gwynns Falls' boundaries extend clockwise from Frederick and the Western Maryland Railroad (east of the Falls) on the rail lines, Wilkens, Dukeland, Maiden's Choice Run, Caton, Hilton, and Frederick Avenue. Within a gentle northwestern slope upward, they enclose a park on the Falls, one church, the Southwest Police Station, and three commercial streets, Frederick, Caton, and Wilkens. The commercial blocks and the Falls in turn enclose brick and frame row houses.

Urban industrial and residential space was carved out of a succession of nineteenth-century estates, much of it property that once formed part of the estate of Charles Carroll and his son-in-law Richard Caton. Victor Gustave Bloede, a city manufacturer, chemist, and banker, and the first president of West Baltimore General Hospital, subsequently owned land at Maiden's Choice Run and Lane (today Caton Avenue); Washington Chew Van Bibber, a physician, medical professor and founder of the Baltimore Pathological Society, between Frederick and Wilkens; banker Harry C. Schnepfe on

Frederick Avenue. St. Mary's Industrial School on Wilkens Avenue, childhood home of Babe Ruth, extended into land on the eastern edge. The Falls and Maiden's Choice Run lured breweries, stockyards, mills, factories, and workers' housing after the Annex of 1888. A woolen mill operated on the Run; a large brewery, the Germania Brewery, owned by German-born Conrad Eurich and Louis Sander, opened on Frederick in 1893. Facilities to make or distribute confectionery and oleomargarine, lumber yards, and automobile service stations opened in the 1920s. Distribution centers replaced industry after World War II.

A row of now-attached Victorian homes and other country frame houses intermixed with Italianate row homes at 2800 Frederick exemplifies the practice of building new structures among old. Stone house structures along 2900 Frederick represent mid-nineteenth-century property converted to industrial-warehouse use. Property on 3200 Frederick has been the site of paint-brush manufacture since 1904, when Rennous Kleinle Company, later Pittsburgh Plate Glass, acquired it from the Germania Brewery. The Great Fire of 1904 prompted the move here of a business formed as the W. A. McGraw Company in 1850. New buildings were added in 1905, 1906, 1910, 1925, and 1952. Using hog bristles imported from Russia, China, and Manchuria, several hundred workers, many neighborhood residents, made hand and power brushes, handle sets, and roller covers. The equipment was designed, made, and repaired on site by skilled machinists, the work force organized in various unions including the United Steelworkers.

Edmondson, Ellicott's Driveway, Frederick, and Hilton Street form boundaries to Carroll-South Hilton, around terrain with a gentle southeastern slope down to the Falls. It includes two commercial stretches along Frederick and Lohrs, one cemetery, two schools, and residences in the northwest quadrant built from 1920 to 1960. Park land along the Falls and Hilton Parkway loops make up sixty percent of the terrain.

Carroll-South Hilton's location on Frederick lured industry, private institutions, and a settlement of country homes in the southern section in the nineteenth and early twentieth centuries. A grist mill, Kinsey's Mill, operated on the Falls as early as 1812; the House of Refuge, a city-funded home for delinquent and needy white children on the site of Southwestern High in 1855; and a school for African-American children north of Mount Olivet after the Civil War. Frame houses, a few extant on Leeds (formerly Carroll Avenue), went up on the high ground overlooking Mount Olivet. A stretch between the cemetery and the Falls acquired the name Skulltown.

Companies which manufacture business paper, including Baltimore Paper, occupied industrial property on Frederick for a half century after World War I, employing as many as 400 workers. Streetcar lines prompted daylight homes, with porches and light tan brick, along Hilton in the 1920s. Many went up on "Elin," the estate of J. H. Frizell, city businessman and once Prohibition Party candidate for governor.

Mount Olivet Cemetery opened in 1849. Methodist chapels had established so-called God's Acres within the city limits as early as 1791.

Beyond the Gwynns Falls

Urban expansion gradually forced their closing. The City Station, representing several congregations, acquired thirty-three acres along Frederick with a commanding view of the Patapsco. City builder Benjamin F. Bennett added a darkstone retaining wall, iron fence, and gabled and arched entryway in the 1870s. For the bereaved who awaited horse-drawn hearses, a so-called mourners' room was placed near the entryway. Methodism's most renowned nineteenth-century missionaries and bishops are buried in the Bishop's (or Preacher's) Lot, set aside in 1854 for itinerant preachers and their spouses. It holds the graves of Francis Asbury, first American ordained bishop, and Enoch George, John Emory, and Beverly Waugh. The remains of Asbury and Emory were transferred from a city plot. The "Bishops Monument," an eighteen-foot monolith of Italian marble with epitaphs on four sides for four bishops, is inscribed "Soli Deo Gloria," from a tablet that commemorates John Wesley. The remains of Robert Strawbridge, first Methodist preacher in the United States, Jesse Lee, an early denominational historian, and Lyttleton Morgan, for whom Morgan State University is named, and the ashes of E. Stanley Jones, world-renowned missionary, are interred near the bishops' graves. Jones, a missionary to India, was converted at revival services nearby in 1901.

Mark of Excellence Academy operated by Faith Christian Center opened in 1985 in the facility of Gwynns Falls Junior High School, built in 1924. Southwestern High School, with a heavily vocational curriculum, opened in 1971.

Boundaries to St. Joseph's, named for the monastery in Irvington, extend clockwise from Caton and Monastery on Monastery, Hilton, Old Frederick, Cathedral Cemetery Road, and Caton. St. Joseph Street runs on the path of a covered-over stream; it once extended through Carroll-South Hilton to the Falls, terrain on each side a gentle ascent to Caton and Old Frederick. St. Joseph's has two churches, one school, and commercial establishments along Caton. Residential housing spans a century of construction and includes country stone dwellings (Monastery), frame duplexes and Tudor houses (Culver and Kossuth), and contemporary row homes (north of Caton).

Streets form a grid built along old southeast to northwest country roads, a departure from the longitudinal-latitudinal pattern of the old city. They were built along Old Frederick, Dorsey's Lane (today Caton), and a north-south street, known by the 1890s as Fairview Avenue, in the area of what is today McCurley Street. In the late nineteenth century, developers dubbed an extreme southern section Fairview and the middle section to Caton White Hall. A private recreation park, called Henry Lohr's Goebel's Park, surrounded a pond along the stream in the area of what is today the 000 hundred block

(OPPOSITE) City public and charitable institutions with needs for large expanses of inexpensive real estate put up the Westside's first edifices. The cornerstone of the House of Refuge, built at the site of today's Southwestern High School close to the Gwynns Falls and Frederick Road, was laid in 1851. Buildings were erected of gneiss from quarries on the property.

of Benkert Avenue, close to a German ethnic community to the south. The well-known Frohsinn Society (German singers), formed in 1878, kept a clubhouse at Old Frederick and McCurley for many years, and Evergreen African Methodist Episcopal had a tiny frame chapel in an alley east of McCurley (formerly Fairview) in 1928.

Wide-scale urban development took place in the 1920s, homes in the 100 blocks of Monastery and Culver built by Donohue Home Building, some with built-in garages. The 500-student-capacity Sarah M. Roach Elementary (#73) was completed on the site of a nineteenth-century elementary school in 1971.

Irvington's boundaries extend clockwise from Hilton and Old Frederick along Hilton, Caton, southwest and northeast roads within Loudon Park Cemetery, Maiden's Choice, a north-south axis along Beechfield Elementary School, Frederick Avenue, Beechfield, Pen Lucy, Hillvale, Mountview, Athol, and Old Frederick. It straddled the city's western boundary, along Augusta, until 1918, much of it an extension of the western slope of the city from Edmondson Avenue south and east to Maiden's Choice Run and the Gwynns Falls. It contains a three-block business district along Frederick, a one block deep shopping center on Collins, five churches, two schools, and one cemetery, all among residences built over a century.

Only forty blocks from downtown, Irvington developed in isolation from both city and county. No southern thoroughfare extended beyond it until Yale was put through to Beechfield in 1950. Consequently, it tended to shelter little neighborhoods within a neighborhood, as park land and spacious private institutions isolated distinct subdivisions of the larger neighborhood. Loudon Park segregates industrial blocks on the east from the patch of row and Victorian houses south of Frederick Avenue and east of Mount St. Joseph's High School. Madonna School and Woodington Woods along Woodington encircle the Victorian village of "Old Irvington"; the Woods and Cathedral cemetery cap the mostly post-World War II row-house housing and garden apartments in the northwest; Mount St. Joseph's and Beechfield Elementary surround a smaller section of new row houses south of Frederick.

Irvington spreads over a section of the seventeenth-century, central Maryland estate of Charles Calvert, third Lord Baltimore, The estate was patented into smaller holdings before the end of the century, notably "Maiden's Choice," a 450-acre tract owned by Thomas Coale, an Anne Arundel Quaker, in 1673, including what is today Loudon Park Cemetery. "Atholl" was the property of James Murray in 1694; "Morning's Choice" was owned by John Scutt by 1700; and "Buck Ridge" was a holding of Christopher Gardiner in 1720.

Inns and wagon repair shops dotted Frederick Turnpike (today Avenue) after it was opened to Catonsville in 1805. Fairview Inn, known also as Three Mile Inn, sat on the site of Memorial Church. It served variously as a slave quarters, slave jail, and tavern and inn with stables for stage and Conestoga wagon drivers. A milestone, smooth and waist-high and marked "3m to B" stands next to the church.

C. Irving Ditty, collector of the port of Baltimore, developed the "Old Irvington" of Victorian dwellings as a planned suburban village in the 1880s. Married to the granddaughter of Dr. Augustus Schwartze, who owned the stately mansion still extant on Euclid Street, Ditty acquired land west of St. Joseph's Street. He laid out three seventy-foot-wide dirt streets from Frederick to Old Frederick, Loudon, Collins, and Augusta, naming the last for a wife or daughter, and another narrow parallel street, Irving, for himself. Four of the development's first houses were put up by city builder Abraham S. Potter on Augusta near the Schwarz mansion. The east-west streets facilitated extensive construction on lots marketed by the Irvington Real Estate Company, construction spreading from Augusta to Woodland.

Frame architecture, large wrap-around open porches, and yards in front and on both sides set the neighborhood apart from the brick, city-like row houses soon put up on three sides. The blocks of wooden detached houses with manicured lawns sat closer to the center city than other "planned" suburbs that had begun to ring Baltimore City, including Roland Park. Yard space between homes, and between houses and streets, symbolized and embodied a turn-of-the-century suburban ideal and upheld the values of family and privacy. Its own neighborhood stores along Frederick, many owned by German ethnic residents, were named for the community and fostered neighborhood isolation by relieving dependence on outside market places. The Irvington Pharmacy opened in 1898, the Irvington Savings and Loan Association in 1905, and an ice house, bakery, grocery store, theatre, and bowling alley were all thriving by 1930.

Planned development quickened development nearby, streetfront Italianate homes and bow-shaped, "swell-front" houses put up on Collins and Loudon by 1906. Blocks east of Yale and south of Frederick within the 1888 annex were developed with daylight row houses, some with stylish bedrooms erected over entryways (as on Rosecroft), by the 1920s. The wooded open land west of Athol yielded to garden apartments after World War II, near a florist and property of the Sacred Heart Mission Center, and to Urban Renewal low-rise housing in the 1980's.

Residential developments all sprang up in isolation from an industrial district east of Loudon Park, variously the locale of many enterprises built near the Stafford Street freight depot. Loudon Park Cemetery isolated lumber yards, lime kilns, the Victor Blodke chemical works, and a coal company and coal distribution center from the 1890s.

The 300-acre Loudon Park Cemetery was incorporated in 1853 on the site of "Loudon," the estate of James Carey, a Baltimore merchant, city councilman, and founder of the Maryland National Bank. With a spacious Roman entry-arch on Frederick, it was built on an elevated plateau. Remains were transferred from city cemeteries, notably old St. Peter's, Whatcoat, and Zion graveyards, taken over by urban construction. The Federal government purchased land on the eastern edge after the Civil War, eventually acquiring the entire cemetery. It was re-designated "Loudon National Cemetery" about the time of World War I. Highly accessible, it received remains transported by rail over the Pennsylvania Railway, or on the "Delores," a hearse trolley car on city lines. The Delores delivered caskets to the Frederick Avenue gate that were then transferred by horse carriage or along the cemetery's own trolley line from the Frederick to the Wilkens side of the cemetery.

Veterans' graves distinguish Loudon Park. "Government Lot" was acquired by the Federal Government in 1861 for the remains of Union soldiers, 2300 eventually being buried there. An army sergeant domiciled in a cemetery cottage kept watch over the plot for many years. Some 275 Confederate soldiers were buried in a section designated "Confederate Hill." Burials began when lot holders donated plots in 1862, midway through the Civil War, the Cemetery subsequently exchanging these plots to insure a uniform section. The statue of a Confederate soldier guarded by two angels with wreath and torch was sculpted on the plot in 1870 by Adalsbert J. Volck. A monument to mothers and widows was eventually erected by The Ladies Confederate Memorial and Aid Society. Veterans' organizations held ceremonies and picnics at the "Hill" on Confederate Memorial Day, June 6th, until the early 1930s. William Wilkens, Mary Pickersgill, flag-maker of the banner hoisted over Fort McHenry in 1812, H. L. Mencken, and Ensign C. Markland Kelly, Jr., the World War II hero shot down while piloting a single-seat plane in the Battle of Midway, are also buried here. Notable monuments included the Ottmar Mergenthaler Monument for the German-born Baltimore inventor of the linotype.

The buildings of St. Joseph's Church and Madonna School were completed between 1893 and the early 1950s. The Passionist Fathers, a European order from Tuscany, Italy, established a small chapel, the Church of the Most Holy Passion, and a monastery on Old Frederick in the 1860s. They erected frame buildings after selling a parcel of land given them by Emily McTavish, granddaughter of Charles Carroll of Carrollton, near the center of Carrollton. Destroyed by fire, the church was replaced in 1886 by a blue granite church in ancient Roman style, itself replaced by the present edifice for a congregation of 1000 in 1931. Built of granite with limestone trim and with a 22-foot cross over the entry door, the sanctuary is adorned with murals. They depict the flight into Egypt and the death of St. Joseph. Stained-glass clerestory windows, with nearly life-size figures of the twelve apostles, dominate an interior of nine altars. Convent buildings, including Whiteford Hall donated by Celinda Whiteford, were built between 1893 and 1923. Over the years, Passionist priests served as chaplains at Bon Secours, St. Agnes Hospital, and St. Mary's Industrial School and as missionaries to China.

The St. Francis Xavier Roman Catholic Brothers opened Mount St. Joseph's, a college, a boarding school, and the first novitiate of the order on Frederick Avenue in 1876. Brick buildings went up on Seven Gates, a twelve acre estate so named because of its accessibility in as many directions; the campus eventually enlarged to thirty-two acres. The college and novitiate closed in 1921, the boarding program in 1958. New buildings—a gymnasium, St. Joseph's Hall, a classroom-science building, and Ryken Hall, housing library, cafeteria, and administrative offices—replaced nineteenth century structures between 1954 and 1967, except for the seven-story tower of Mount St. Joseph's, the school emblem.

Church edifices reflect two eras of in-migration, the suburban buildup before and after World War I and the African-American migration of the 1950s. An "English" Lutheran Church, the Church of the Redeemer, for second and third generation Germans, opened on Vermont in 1897, with a parsonage constructed in 1905. St. James Episcopal was built in 1908. Yards characteristic of suburban institutions surrounded both. Memorial Methodist was formed as Mount Olivet Mission Chapel in 1867 and served by circuit riders. It was renamed Memorial, in honor of bishops buried in Mount Olivet Cemetery, in 1900, and located in a stone chapel at Frederick and Mount Olivet (Carroll-South Hilton) in 1900. The new stone church with its thirty-two foot tower went up in the 1920s; old cornerstone and a portion of the altar rail where E. Stanley Jones was converted were brought to the new sanctuary. A portrait of Jones, who wrote *Abundant Living* and twelve other religious books, and the manuscripts of his religious books and other mementos are maintained in the church parlor. Pleasant Grove Baptist Church, formed in 1923, moved to 200 Loudon in 1983.

The Walter P. Carter Center of the Department of Health and Mental Hygiene in the St. Joseph's property on Morley was named for the North Carolina-born Baltimore civil rights activist and officer of CORE (Congress of Racial Equality).

Beechfield, Frederick, Wickham and Pen Lucy Roads bound the five blocks of Tremont, part of the 617 acre, late-seventeenth century estate of "Atholl." It takes its name from the late nineteenth-century estate formed from "Atholl" and owned successively by Charles D. Deford, William Baker, and William Baker, Junior. The Annexation of 1918 inspired the development of daylight row houses between the wars along the flat land of Amberly, Dunkirk, Dartford, and Frederick. Flat, spread-out apartment construction surrounded by green space is represented by the older Beechfield Apartment units at Beechfield and Sayer, and the newer Hunting Hills units, at Sayer and Wickam. By 1980 Tremont was a racially integrated neighborhood of one thousand residents.

(OVERLEAF - LEFT) "Athol," on a 617 acre estate patented as "Atholl" north of Frederick Road in the area of Tremont.

(OVERLEAF - RIGHT) Artists view of St. Joseph's Monastery. The first edifice was built on Old Frederick Road about 1860.

Beyond the Gwynns Falls

Greater Edmondson

Six neighborhoods along Edmondson to Hunting Ridge built up on the high ground beyond the Gwynns Falls between 1910 and 1930. They comprise Baltimore's most distant suburb of daylight row homes. Begun as residences for streetcar commuters—developers advertised them as a half hour from downtown Baltimore—these neighborhoods were completed with houses built with garages. New residents traveled neighborhood thoroughfares into the city and County. Elevation, and natural and built boundaries, bequeathed an identity to the residential construction very similar to that of rowhouse architecture elsewhere. Cathedral Cemetery, which isolated the neighborhoods from Frederick Road industry and detached estates and country houses built in the county, and the Gywnns Falls, hemmed them in on the east and south.

Boundaries of Edmondson extend clockwise from the intersection of the Western Maryland Railway and Edmondson along Edmondson, Woodington, Rokeby Road to just east of Seminole, thence north-northwest west to Gwynns Falls, and along the Falls and Railroad. Entirely residential, it includes five large churches, two schools, and one playground; forty percent of the acreage is green space and wooded land within Gwynns Falls Park.

These blocks formed part of the late seventeenth century estates of "Morning's Choice" and "Parker's Place," the latter a 1695 grant to Robert Parker. "Bonnie Brae," property of Charles H. McBlair, spread over southern sections in the middle of the nineteenth century. Acreage north of Edmondson made up part of "Lyndhurst" and of "Gelston," the property of Hugh Gelston eventually called Gelston Heights and having access to Franklintown Road. Reverdy Johnson, lawyer, Attorney General of the United States during the presidency of Zachery Taylor, United States Senator, and ambassador to Great Britain, owned "Lyndhurst."

A scattering of craftsmen, farm laborers, and quarry workers made up a tiny settlement close to the Falls before development. The extension of a trolley line in 1899, opening of the new Gwynns Falls span, and extension of city water and sewage systems, prompted construction before and after World War I. Daylight row and duplex houses with porches lined Edmondson by 1914, streets one block north of Edmondson during the 1920s, and three blocks beyond Edmondson and on Lyndhurst during the 1930s. Many were put up by builder James Keelty. He acquired property along Edmondson by 1922, and the Gelston and Johnson property in 1926 and 1928.

Advertisements highlighted the green space features of Keelty built homes. Houses sat on a hilltop and overlooked the scenic Falls. A fifteen-foot green park strip distinguished Wildwood, where houses were built wider and deeper, twenty-two by thirty-seven feet. Half-attics there added extra room, and garages defined homes as modern. Fireplaces, tile porches, and exterior variety within rows distinguished the homes from typical Keelty-built rows.

Edmondson Avenue was widened to facilitate automobile traffic in the 1920s, sycamore trees were planted along many streets, and Lyndhurst Elementary School was opened in 1928. A neighborhood of young families was sometimes dubbed "Mortgage Hill." Northern sections of Edmondson were finished with plainer rows in the 1940s and 1950s after Keelty's death, by his sons. Edmondale Apartments, spreading over four-and-one-half blocks north and west from Stokes and Wildwood, and comprising 262 units of two bedrooms each, was built by 1950. African Americans moved to Edmondson in large numbers in the late 1950s and 1960s.

Mount Olivet Baptist Church, a congregation formed in 1922, occupies a facility that once housed the Edmondson Theatre; Mount Olive Holy Evangelical Apostolic, Lyndhurst and Edmondson, the sanctuary put up by All Saints Evangelical Lutheran. Keelty contributed the sanctuary of St. Bernadine, built in 1929. A shrine to the Immaculate Heart of Mary, made of Carrera Italian marble and dedicated to the fallen and the survivors of the two World Wars, was put up in 1948. Edmondson Avenue Methodist is formed from two Methodist Protestant congregations, one at Edmondson and Grantley, and the other, Christ Methodist Protestant, originating on Baker near Fulton.

(OVERLEAF) Builder James Keelty was a benefactor to St. Bernadine's Roman Catholic Church, erected for newly developed Edmondson in 1929.

Beyond the Gwynns Falls

Allendale, bounded by Hilton, Monastery, Caton, Mt. Holly Street, and Edmondson, slopes downward toward the Gywnns Falls Parkway which it borders. Mostly blocks of row homes, it contains two schools, one church, one senior citizens apartment complex, and scattered shops. Its high ground, accessible to the city along a country road (Dorsey's Lane, today Caton Avenue), attracted city merchants who located spreading estates here, "Allendale," the property of William Heald north of Cathedral Cemetery, being the largest. John Marr and Louis Zaiser owned land east of Heald's property.

Blocks north of Mulberry developed with Edmondson, many made up of daylight row houses also built by Keelty. Row houses were put up on 3300 and 3400 Edmondson and on 300 and 400 Hilton in the 1910s, and 500 Denison and Edgewood in the 1920s. Keelty kept a real-estate office on Edmondson Avenue in the 1920s, close to the American Legion Hall and Thomas Jefferson Democratic Club. Mary E. Rodman School on 3500 Mulberry, with a celebrated boys chorus under the directorship of Ruth Thornton Hawkins for many years, was erected in the late 1960s to serve a largely African-American neighborhood of young parents and children. The 12-story, 164-unit dwelling of Allendale, A HUD-financed housing development for elderly and disabled citizens, went up in 1985 near the site of Heald's estate house.

West Mulberry's boundaries extend from Edmondson and Mount Holly clockwise along Mt. Holly, Caton, the southwestern boundary of Cathedral Cemetery, Old Frederick, and Edmondson. Property of Edmondson High School formed much of the late nineteenth-century estate of James A. Wilson. Housing plots in the northeast corner were laid out by the Lyndhurst Improvement Company in the 1890s, its row houses developed with Edmondson. Housing lined four blocks of Edmondson Avenue and one block of Loudon Street by 1921 and spread over every residential block by 1931.

Cathedral, or "New Cathedral", Cemetery opened in 1870 with an entry from Old Frederick Road on fifty acres of the estate of "Bonnie Brae." Remains transferred from the Sandtown-Winchester cemetery included those of Charles Carroll of Carrollton and thirty-six nuns who had perished in an early-century cholera epidemic. The burial vault for the latter had been presented to the order of the Sisters of Charity in recognition of their services to the city. The Gothic, solid granite mortuary chapel was built soon after the cemetery opened.

Planned as a small public high school in 1954, Edmondson-Westside Senior High was expanded as it was built (1954 to 1960) to accommodate the large population influx of the late 1950s. The two- and three-story red brick facility was put up with an additional story to accommodate 1,850 students.

Bisected by the western boundary of the city in the Annex of 1888, Rognel Heights is bounded by Edmondson, Athol, a line parallel to and southwest of Walnut, Seminole, Rokeby Road, and Woodington. It is named for two nineteenth-century owners of the Baltimore county section, William F. Rodgers and William O. Nelson. One playground, a mini-park, and a school are situated among frame houses built within Baltimore County before 1918. Contemporary row homes spread along rolling high ground. Rognel Heights has no industry or commercial dwellings.

Acreage formed part of "Hunting Ridge" in the seventeenth century, and "Morning's Choice," bordering "Atholl" to the south. General John Swan and Reverdy Johnson owned nineteenth-century tracts. The oldest development spread out over western blocks at an angle to the orderly grid of the 1888 annex, on land developed by investor William T. Pfeiffer. Detached, brown-shingled homes heightened the sense of a country environment. Pfeiffer also marketed water from a well-known natural springs just north of development. Artesian wells were drilled there, and a water tower built over a natural ravine and rocky aquifer on Sixth Avenue (now Sidehill). Pfeiffer bottled and marketed the water to downtown grocers and offices as "Rock Crystal Spring Water." The cisterns and wells were leveled in 1918 as a hazard.

Two-story brick duplex and row houses went up on Woodington, Wicklow, Kevin, Colborne, Flowerton, and Seminole in the 1940s and 1950s. Westside Methodist built Rognel Heights Methodist at Walnut and Colborne in 1949 for a congregation formed there in 1914 and merged in 1928 with Franklin Street Methodist. An exterior seventeen-foot cross in a perennial garden, a memorial to Emma Meredith Nichols and the gift of her son Thomas Steele Nichols, honors historic Methodism. Fifty-nine stones, collected from forty-eight states, three Federal territories, and six continents, commemorate Christian brotherhood. The Maryland stone was taken from St. Mary's City; others came from Holy land sites—the Galilean Sea, the alleged tomb of Jesus, and the slope of the Feeding of the Five Thousand. Georgian Etowah pink marble at the center recalls the missionary trip of denomination founder John Wesley to Georgia from 1735 to 1737. At its center are stones collected by a Belgian Congo nurse and missionary, Kathryn Eye. Enoch Pratt opened a branch at Edmondson and Athol in 1951. Rognel Heights Elementary, #89, was built for 750 students in 1970.

Boundaries to Edmondson Village run clockwise from Athol and Old Frederick on Old Frederick, Pen Lucy, Uplands Parkway, Edmondson Avenue, Swann, Rokeby Road, northeast on a line parallel to and southwest of Walnut, and Athol to Old Frederick. A shopping center and school cover one-third of the area in the northeastern section, garden apartments and row houses on rolling hills the rest. Much of its acreage stood on the eighteenth-century estate of General John Swan and mid-nineteenth-century estate of William Frick. Scottish born Swan, an Anne Arundel County estate owner, secured a 1000 acre section of the estate of Tory Daniel Dulaney. He eventually helped organize the Franklin Road Turnpike Company. A part of the property passed into the hands of Edward Austin Jenkins in 1881. A stone lodge house built either by Dulaney or Swan near Old Frederick Road sat on the site of Edmondson Shopping Center until 1946. Its unusual cypress and pecan trees and the wainscoted dining room of the estate house won it local renown.

Some 997 units of the Uplands Apartments spread over eight irregularly shaped blocks south of Edmondson in the early 1950s, a complex remodeled in the 1980s as subsidized housing. The Edmondson Village Shopping Center went up on an eleven acre site in 1947 as one of the nation's first planned suburban shopping centers. Local builders Joseph and Jacob Meyerhoff built it in the style of Colonial Williamsburg. Its architecture suggested stability and tradition even as the project encouraged entirely new consumer behavior and habits on the Westside. Twenty-nine stores built back from the street and a sunken garage to hold 700 automobiles accommodated commuters. Recreation places—a theatre and bowling alley—were located among the stores. The architectural features lent a distinctly non-commercial, residential quality to shopping. Trees and shrubbery surrounded the area; chimneys were placed for decorative purposes alone; and slate roofs and a variety of bay and dormer windows were put on upper floors to resemble private homes. To acquaint and adjust consumers to the new mode of purchasing, a clubroom for neighborhood activities was opened. Local department stores maintained branches, Hochschild Kohn within the center, the Hecht Company across from it on Edmondson; the latter facility was eventually acquired by the city and converted to a vocational skills center to serve six high schools.

Mountainview Road, Pen Lucy, Old Frederick Road, and Athol bound Uplands, a community of 800 named for the estate of William Frick, grandson-in-law of John Swan. Wed to Ann Elizabeth Swan before the Civil War, Frick practiced law in Baltimore City for sixty-three years. This acreage formed part of the seventeenth-century estate of "Hector's Fancy" and was once called "Bleake Hill."

The estate served as summer residence for Frick's daughter, Mary Sloane Jacobs, until 1926. A premier Baltimore socialite, and once married to a Garrett, Jacobs also resided in the city (Mount Vernon Place, in the edifices that today comprise the Engineer's Club) and in Newport, Rhode Island, and was a benefactor to the Baltimore Museum of Art.

Daylight row houses went up on Pen Lucy and Athol in the 1920s, unadorned, brick-faced row houses elsewhere after World War II.

At the Western Edge

Formed entirely from the Annex of 1918, neighborhoods which hug the west and southwest city boundaries developed as automobile suburbs to the city and villages and suburbs within Baltimore County. They were built "over the hill" from the western ascent along the Gwynns Falls and exhibit the tendency of early home architecture to influence later construction. Frame houses built before 1918 inspired cottages and detached homes which blended with them. Developments went up farther from thoroughfares and with greater wooded and green space than anywhere else within the Westside.

Hunting Ridge nestles between Leakin Park and built-up sections of Edmondson. Clockwise from Swann and Edmondson, its boundaries extend along Edmondson, Cooks Lane, Briarcliff, Winans Way, a zigzag path near the approach of Winans Way and Dead Run (close to School #89), Seminole Avenue, and a line parallel to and southwest of Walnut, Rokeby Road, and Swann. It has one church, a public school, and a fire house, and no industry or commercial establishments. It takes its name from the 25,000-acre seventeenth-century colonial tract which spread over much of Baltimore County, owned variously by John Bailey, father-in-law of John Calvert and son of George Calvert, and Benjamin Tasker, founder of the Baltimore Iron Works Company. Daniel Dulaney, James and John Swan, and William and Mary Frick also owned sections once designated "Frederickstadt." In the mid-nineteenth century much of the neighborhood formed the southern part of Crimea, the estate of railroad engineer Thomas Winans along Franklintown Road, the bulk of it today Leakin Park. "Crimea" acquired fame during the

Civil War when mock fortifications erected by Confederate sympathizer Ross Winans failed to deter union troops from invading it and capturing him. Winans was imprisoned in Fort McHenry. His granddaughter, Celeste Marguerite Winans Hutton, resided at the estate until at least 1916. Property west of Brockwood formed the orchards and nursery of "Breisgau" in the late nineteenth century. It was owned by horticulturalist John Cook, landscape architect to a number of Westside estates. Cook allegedly developed a hybrid tea rose on his thirty acres in 1873.

The blocks near Edmondson developed in the 1920s as an automobile suburb of detached homes with garages. A public school, Ten Hills-Rognel Heights (today Thomas Jefferson #232), the sanctuary and educational building for Lafayette Square Presbyterian, renamed Hunting Ridge, and an auto sales and service establishment on Edmondson, all went up before 1930. Duplex and row houses lined northern blocks after World War II. An influx of African-American home buyers and renters formed it into a racially integrated neighborhood in the 1970s and 1980s.

Boundaries of Ten Hills extend clockwise from Edmondson and Uplands Parkway on Uplands, Pen Lucy, Wickam, Frederick Avenue, Rock Glen Road, a line northeast from the intersection of Rock Glen and Wendley Road, Westgate, Brookgreen Road, Stamford, and Edmondson. One church, a hospital, and a swimming club stand among detached homes and garden apartments. Ten Hills is formed from "Hunting Ridge," the nineteenth-century property of Frick and Jacobs, and "Atholl" on the south and east and "Bellview" (or "Bellevue") close to Edmondson. The last, a 200-acre estate, was owned by Phillip Chappell, a city chemical manufacturer and banker. Chappell's son, Thomas, raised prize livestock here for many years.

The 125 acres of Bellview were acquired by the Ten Hills Corporation, a syndicate of 50 investors including real-estate broker Charles H. Steffey, in 1909. Spacious houses of brick and frame went up on lots 100 by 200 feet. Much like Guilford in north Baltimore and Stoneleigh in Baltimore County, it eventually numbered 200 homes, many with 10 to 14 rooms. Strict development plans required Corporation approval of home design, and restrictive covenants governed property transfer. Streets were laid out in curved patterns to heighten a sense of privacy.

The Ten Hills Civic Club was organized in the 1920s, the Ten Hills Community Association in 1936, and a private swimming club opened along Nottingham in 1957. Apartments were built along Nottingham and Rock Glen in the 1970s. The wooded acreage along Uplands Parkway, which opened in the 1940s, is formed from the Frick-Jacobs estate. St. Bartholomew's Episcopal, built in 1928, grew from three city and county congregations, Trinity, with a chapel on Edmondson before the development of Ten Hills, St. Bartholomew's, a nineteenth-century parish in "Druid Heights," and old Holy Trinity from "Greenlawn." Gundry Hospital, once the Gundry Sanatorium, founded at Baltimore and Payson in 1900 as a private institution for mental disorders, has occupied the mansion house on the estate of "Sorrento" (south Athol) since 1936.

The seventeen blocks of West Hills are bounded by the Baltimore National Pike, the city line, Dead Run, Winans Way, Briarcliff, and Cooks Lane. Gentle hills spread over a part of Hunting Ridge surveyed as "Hector's Fancy" in 1695. Nineteenth-century landowners included William Wilkens and Hollins McKim in the southern sections, and George E. Page, in the northern. It developed after World War II with unadorned daylight row homes and duplexes, many with formstone trim, lining nearly every block. St. William of York, established in 1914, built a convent and school, between 1948 and 1950. Second English Lutheran, organized in 1841, moved from property now occupied by University Hospital, downtown Baltimore, into a Colonial brick building on spacious grounds at the Pike and Briarcliff in 1952.

Boundaries to Westgate extend clockwise from Rock Glen and Frederick Avenue along Frederick, the city line, Baltimore National Pike, Edmondson, Stamford Road, Brookgreen, Westgate, a southwesterly line to the intersection of Rock Glen and Wendley, and Rock Glen. Regarded as the eastern end of Catonsville, it reflects the influence of rural frame architecture. Nineteenth-century pillared frame houses sit back from the road along North Bend. Small frame cottages spread along Westgate, Charing Cross, Kristin, Wendley, Mallory Hill, and North Bend close to modern apartments. The northeastern blocks are an extension of Ten Hills. It has two churches and two schools.

Many blocks were formed from "Slade's Camp." North Bend Lane (today Road) extended from Frederick since at least 1877, and small estates, many owned by city bankers and businessmen, built up on both sides of it. A stream into Maiden's Choice Run ran in the direction of Rock Glen Road before development. Northern sections close to the Ellicott City car line built up in the 1920s. It is the third and fourth location on the Westside to its two churches. West Baltimore Methodist, Greenwich and Charing Cross, dates back to 1843 and occupied a facility at Greene and Lombard. A Methodist Protestant congregation, it put up a stone edifice at Lafayette and Gilmore (Harlem Park) in 1885, replacing the frame building called Memorial Chapel. It was disassembled and moved stone by stone in 1930 for the current structure. An educational building went up in 1957, a parsonage in 1966. Brantly Memorial Baptist, formed in 1848, met in a small chapel near Pierce and Fremont after the Civil War. A chapel was built at Schroeder and Pierce in 1884, a lot acquired in 1888 at Schroeder and Edmondson (Harlem Park) for open-air meetings and a church completed in 1892. Named for W. T. Brantly, pastor of Seventh Baptist, it moved to the Baltimore National Pike in 1943. West Baltimore Middle, originally Rock Glen Junior High and one of Baltimore's largest intermediate schools, and North Bend Elementary, went up in the late 1960s to serve a large suburban influx.

Boundaries of the hilly terrain of Yale Heights run clockwise from an intersection formed by Maiden's Choice Run and the southwest boundary to Loudon Park Cemetery, along the Cemetery's edge, Beechfield, Colleen Road, Beechfield, Frederick, a line extending southward through Beechfield Elementary School property, to Maiden's Choice Run, thence to Loudon Park. It includes detached hilltop estate houses on Thornfield and Cedar Gardens, row houses and apartments built after World War II, and one church. The blocks are carved from "Maiden's Choice." "Airy Hill," a 100-acre, nineteenth-century estate with several streams, spread over part of it in the nineteenth century. The Catonsville Short Line Railway ran a path along it in 1860, its engines converted to steam in 1874.

Large, ten- to fourteen-room houses of frame and brick had been built to overlook the valley of Maiden's Choice Run by 1928, in a small development which resembled Ten Hills. But urban build-up was delayed until Yale Avenue was extended southwest from Potter to Beechfield with winding streets built westward. Newer houses and apartments exemplify modern trends in row-house architecture. Made of modest brick with cement trim, they were put up away from the street on courtyards and sidewalks perpendicular to it. They were built five or six to a group, the amenity of an "end of the group" house less often a different, more decorative style, as in older row houses, than affording extra yard space. The College Gardens Corporation built College Gardens Apartments on 4300 Parkton.

The ranch-style sanctuary of Beechfield Methodist was built in 1959 for a new congregation with many charter members from Fayette Bennett Church, near Fayette and Fremont, which closed with the opening of the new church. The congregation met in a bungalow parsonage before the church was completed. Buildings for Beechfield Elementary went up in 1954 and 1970. African-American in-migration of the 1970s transformed the blocks into a racially heterogenous neighborhood.

The southwestern boundary to the city, Frederick Avenue and the continuous path of Beechfield, Coleen Road, and Beechfield form the boundary of the wedge-shaped neighborhood of Beechfield. It contains one church, cemetery, school and rehabilitation institute for children, and housing built over a century. Its western acreage was once part of the eighteenth-century estate "Cloud Capped," known by 1800 as "Cloud Cap," the property of Charles Carroll of Carrollton. The Baltimore Iron Ore Works, whose investors included Carroll, Samuel Chase, members of the Dulaney family and several others, acquired the land during the Revolution. Allegedly, the British fleet of fifty vessels was spotted from the hilltop estate house in September 1814, one day before the Battle of North Point. Owned variously by James Cox, Talbott Taylor, and Orville Horowitz, it was acquired in 1890 by Blanchard Randall, a city grain commission merchant, also owner of Tower Hill, north of Frederick Avenue. Randall enlarged the estate house with terraces built from a demolished city bank.

The eastern blocks were developed as Norwood or Norwood Heights before and after the Annexation of 1918. Detached, frame homes lined hilltops in blocks bounded by Williston, Hazleton, Overton, and Chapelgate, and along Taylor Avenue near nineteenth-century estate homes built of stone near the southern part of Chapelgate. Plain, unadorned row homes went up on and off Frederick after World War II.

RICA, the Regional Institute for Children and Adolescents, an agency of the Maryland Department of Health and Mental Hygiene, occupies buildings that once housed St. Charles College and St. Mary's Seminaries. "Cloud Cap" owner and prominent University of Maryland professor of Obstetric Surgery Nathan Smith bequeathed fifty-five acres to St. Mary's in the mid-nineteenth century. Founded in 1791 by the Fathers of St. Sulpice, St. Mary's established a clergy retreat there. The pre-Seminary program of St. Charles, originally set up in Ellicott City, and St. Mary's Seminary were located there between 1911 and 1969.

The Baltimore National Cemetery, Maryland's "Little Arlington," was formed from "Cloud Cap" in the 1930s and 1940s to alleviate the overcrowding of Loudon Park. The WPA and the Department of Army surveyed and built roads, demolished the mansion house, and erected a lodge, gates, and fences. Fellowship Baptist Church, built at Melbourne and Beechfield to accommodate suburban influx, blends with the yards and one-story residences south and west.

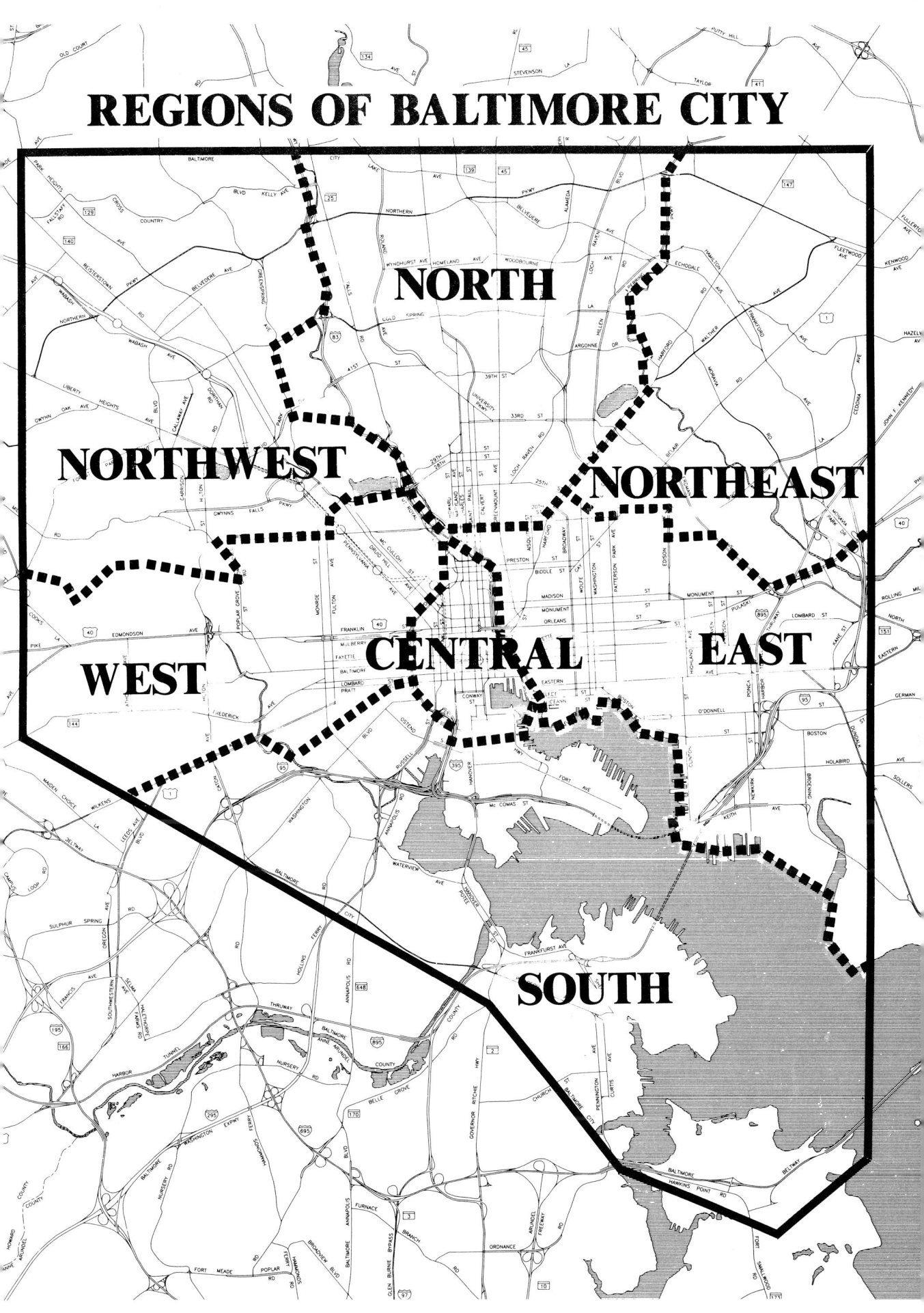

West Baltimore

MOUNT ROYAL AND MADISON

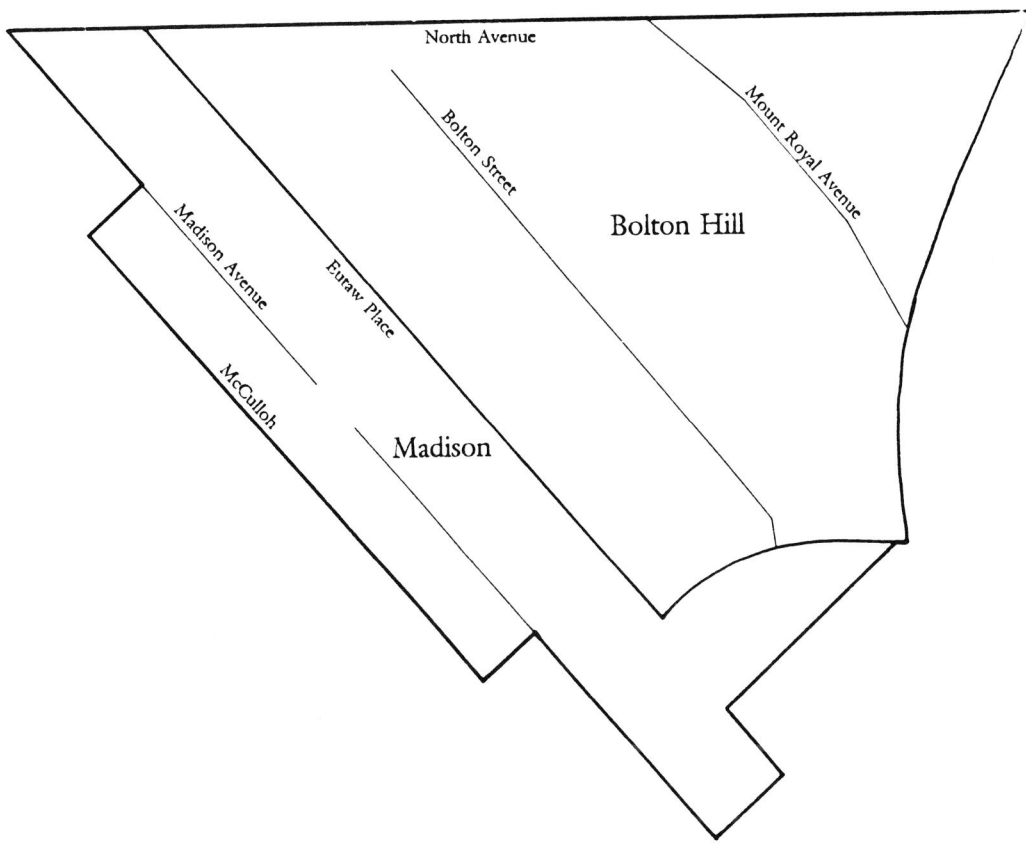

The "Bottom to Sugar Hill"

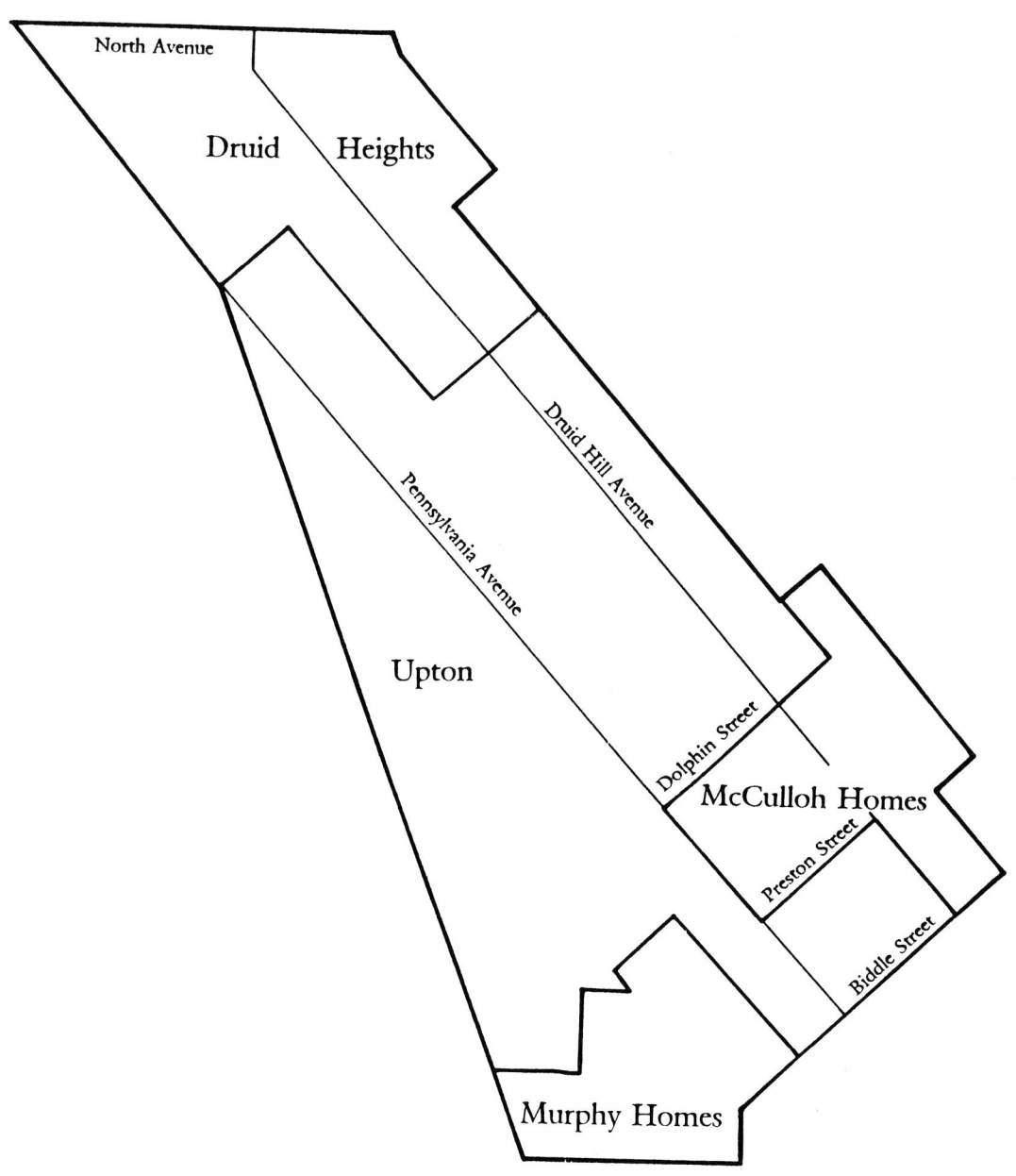

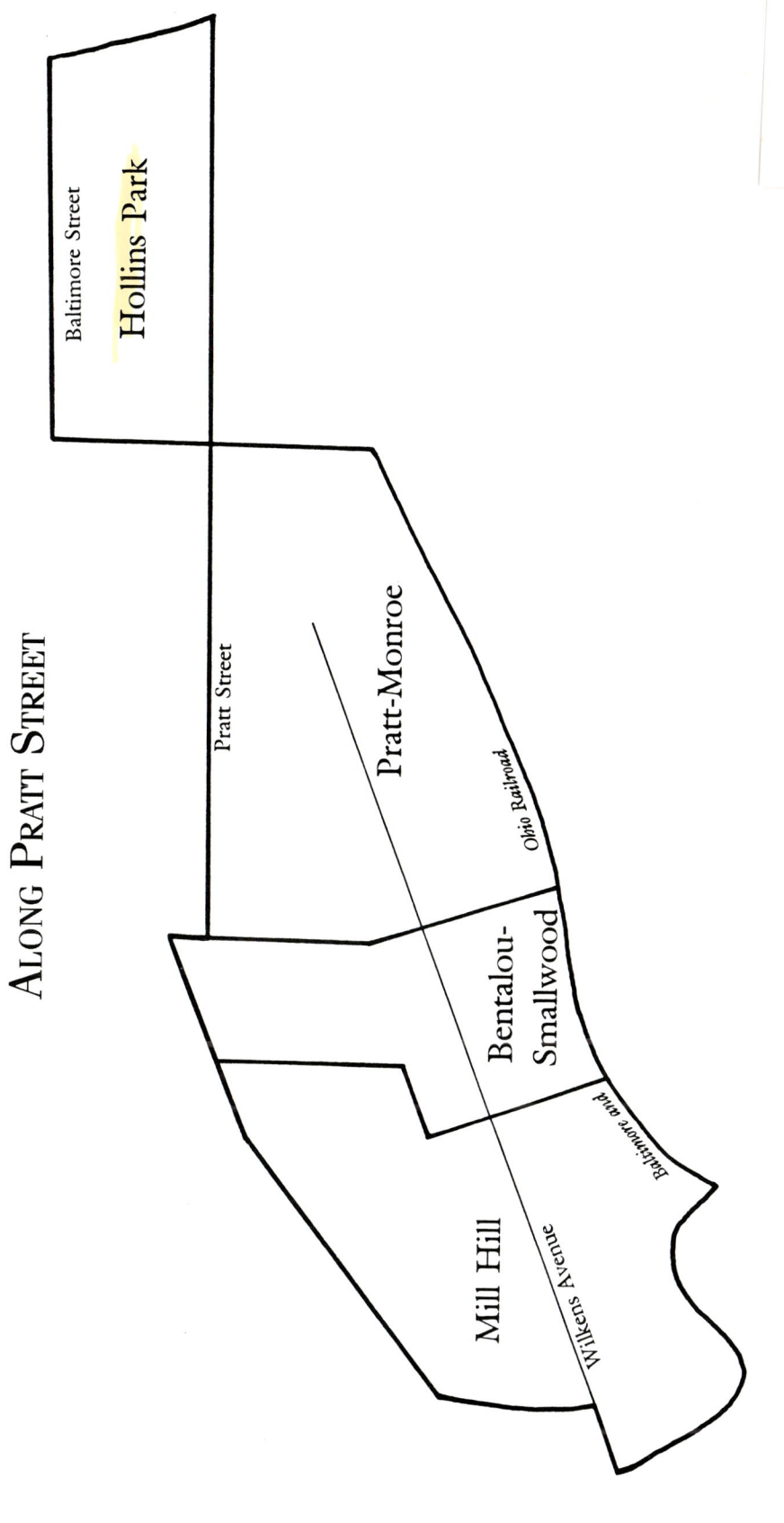

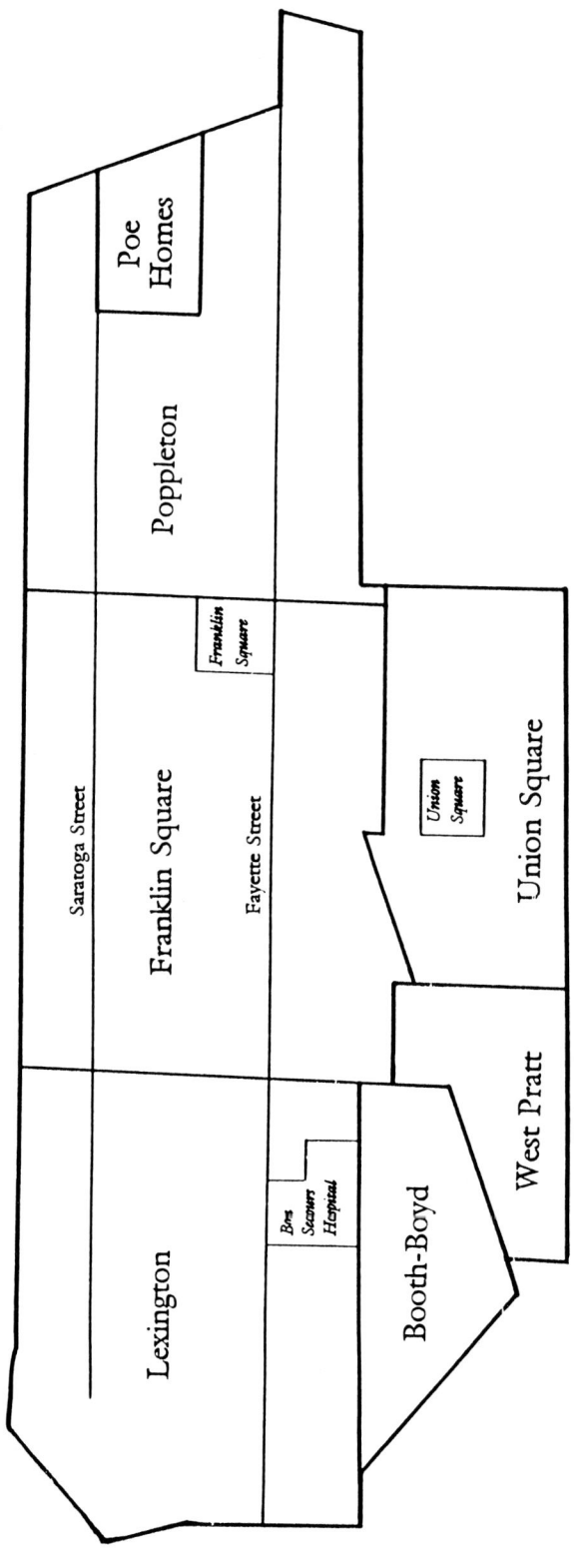

SANDTOWN-WINCHESTER

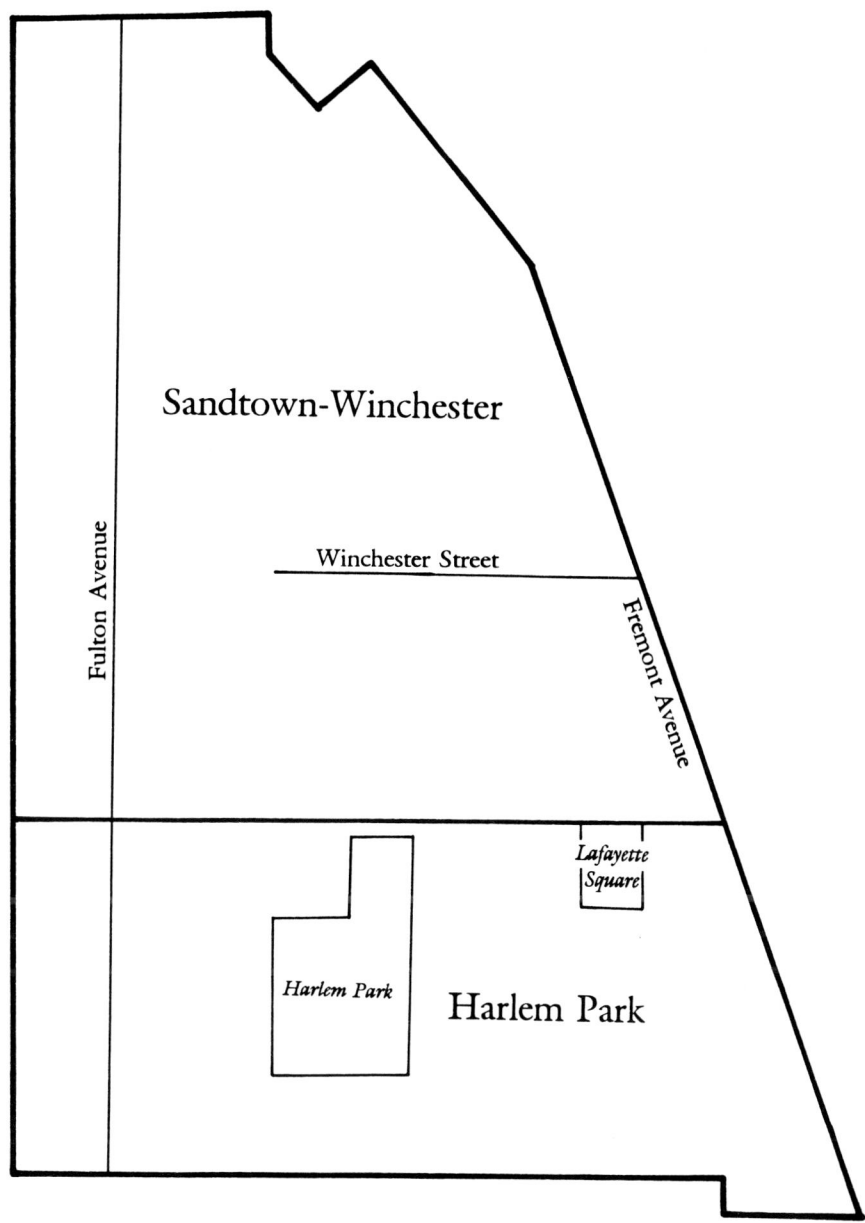

Neighborhood Maps

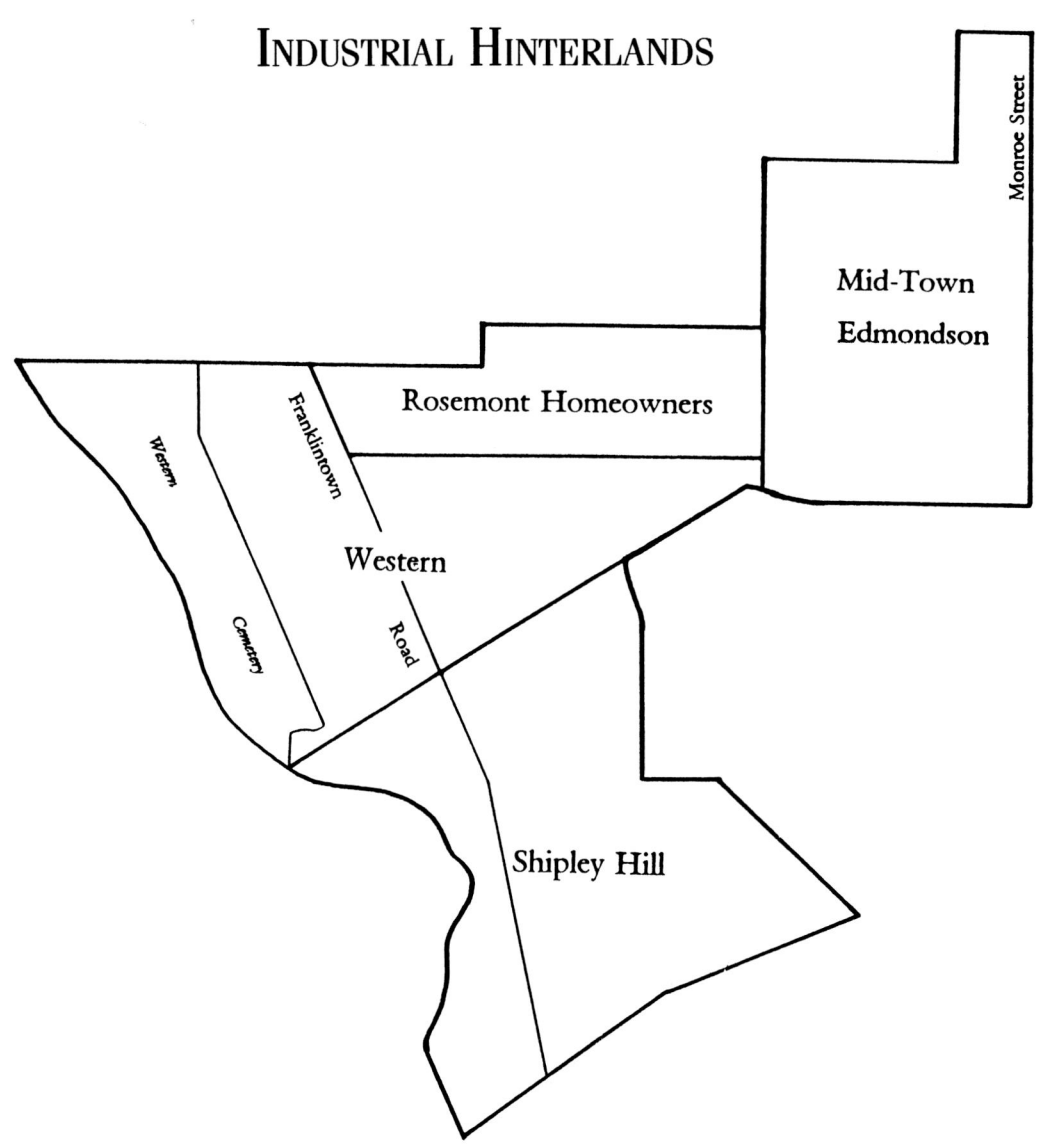

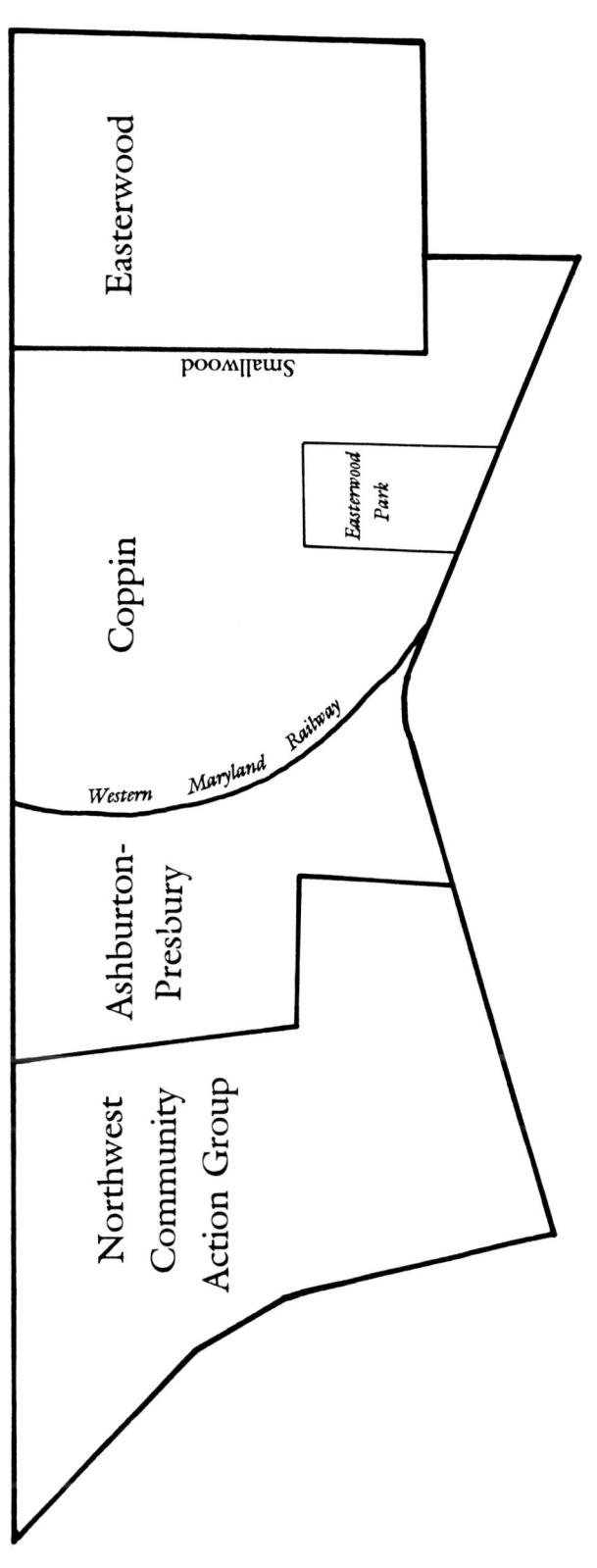

Neighborhood Maps

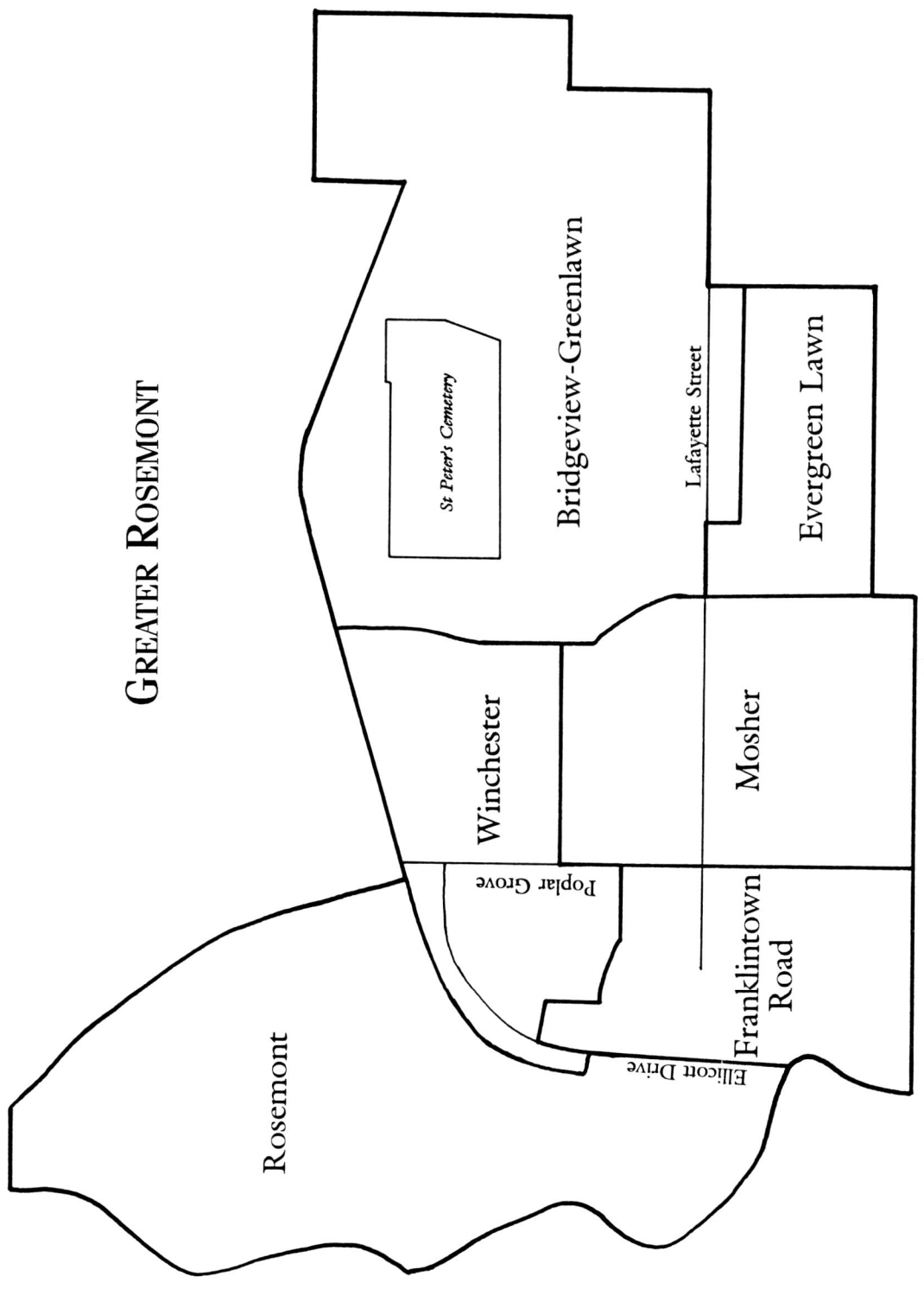

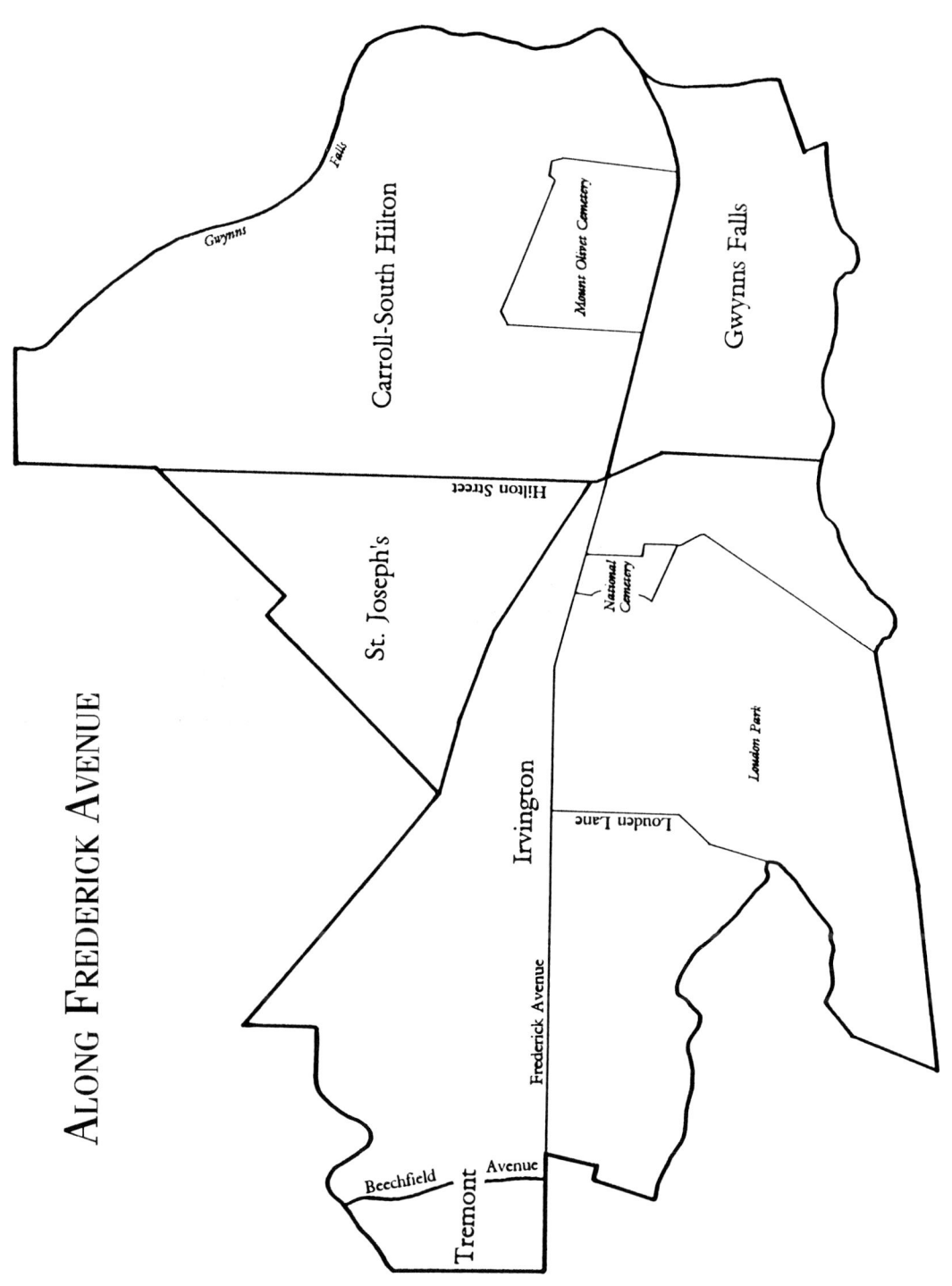

Greater Edmondson

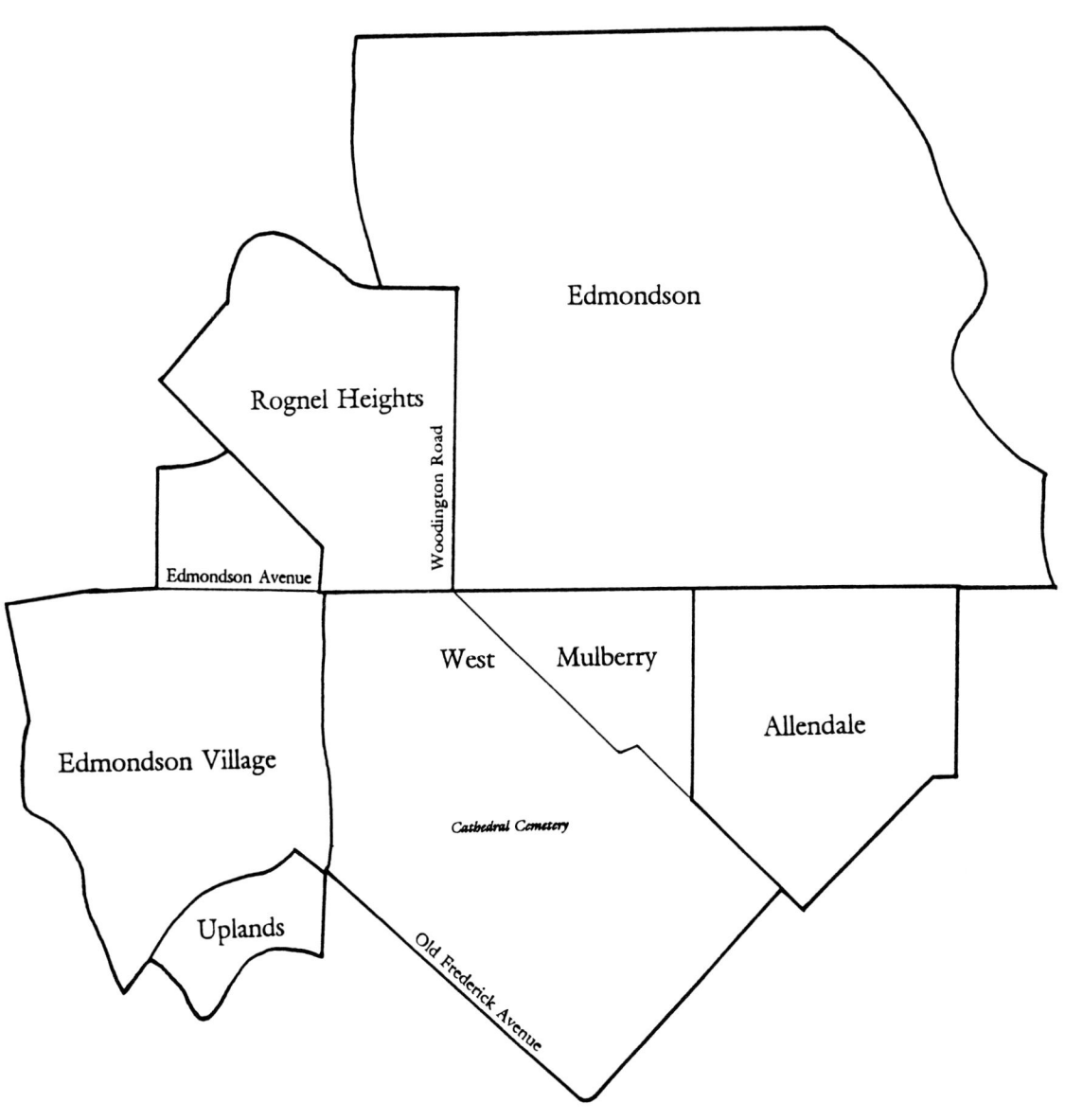

At the Western Edge

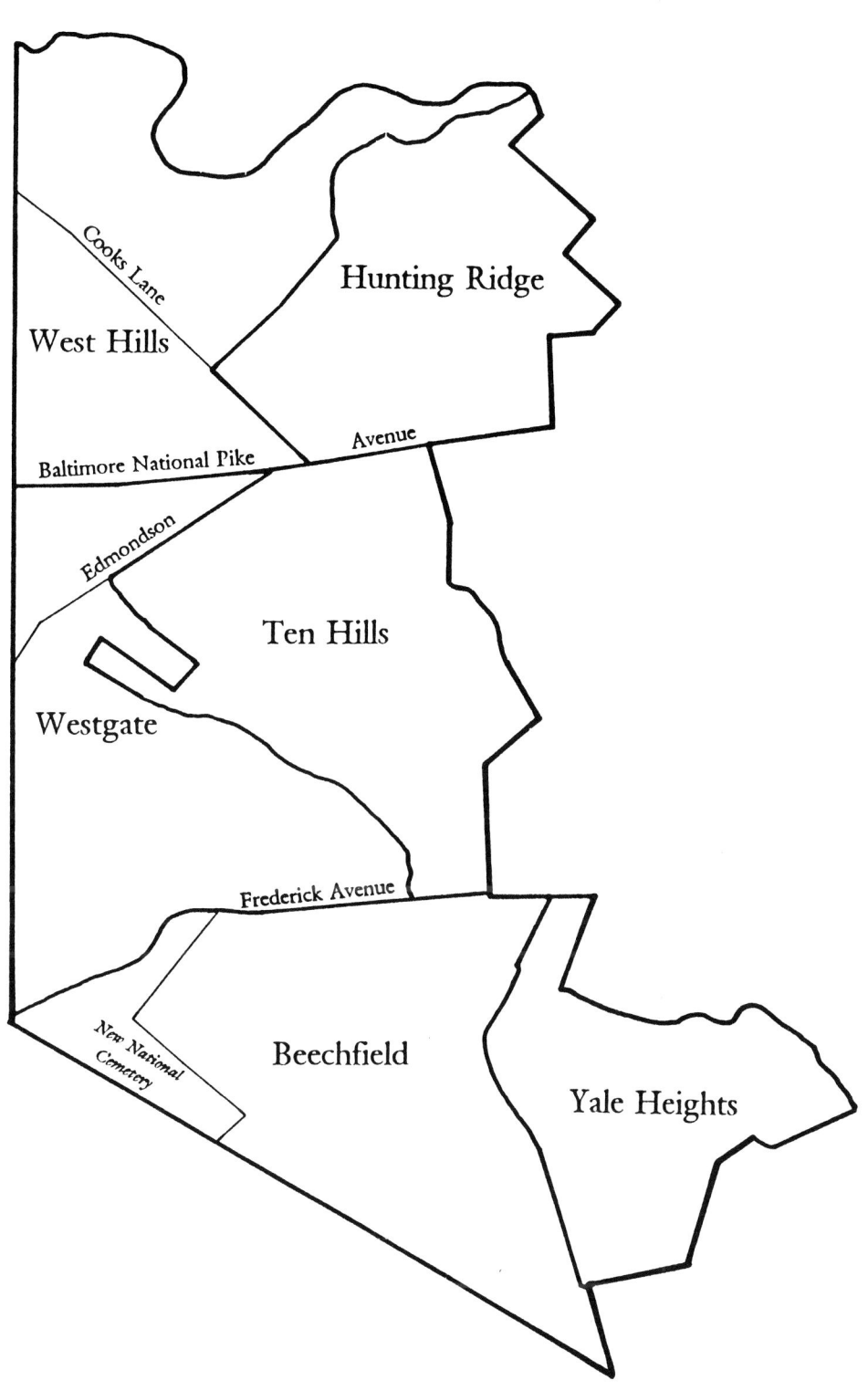

Index

Afro-American, 25, 34, 83, 110, 111, 113, 127
"Alexandrofsky," 61, 62
Allendale, 173
Altamount Hotel, 16
Amalgamated Clothing Workers Building, 22
Amtrak Lines, 106, 125, 138, 148
Ashburton-Presbury, 144, 145
"Atholl," 164, 167, 168, 174

B and O Railroad Yards
 Mount Clare, 9, 58, 59-61, 62-63, 65, 68-69, 76
Bailey, Pearl, 24-25, 47
Baker Circle, 126
Baltimore
 annexations and annexes, 7, 10, 104, 106, 126, 131-33, 136, 142, 155-56, 164, 167, 169, 176, 179
 civil rights agitation, 28, 43, 91, 111, 136
 labor unions, 27, 29, 46, 56, 61, 73, 109, 111-12, 134
 middle classes, 17-18, 39, 80-81, 132;
 racial segregation, 26-30, 38, 43, 46, 52, 82-83, 109, 127, 136;
 upper classes, 2, 3, 16, 18-19,
 working classes, 2, 3, 4, 7, 10, 16-17, 27, 29-30, 31, 32, 46, 47, 55-58, 61, 69, 70, 72-73, 82-83, 84, 100, 103, 109-112, 118, 125, 132, 150.
Baltimore and Catonsville Passenger Railway, 72, 96
Baltimore and Ohio Railroad, 2, 56, 59-61, 95, 100
Baltimore and Potomac Railroad, 9, 38, 106, 125, 139
Baltimore and Randallstown Railway, 125
Baltimore, Calverton and Powhatan Railroad, 104, 146
Baltimore Female College, 10
Baltimore Hebrew Orphan Asylum, 151
Baltimore National Cemetery, 180
Baltimore Urban League, 40, 46, 136
Bartlett and Hayward, Co., 60, 65, 91, 93
Beechfield, 179-180
Bentalou-Smallwood, 71-77
Bethel AME Church, 46, 49
Bishop's Lot, Mount Olivet Cemetery, 162

Black Panthers, 127
Bloomingdale Turnpike, 145-146, 150, 152
"Bolton," 5, 6
Bolton Hill, 1, 4, 5-14
Bolton Station, 7
Bon Secours Hospital, 107
Booker T. Washington Junior High School, 19, 38
Booth-Boyd, 104-05
"Boston Fear," 145
"Bottom," 25-26, 30, 31, 38, 40, 46
"Boxer's Church," 87-88
Brewster, Cora and Flora, 18
Bridgeview-Greenlawn, 148
Brotherhood of Liberty, 43
Brown Memorial Church, 7, 12, 13
"Butcher's Church," 87-88

Calloway, Cab, 38-39, 48
Camp Druid Hill, 40
Camp Hoffman, Lafayette Square, 119-120
Carey Theatre, 112, 113, 115
Carroll, Charles, of Carrollton, 60, 100, 166
Carroll-South Hilton, 161
Carrollton Viaduct, 57
Carrollton (Village), 160
Carver High School, 145
Cathedral Cemetery, 125, 170, 173
Chatsworth Run, 34, 38, 124
Children's Fountain, 16
Churches and Synagogues, 7, 9, 11, 12, 13, 15, 22, 32, 34, 38, 48-50, 51, 52, 61, 69, 71, 73, 76, 87-88, 89, 90, 92, 94, 95, 96, 97, 102, 103, 104-05, 107, 111, 113, 116, 117, 118-19, 122-23, 126, 127, 136, 139-40, 141, 142, 144, 145, 146-47, 149, 150, 151, 152, 153, 162, 164, 166-67, 171, 174, 178, 179
Citizens' Passenger Railway, 3
City-Wide Young People's Forum, 46
"Cloud Cap," 180
Colored Law and Order League, 40
Colored Men's Progressive and Co-operative Union, 29
Colored Women's Suffrage Club, 40

Cone, Joseph, 117
"Confederate Hill," Loudon Park, 166
Confederate Memorial, 14
Coppin, 144
Coppin, Fannie Jackson, 97
Coppin Normal School, 97-98
CORE, 91, 167
Cummings, Henry S., 43

Deaver Smith Tea Company, 40
Delaware Row, Franklin Square, 96
"Delores," 166
Democratic Party, 42, 90, 96, 173
Diane Theatre, 50
Ditty, C. Irving, 165
"Doctor's Row," 18
Douglass High School, 40, 46, 111, 127-28
Douglass Theatre, 46, 97
Druid Heights, 51-52
Druid Hill Park, 3, 4, 10, 18, 51
DuBois, W. E. B., 40
DuBois Club, 40

Easterwood, 143-44
Easterwood Park, 143, 144-45
Edmondson, 170-72
Edmondson, Thomas, Jr., 117
Edmondson Village, 174-75
Edmondson-Westside Senior High School, 173
Enoch Pratt Library, branches, 38, 52, 105,
Eutaw Place, 15-16, 17, 18, 19-21, 69
Evergreen Lawn, 126, 149-150
Expressway I-170, 91-92

Fitzgerald, F. Scott, 10
Franklin Square, 95-98
Franklin Square (Park), 80, 90, 92, 97, 100
Franklin Square Hospital, 90, 96
Franklintown Road, 151-52
Frick's Folly, 11
Frick's Run, 6

Friends School, 7, 14

Garrett, John W., 95
Garrett Park, 97
Garvey, Marcus, 40
Gary, James A., 9
Gilmor, Robert, Sr., 116
Gilmor Homes, 128-29
"Gin Belt," (Bolton Hill), 10
Good Shepherd Home, 100, 101
"Goose Hill," 149
Goucher, John F., 118-19
Great Glade, 6
Gwynns Falls, 56, 57, 125, 131, 132, 133-34, 137, 152, 153, 154, 155, 156, 164, 170, 171, 176
Gwynns Falls (neighborhood), 160-61
Gwynns Run, 73, 106, 132, 137, 138, 141, 148, 152

"Harlem," 117, 124
Harlem Park, 116-123
Harlem Park (park), 108-09, 116, 117-18, 122
Hawkins, Ashbie, 43
"Hell's Kitchen," Baltimore, 69
Hibernian Society, 61
Holiday, Billie, 47, 50
Hollins, John Smith, 59
Hollins Market, 54, 57, 66, 67
Hollins Park, 59-66, 90
Hooper, William E., 16
House of Refuge, 162-63
Housing
  italianate, 3, 39, 51, 59, 71, 81-83, 91, 96, 99, 100, 103, 117, 135, 138, 144, 146, 149, 150, 156, 161, 165
  public, 32-33, 34, 36, 83-85, 87, 128-29
  row, "daylight," 51, 68, 71, 107, 135-36, 138, 141, 142, 143-44, 146, 149, 150, 152, 155, 167, 170, 171, 175, 176, 179, 180
Howard, John Eager, 6, 15, 86, 89
Hunting Ridge, 176-77
"Hunting Ridge," 174, 176-77

Immigrants, 27, 29-30, 56, 58, 61, 64-66, 69, 72, 80, 139
Irvington, 164-67
Isaac Newton Academy, 90, 91
Ivanhoe Terrace, Franklin Square, 96

Jackson, Howard, 87
Johnny Jump-up Hill, 6
Johnson, Harvey, 43, 46
Jones, E. Stanley, 162, 167
Jones Falls, 1, 2, 6

Keelty, James, 106, 141, 171
Keely, Patrick Charles, 12
Keerl, Thomas M., 142
Kelly, John S. (Frank), 90
Key Monument, Eutaw Place, 15
Knapp Institute, 64

Lafayette Market, 38, 112, 113, 114
Lafayette Square, 119, 120-21
"Latin Quarter," Baltimore, 32
Lee, Jesse, 162
Lexington, 106-07
Lincoln Theatre #2, 32, 47
Linden Terrace, 96
Lithuanian Democratic Club, 64
Lithuanian Hall, 64, 68
"Little Appalachia," 10
"Little Lithuania," 64-65
Long, Robert Carey, 65-66
Loudon National Cemetery, 164, 165-66, 179
"Lung Block," 32
Lutheran Health Care Facility, 151

Madison, 1-5, 15-22
Maiden's Choice Run, 160, 164, 178, 179
Malachi Mills House, 96
Marshall, Thurgood, 38
Maryland Baptist Orphanage, 40
Maryland Freedom Union Local #1, 91

Index

Maryland Institute for Art, 14
Maryland State Normal School, 117, 126, 145
Maryland Suffrage League, 46
McCulloch, James H., 31
McCulloh, James W., 31
McCulloh Homes, 31-33, 37
McCullough, John, 31
McGovern, Terry, 87
McMechen, George, 38
McTavish, Emily Caton, 100, 166
Melvin H. Cade Armory, 149
Mencken, Henry. L., 64, 80, 97, 100-01, 102-03
Meyerhoff, Joseph and Jacob, 175
Midtown Edmondson, 142
Mill Hill, 57, 71-77
"Millionaire's Row," 100
Ministerial Alliance, 46
Moore Institute, 90
Morgan, Lyttleton F., 118, 162
Morgan College, 118, 119
Mosher, 150-51
Mount Olivet Cemetery, 161-62, 167
Mount Royal, 1-3, 9
"Mount Royal," 2
Mount Royal Protective (Improvement) Association, 10
Mount Royal Station, 2, 7, 8
Mount Royal-Fremont Urban Renewal District, 4, 10
Mount St. Joseph's High School, 164
Mt. Hope Asylum, 10
Mt. Hope College, 10
Murphy, George B., 34
Murphy Homes, 34-36, 142

NAACP, 43, 126, 136
National Temperance Hospital, 90
Newington Park (Peabody Fields), 126
Northwest Community Action Group, 145-47
Norwood Heights, 179

Olmsted, Frederick L., Jr., 134

Olmsted Commission, 134, 144
Omega Psi Phi Fraternity, 144
Omnibuses, 80

Pennsylvania Avenue, 24-26, 30, 31, 38, 40, 43
46-48, 50, 51-51, 109, 112, 144
Pennsylvania Railroad, 125
Perkins Square, 35, 36
Phoenix Club, 16, 22
Poe, Edgar Allen, 87
Poe Homes, 86-88
Poe House, 87
Poppleton, 80, 89-94
Poppleton Survey, 68
Pratt-Monroe, 68-70
Provident Hospital, 40, 42
Public Baths, Argyle Avenue, 40, 44

Rear View Park, 107
Regent Theatre, 46
Regional Institute for Children and Adolescents, 180
Reisterstown Turnpike, 6, 26, 31, 124, 143, 151
Republican Party, 28, 43
Rognel Heights, 173-174
Roosevelt, Eleanor, 128
"Rose Hill," 15
Rosemont, 152-53
Rosemont Homeowners, 141
Royal Theatre, 46-47, 112
Rutter's Run, 6

Sandtown, 109
Sandtown-Winchester, 124-29
Sandtown-Winchester Community Association, 129
Santo Domingoans, 26, 30
Seven Gates, 166
Sharp Street Methodist Church, 46, 49
Shipley, Charles, 138, 139, 141, 151
Shipley Hill, 138-40
Slaughter houses, 106, 139
Smith, Bessie, 96

"Snake Hollow," 72, 73
Spicer's Run, 6, 51
St. Bernadine's Church, 171-172
St. Joseph's, 162, 164
St. Joseph's Monastery, 167, 169
St. Katherine's Home for Little Colored Girls, 40, 41
St. Luke's Episcopal School for Boys, 90
St. Mary's Episcopal Home, 32, 40
St. Peter the Apostle Cemetery, 149
Steuart, George Hume, 95-96
Steuart Hill, 95, 104
Stockyards, 76, 139
Streetcars, 9, 10, 51, 52, 111, 118, 134, 136, 141, 146, 149, 152
"Sugar Hill," 25-26

Ten Hills, 149, 158, 176
Thomas, M. Carey, 18, 143
Three Mile Inn, 164
Tiffany, Henry, 15, 16, 19
Tipman, Joe, 86-87
Tremont, 167
Trolleys, horse-drawn, 3, 7, 10, 37, 51, 56, 80, 96, 117, 142

Union Baptist Church (Upton), 43, 49, 50
Union Square, 99-103
Union Square (park), 101-02
Union Square Preservation District, 65
Uplands, 175
Upton, 37-50, 51, 52
"Upton," 37
Urban Renewal, 10, 11, 16, 22, 26, 34, 48, 49, 123

Valck, Adrian, 116-17
Viva House, 102-03
Voshell, James, 141

Walter Greene Post, American Legion, 40
Washington, Booker T., 40
Waverly Terrace, Franklin Square, 96

West Baltimore General Hospital, 151
West Hills, 178
West Mulberry, 173
West Pratt, 99-103
Western, 141
Western Cemetery, 141
Western Maryland Railroad, 125, 143, 144, 148, 152, 160
Westgate, 178
Westphal, Walter, 76, 106
White, Levi Stratton, 32
Wilkens, William, 69, 72-75, 138
Wilkens Avenue, 69-73, 76
Wilkens Hair Factory, 72-73
Willow Brook, 97
Wilson, Franklin, 142
Winans, Ross R., 59, 61, 177
Winchester, 152

Yale Heights, 158, 178-79
YMCA
    Druid Hill Ave., 39-40, 45, 46,
    West End, 90